AF600325

THE CATHOLIC UNIVERSITY OF AMERICA
CANON LAW STUDIES
No. 314

HOLY VIATICUM

A HISTORICAL SYNOPSIS AND A COMMENTARY

by

THE REVEREND JAMES J. HANNON, J.C.L.

Priest of the Diocese of Natchez

A DISSERTATION

Submitted to the Faculty of the School of Canon Law of the Catholic University of America in Partial Fulfillment of the Requirements for the Degree of Doctor of Canon Law

THE CATHOLIC UNIVERSITY OF AMERICA PRESS
WASHINGTON, D. C.
1951

NIHIL OBSTAT:

CLEMEUS V. BASTNAGEL, J. U. D.
Censor Deputatus

Washington, D. C., die 25 Maii, 1950.

IMPRIMATUR:

✠ RICHARDUS O. GEROW
Episcopus Natchetensis

Jackson, Mississippi, die 29 Maii, 1950.

Printed by The Abbey Press, St. Meinrad, Indiana

TO HIS EXCELLENCY
MOST REVEREND RICHARD O. GEROW
BISHOP OF NATCHEZ

TABLE OF CONTENTS

FOREWORD vii

Part One

HOLY VIATICUM FROM THE FIRST CENTURY TO THE CODE OF CANON LAW (1918)

CHAPTER

I. THE MEANING OF THE TERM "VIATICUM" 1

II. LEGISLATION AND PRACTICE PRIOR TO THE COUNCIL OF TRENT (1545-1563) 8

ARTICLE 1. Early Beginnings of the Practice 8

ARTICLE 2. Special Legislation Concerning Dying Penitents . 14

ARTICLE 3. The Beginnings of Current General Legislation . 20

III. HOLY VIATICUM FROM THE COUNCIL OF TRENT (1545-1563) TO THE CODE OF CANON LAW (1918) ... 35

ARTICLE 1. The Legislation and Catechism of the Council of Trent 35

Section 1. The Legislation of the Council of Trent 35

Section 2. The Doctrine of the Catechism of the Council of Trent 37

ARTICLE 2. Legislation after the Council of Trent 39

Section 1. The Obligation to receive Holy Viaticum 40

A. The nature of the obligation 40

B. The temporal element in the obligation 45

Section 2. The Proper Minister of Holy Viaticum and the Manner of Administration 51

A. The proper minister 51

1. The Parish Priest 52

2. Hospital Chaplains 54

3. The Superior of Clerical Exempt Religious 57

4. The Minister for the Bishop and the Pastor 59

B. The manner of administration 65

Section 3. The Recipient of Holy Viaticum 65

A. Recipients in general 65

B. Children as the recipients 69

C. Persons under capital punishment 72

Part Two

CANONICAL COMMENTARY

IV. THE CANONICAL PRECEPT TO RECEIVE HOLY VIATICUM 76

ARTICLE 1. The Nature of the Precept 76

ARTICLE 2. The Manner of its Fulfillment 84

▼

Section 1. The Danger of Death 84
Section 2. The Element of Time 91
Section 3. Relaxation from the Law of the Eucharistic fast 96
V. THE MINISTER OF HOLY VIATICUM 102
ARTICLE 1. Holy Viaticum in Its Administration a Reserved Parochial Function 102
ARTICLE 2. Exceptions to the Right of the Pastor 107
Section 1. The Minister of Holy Viaticum in a Case of Necessity 107
Section 2. The Minister of Holy Viaticum in Religious Houses 112
Section 3. The Minister of Holy Viaticum in Hospitals ... 117
Section 4. The Minister of Holy Viaticum to the Bishop and to the Pastor 120
ARTICLE 3. The Obligation to Administer Holy Viaticum . 121
VI. THE RECIPIENT OF HOLY VIATICUM 126
ARTICLE 1. Adults as the Recipients 126
Section 1. General Legislation 126
Section 2. Abnormal Cases 136
A. Abnormal cases arising from mental disorders 136
B. Abnormal cases arising from physical disorders 141
ARTICLE 2. Children as the Recipients 146
VII. THE ADMINISTRATION OF HOLY VIATICUM 150
ARTICLE 1. The Manner of Bringing Holy Viaticum to the Sick 150
ARTICLE 2. The Process of Actual Administration 156
Section 1. Liturgical Prescriptions 156
Section 2. The Factors of Time and Place in the Administration of Holy Viaticum 161
ARTICLE 3. The Rite in which Holy Viaticum is to be Administered 166
CONCLUSIONS 170
BIBLIOGRAPHY 173
ABBREVIATIONS 182
ALPHABETICAL INDEX 184
BIOGRAPHICAL NOTE 183
CANON LAW STUDIES 187

FOREWORD

Little need be said by way of introduction to the subject matter of this dissertation. All Catholic priests and even the average Catholic layman are familiar in some degree with most of the problems that come up for discussion. There is no more important moment in the immortal existence of the soul than the moment in which it parts with the mortal body in death. On its state at that moment will depend an eternity of bliss or misery. And there is no better way in which the faithful can prepare themselves for that moment than by a devout reception of the Eucharist. Recognizing the potential source of comfort and strength to the dying in this sacrament, the Church realized from the beginning its responsibility in providing the faithful with It. This solicitude is evidenced in many aspects of the Church's legislation relating to this last reception of the Eucharist.

In the first part of this dissertation, the writer proposes to trace the trend of legislation from the early days of the Church's existence to the publication of the Code of Canon Law. The history of the subject falls naturally into two periods: Holy Viaticum up to the time of the Council of Trent, Holy Viaticum from the Council of Trent to the Code of Canon Law. In the former period many references are made to Patristic writings and to other non-canonical sources. This was done with a view to indicating the practice of the time, in lieu of clear legislation, and is not intended to be an exhaustive survey. In the tracing of the historical development of the later period, special consideration will be given to the legislation enacted by the Council of Trent itself, while in the post-Tridentine period many decrees and instructions of the Roman Curia will be cited. It will be seen that the pre-Code legislation relative to the canonical institute of Holy Viaticum is of paramount importance inasmuch as it forms the immediate basis for the canons of the Code which now regulate that same institute.

The second part of this dissertation consists in a commentary on the relative canons of the Code. Canon 864 states the obligation to receive Holy Viaticum, and therefore it is treated at length. The subject of Holy Viaticum, however, is one which is not restricted solely to the field of Canon Law; it is rather a canonico-moral question. This is very evident from the fact that both canonists and moralists treat this matter, and in fact the latter often present a more detailed and comprehensive commentary than do the former. In view of this, the teaching of many moral theologians will be freely utilized.

The writer takes this occasion to extend a most sincere expression of gratitude to His Excellency, the Most Reverend Richard O. Gerow, D.D., Bishop of Natchez, for the opportunity of advanced study in Canon Law; to the members of the Faculty of the School of Canon Law for their guidance and assistance; and to all others unnamed who have given of their time and talents towards the completion of this work.

PART ONE

HOLY VIATICUM FROM THE FIRST CENTURY TO THE CODE OF CANON LAW (1918)

CHAPTER I

THE MEANING OF THE TERM "VIATICUM"

Long before the institution of the Sacrament of the Eucharist by Christ, the term "viaticum" was widely used in ancient Greek and Latin culture. Among the Greeks there existed the custom of providing a supper for those about to undertake a long journey. Such a meal was referred to as the ἐφόδιον. The provision of all things necessary for the journey, such as food, clothing, and money, were referred to as the ὁδοιπόριον. A similar custom existed among the Romans, and in their classical writings there is to be found the corresponding term "Viaticus," which means of or pertaining to a journey.[1]

Among the pagan writers also there prevailed an added significance of the term as indicating the fare for the voyage to the after life. The practice of burying money (*viaticum*)

[1] Cf. A. J. Schulte, "Holy Viaticum," *The Catholic Encyclopedia* (15 vols., and 2 supplements, New York, 1907-1922), XV, 397-399. The author here cites the foregoing use of the term by Pliny, *Ep. 12, in fine*: "Vide ut mihi viaticum redes quod impendi." A. C. Rush, *Death and Burial in Christian Antiquity*, The Catholic University of America Studies in Christian Antiquity, n. 1 (Washington, D. C.: The Catholic University of America Press, 1941), p. 93, where a similar usage is attributed to Plautus, *Bacchides*, I, 94: "Ego sorori meae coenam hodie dare volo viaticum," and to Horace, *Ep. I*, 17; A. Bride, "Viatique," *Dictionnaire de Théologie Catholique* (15 vols., Paris, 1903-1948), XVI, 2842-2858; N. G. Liddell-R. Scott, *Greek-English Dictionary* (2 vols., Oxford: The Clarendon Press, 1925), ἐφόδιον I, 476, ὁδοιπόριον II, 1198; A. Forcellini, "Viaticus," *Lexicon Totius Latinitatis* (6 vols., Patavii, 1940), IV, 976. Etymologically, the term "Viaticum" is derived from neuter form of the adjective "viaticus," which in turn is derived from *via* and *iticus*.

with the dead with a view to providing them with this fare was a practice much in vogue in ancient times and was common in the sixth century B. C. It arose out of the belief that the attainment of the after life entailed a crossing of the mythical river Styx through the services of Charon for whom the fare was intended.[2]

It is probable that the idea of "*Viaticum*," both as a parting meal and as money for a journey was present to the Christian mind when they called the reception of the Eucharist at death the "*Viaticum.*" This was to be the Christian substitution for similar practices of pagan times. On the one hand, It was to be the meal for the journey to eternity, inasmuch as the dying person would be nourished with the Body and Blood of Christ; on the other hand, there are traces of an ancient Christian practice of burying the Eucharist with the dead in keeping with the pagan idea of providing them with the requisite money for the journey.[3]

Among the early Christian writers, however, the term "*viaticum*" was given a variety of meanings. Phileas, Bishop of Thmuis (†304), in a letter to his flock, applied it to the means of salvation in general.[4]

In the fourth century, St. Basil, Bishop of Caeserea (370-379), applied it to anything that gave spiritual strength and comfort to the dying.[5] In a more specific way he also applied the term to the sacrament of baptism, and to good counsel and to prayer.[6]

In similar fashion, St. Gregory of Nazianzen (†391), who for a time was bishop of Constantinople, applied the term to

[2] Cf. Rush, *loc. cit.*

[3] Cf. *infra*, pp. 8-10.

[4] Eusebius, *Historia Ecclesiastica*, Lib. VIII, cap. 10—*Die griechischen Christlichen Scriftsteller der eresten drei Jahrhunderte* (7 vols. in 10), VII, pars II (*Eubebius Werke*, ed. Schwartz: Leipzig, 1908), p. 761 (hereafter cited *GCS*).

[5] *Homilia de Spiritu Sancto*, n. 66—P. J. Migne, *Patrologiae Cursus Completus, Series Graeca* (161 vols., Paris, 1857-1866), XXXI, 650 (hereafter cited *MPG*).

[6] *Homilia XIII*, 5 —*MPG, XXXI*, 423; *Ep. LVII* et *CLXXII*, —*MPG*, 406 and 650.

the administration of the sacrament of baptism to the dying.[7]

Among the writings of the Latin Fathers prior to the fourth century, there is to be found the same broad application of the term with scarcely any trace of its present-day specific meaning. St. Cyprian (200-258), in giving it a connotation embracive of prayers and good works of all kinds, typified the Christian notion of the term among his contemporaries.[8]

In the conciliar legislation of the early centuries, the term "*viaticum*" is again found, but again there is lacking that precision of meaning with which it is characterized in current ecclesiastical terminology. What seems to be the earliest reference to it is found in the I General Council of Nicaea (325). This council, in defining the law of the Church relative to that class of persons referred to as *lapsi*, stated they were not to be deprived of "the last and most necessary viaticum."[9]

[7] *OratioLX, De Baptismo*, n. 11—*MPG*, XXXVI, 374.

[8] *De Lapsis*, n. 25—P. J. Migne, *Patrologiae Cursus Completus, Series Latina* (221 vols., Parisiis, 1844-1864), IV, 485 (hereafter cited *MPL*).

[9] Can. 13: "... si quis egreditur e corpore, ultimo et necessario viatico minime privetur...."—C. H. Turner, *Ecclesiae Occidentalis Monumenta Iuris Antiquissima. Canonum et Conciliorum Graecorum Interpretationes Latinae*, Tom. I, fasc. I, pars altera, (Oxonii: e Typographia Clarendiana, 1904), 267. This is the text according to Dionysius the Little, and the one which is used here. Cf. J. Mansi, *Sacrorum Conciliorum Nova et Amplissima Collectio* (53 vols. in 60, Paris-Leipzig-Arnhem, 1901-1927), II, 681 (hereafter cited Mansi); Jean Hardouin, *Acta Conciliorum et Epistolae Decretales ac Constitutiones Summorum Pontifium* (12 vols., Parisiis, 1714-1715), I, 331 (hereafter cited Hardouin); H. J. Schroeder, *Disciplinary Decrees of the General Councils* (St. Louis: Herder, 1937), p. 42; *Codicis Iuris Canonici Fontes*, cura Emi Petri Card. Gasparri editi (9 vols., Romae, [postea Civitate Vaticane]: Typis Polyglottis Vaticanis, 1923-1939, [Vols. VII-IX, ed. cura Emi Card. Serédi]), n. 1 (hereafter cited *Fontes*); C. Hefele-H. Leclercq, *Histoire des Conciles* (10 vols. in 19, Paris, Letouzey et Ané, 1907-1938), I, 593; H. Denzinger-C. Bannwart-J. Umberg, *Enchirdion Symbolorum Definitionum et Declarationum de Rebus*

Considerable doubt has been raised with regard to the precise meaning of the term as contained in the thirteenth canon of the I General Council of Nicaea. Van Espen (1646-1728), in giving expression to this doubt, adverted to the fact that emerges from the foregoing paragraphs, namely that the writers of antiquity used the term *"viaticum"* only in a very loose sense. In his effort to resolve the doubt, he cited an older author, Gabriel de l'Aubespine (1579-1630), who held that, whenever the term was applied to the Eucharist when received in danger of death, it was usually qualified by such phrases as "the most safe," the most absolute," or "the most powerful" viaticum. The phrase "most necessary viaticum" was used only with reference to the sacrament of baptism in respect to catechumens or with reference to the sacrament of penance with respect to dying penitents. Van Espen, however, was of the opinion that the more usual significance of the term was with reference to the sacrament of the Eucharist when administered to those who were dying. The faithful of the first ages of the Church looked upon the Eucharist as the complement of Christian perfection and as the last seal and hope of salvation. It was for this reason that at the beginning of life, after the reception of baptism and confirmation, the Eucharist was given to infants, and at the close of life Its administration followed upon the reception of the sacraments of reconciliation and extreme unction, so that properly and literally It could have been styled by the Fathers of the Council of Nicaea as "the last and most necessary viaticum." In support of his view he pointed to older authors, such as Balsamon and Zonaras, both of the twelfth century, who, he asserted, indicated a preference for his own view.[10]

Schroeder (1875-1942) likewise inclined to the opinion that the term as used in this context had reference to the Eucharist when received in danger of death. He added,

---

Fidei et Morum (18-20. ed., Friburgi Brisgoviae: Herder and Co., 1932), n. 57 (hereafter cited Denzinger).

[10] *Ius Ecclesiasticum Universum* (2 vols., Lovanii et Lugduni, 1753), Pars II, sect. I, tit. IV, cap. IV, nn. 1-4—I, 403.

however, that the corresponding Greek term ἐφόδιον already referred to, could be taken to mean not only the Eucharist, but also penance and extreme unction.[11]

In the *Statuta Ecclesiae Antiqua*, once supposed to contain the legislation of the IV Council of Carthage (398), the term is again found. Canon 77 stated that the sick penitents were to be given "Viaticum," and the following canon added that such penitents who had received the "Viaticum of the Eucharist" should be absolved with the imposition of hands if they recovered.[12] An examination of the text of those two canons seems to indicate that the Fathers of the Council had in mind the reception of the Eucharist only. At any rate, there is indicated a more restricted use of the term "viaticum."

In the following century the I Council of Orange (441) decreed that dying public penitents were to be admitted to Communion, a Communion which was for the consolation of the dying person, and for that reason was aptly called by the Fathers a "viaticum."[13] The reference made by the Council is indeed important as indicating a new definition of the old classical term according to the mind of the Church. In the light of this fragment of conciliar legislation the term "viaticum" did signify the Eucharist as received by those in danger of death.

The Council, however, was a local one, and its precise application of the term was not as yet universally adopted. In the following year, (442) the I Provincial Council of Vaison spoke of penitents who died suddenly as being cut off from the "Viaticum of the sacraments."[14] Such a use of

[11] *Op. cit.*, p. 43.

[12] Mansi, III, 957; H. T. Bruns, *Canones Apostolorum et Conciliorum Saeculorum IV-VII* (2 vols., Berolini, 1839), I, 148 (hereafter cited Bruns).

[13] Can. 3: "Qui recedunt de corpore poenitentia accepta, placuit sine reconciliatoria manus impositione eis communicare, quod morientes sufficit consolationi secundum definitiones patrum qui huusmodi communionem congruentur viaticum nominarunt."—Mansi, VI, 437; Bruns, II, 122.

[14] Can. 2 —Bruns, II, 127.

the term, inclusive as it was of, not only the sacrament of the Eucharist, but also of the sacraments of penance and extreme unction, affords a basis for the conclusion that as late as the middle of the fifth century, there was yet wanting the present-day technical and uniform significance of the term.

In the light of the foregoing testimonies it can readily be seen that the practice itself of providing dying Christians with the sacrament of the Eucharist was of very early origin. Furthermore, they show the importance, attached to the reception of Holy Viaticum. But while the practice did exist, it was not always exclusively designated by that term. It is not surprising, then, to find such a variety of meanings in the early Christian writings and legislative enactments. On the contrary, such varying applications were rather to be expected. The term itself was old, having been coined by the pagan writers of pre-Christian times. When lifted out of its pagan context, it brought with it many of its pagan meanings, a factor which must have been at least in part responsible for its wide application in its new and Christian setting.[15]

It is difficult to determine at what precise time the term came to be applied solely to the Eucharist when received by persons in danger of death. From the fifth century onward it seems to have lost many of its former applications, and throughout the early middle ages its generally accepted usage was in reference to the Eucharist only. Apart from the definition of the Council of Orange (441),[16] there does not appear to have been any other attempt to officially define it.

From the sources studied, it is the conclusion of the writer

[15] An example of that wide application is its one-time usage with regard to the portable altar of a bishop. Cf. J. Cavalieri, *Opera Omnia Liturgica seu Commentaria Authentica Sacrae Rituum Congregationis Decreta ad Romanum praesertim Breviarium, Missale et Rituale quomodolibet Attinentia* (5 toms. in 1 vol., Basani, 1778), Tom. IV, cap. V, p. 48 (hereafter cited *Opera Liturgica*).

[16] Cf. *supra*, p. 5.

that the term was generally restricted to its technical meaning in the years that preceded the compilation of the *Decree* of Gratian (ca. 1140) inasmuch as the legislation contained therein seems to take for granted such a restricted usage. St. Thomas Aquinas (1225-1274), in defining the various aspects of the sacrament of the Eucharist, stated that in so far as the sacrament was prefigurative of the enjoyment of God it was called the Viaticum, since it offers us the grace of attaining heaven.[17]

The essential differences that obtain between simple Holy Communion and Communion administered by way of Viaticum lie in the accompanying relaxation of the law of the Eucharistic fast with regard to the latter, and in the different formulas prescribed by the Roman Ritual for the administration of the two. The formula for simple Holy Communion is:

> Corpus Domini Nostri JesuChristi custodiat animam tuam in vitam aeternam. Amen.[18]

The formula for the administration of Holy Viaticum reads:

> Accipe, frater (vel soror) Viaticum Corporis Domini Nostri Jesu Christi, qui te custodiat ab hoste maligno, et perducat in vitam aeternam. Amen.[19]

[17] *Summa Theologica* (6 vols., 12. ed., Taurini: Marietti, 1937-1938), Pars III, q. 74, art. 4 (hereafter cited *Summa*).

[18] *Rituale Romanum Pauli V Pontificis Maximi editum aliorumque Pontificum cura Recognitum atque Auctoritate Pii Papae XI ad normam Codicis Iuris Canonici accomodatum* (2. ed. iuxta Typicam Vaticanam amplificata I, New York: Benziger Brothers, 1925), Tit. IV, cap. 2, *de sanctissimo Eucharistiae Sacramento*, n. 5 (hereafter cited *Rituale Romanum*).

[19] *Rituale Romanum*, Tit. IV, cap. 4, *de communione infirmorum*, n. 19.

CHAPTER II

LEGISLATION AND PRACTICE PRIOR TO THE COUNCIL OF TRENT (1545-1563)

Article 1. Early Beginnings of the Practice

In the light of the ancient pagan practices which form the cultural and historical background for the Christian concept of Viaticum, it is rather to be expected that the first indications of the existence of the practice of administering the Eucharist to the dying would be of early origin. Doubtless those practices of supplying the dead with material helps were still fresh in the minds of the early Christians in a manner explanatory of this early origin.

As far as can be ascertained from the sources, the Christians did not adopt the custom of placing a coin in the mouth of the dead. There are, however, traces of an ancient practice of burying the Eucharist with the dead. This abuse was especially prevalent from the fourth to the seventh century, and the sources show that it was not confined to one locality, but was somewhat general. The widespread existence of the abuse is testified to mainly by the prohibitions of various councils, for such prohibitive conciliar legislation would have been called for only by reason of a public and widespread abuse.

The prohibition is met with as early as the Council of Hippo (393). In order to have arrested the attention of the Fathers of the Council, the practice itself must have been in existence sometime prior to that date.[1]

The continuance of the abuse is seen, when four years later, the III Council of Carthage (397) issued a similar condemnation of it, pointing out that the command of Christ as contained in the words: "Take and eat," could in no way be fulfilled by the dead.[2]

[1] Can. 4: "Corporibus defunctorum Eucharistia non detur."—Mansi, III, 919.

[2] Can. 6: "Item placuit, ut corporibus defunctorum Eucharistia non detur; dictum est enim a Domino: accipite et edite. Cadavera autem nec accipere nec edere possunt."—Bruns, I, 123.

Contemporaneous with the prohibitions of the African councils, the denunciation made by St. John Chrysostom (†407) shows that the practice likewise existed in the East.[3] Towards the close of the sixth century, the Council of Auxerre (578), in legislating against certain abuses relative to burial practices, stated that it was not allowed to give the Eucharist to the dead.[4] This reflects the existence of the abuse in Gaul, and at the same time shows how tenacious a hold the practice must have had in the early Church.

Finally, the Trullan Synod (692) repeated the earlier legislation found in the III Council of Carthage, and like it referred to he selfsame words of Christ.[5]

Regarding the practice itself, Ménard (1585-1644), in his *Notes on the Gregorian Sacramentary,* stated that at times the Eucharist was placed in the mouth of the dead person; at other times It was placed upon the breast and buried with the body.[6] The ancient custom of allowing the faithful to reserve the Eucharist in their own homes undoubtedly lent facility to the practice. Rush maintains that it was customary among the Romans to have the Communion of the Lord in the mouth at the moment of death and states that the Roman Ritual at one time specifically demanded such a procedure.[7]

The writings of the early Fathers and the legislation of the early councils demonstrate clearly that the practice of administering Holy Viaticum to the dying was generally in vogue at an early date. Perhaps the earliest mention of it is to be found in the writings of Dionysius of Alexandria (248-264/5). In a letter to Pope Fabius (236-250) he related the incident concerning a dying man, Serapion by name, who requested a priest that he might receive the last sacraments before his death. The priest, being sick, could

[3] *Homilia 40* (in I Cor.), n. I—*MPG,* LXI, 347.

[4] Can. 12: "... non licet mortuis nec eucharistiam nec osculum tradi."—Bruns, II, 238.

[5] Can. 83—Bruns, I, 60.

[6] *MPL,* LXXVIII, 473.

[7] *Death and Burial in Christian Antiquity,* p. 92.

not come. Accordingly he gave the messenger a small portion of the consecrated bread, bade him soak It in water or wine and let the drops fall into the sick man's mouth. The aged Serapion having thus received the Viaticum at once gave up his soul.[8]

Weighty evidence of the early origin of the practice of administering Holy Viaticum may be gathered from the I General Council of Nicaea (325). In the thirteenth canon this Council referred to it as being already "an ancient and canonical law," and demanded that it be observed even in the case of dying penitents, for these were not to be deprived of "the last and most necessary Viaticum."[9] This conciliar legislation shows the importance that was attached to the reception of Holy Viaticum by the early Christians, a factor which further demonstrates its early origin.

Paulinus, Bishop of Nola (409-431), in his life-story of St. Ambrose (†397), recounted that when the saint had taken the Body of the Lord he breathed forth his spirit, bearing with him the good Viaticum.[10]

St. Gregory the Great (590-604) is a later witness to the practice. He related that St. Benedict (†ca. 547), on the sixth day of his illness had himself carried into church by his deciples, and there fortified himself in death by his reception of the Body and Blood of the Lord.[11]

There are other sources which show that the repeated reception of Holy Viaticum was an accepted practice. St. Gregory Nazianzen (†391), when describing the last illness of his father, who was likewise a bishop, stated that through

[8] Eusebius, *Historia Ecclesiastica,* Lib. VI, cap. 44, nn. 4-5—*GCS,* II, pars 2, 625; *MPG,* XX, 630.

[9] Can. 13: "With regard to those dying, the ancient canonical law shall continue to be observed, namely, if anyone be near death let him not be deprived of the last and most necessary Viaticum.... In general, and in the case of anyone dying who wishes to receive the Eucharist, let the bishop give it to him after due investigation."—Schroeder, *op. cit.,* p. 42.

[10] *Vita S. Ambrosii*—*MPG,* XIV, 43.

[11] *Dialogi,* II, 37—*MPL,* LXVI, 202.

his own hands the aged bishop strengthened himself many times daily with the Liturgy.[12]

Further examples of the repeated reception of Holy Viaticum are given by Rush. He states that St. Melania (†400) received the sacrament three times during her last illness, and that this was an indication that the practice existed in the Roman Church.[13]

The kindred practice of reserving the Eucharist for the purpose of administering Holy Viaticum to the dying merits some consideration. At first the motive which prompted it was rather a liturgical one. It was a matter of importance to the early Christians that the Eucharistic ritual should contain a clear and striking example of the mark of unity given by Christ to His Church. Thus arose the custom of sending a portion of the bread consecrated at the Pope's Mass to the priests whose duty it was to offer the Christian sacrifice in the titular churches of Rome. Such also was the motive underlying the practice of reserving part of the Host from the Mass of the previous day. These particles thus reserved were referred to as the *Sancta*.[14]

But it cannot be ignored that the added motive of having on hand at all times the sacrament of the Eucharist arose from the needed preparadeness for administering It to dying Christians. It too played an early and important part in the adoption of the practice of reserving the Sacred Species. The incident concerning the aged Serapion[15] gives some indication that even at this early date the Eucharist was reserved either in the church or in the house of the

[12] *Oratio 18*, n. 38—*MPG*, XXV, 1035.

[13] *Death and Burial in Christian Antiquity*, p. 97.

[14] J. Henry, *The Mass and Holy Communion: Interritual Law*, The Catholic University of America Canon Law Studies, n. 235 (Washington, D. C.: The Catholic University of America Press, 1946), p. 30; A. Fortescue, *The Mass: A Study of the Roman Liturgy* (New York: Longmans, Green and Co., 1922), pp. 174-175; Duchesne, *Christian Worship: Its Origin and Evolution* (translated from the French by M. L. McClure, London: Society for the Promoting of Christian Knowledge, 1903), p. 163 (hereafter cited *Christian Worship*).

[15] Cf. *supra*, p. 9.

priest for the purpose of providing Holy Viaticum for the dying. If further points to the fact that lay people were allowed to administer the sacrament.

A later incident described by St. John Chrysostom (†407) may beregarded as giving added credence to the theory that the practice was of early origin and was widely adopted at the beginning of the fifth century. He described the incident as taking place in Constantinople in 405; how the soldiers entered the church and spilt the Precious Blood from the chalice.[16] This points to the fact that the Eucharist was reserved, not only under the species of bread, but also under the species of wine.

A contrary argument is not to be deduced from a decretal of Gregory IX,[17] which stated that the priest was the while he was still fasting to visit the sick in order that he might minister to their needs. One might infer from this that the underlying reason for the prolonged fast was the possible necessity of having to celebrate Mass in order to provide Holy Viaticum for the dying. But in his commentary on this decretal, Gonzalez-Tellez (†after 1673) pointed out that in ancient times the observance of the Eucharistic fast was required not only for the celebration of Mass but also for the administration of the sacraments.[18]

Many references to the practice of the private reservation of the Eucharist in the homes of the faithful are to be found in the patristic writings.[19] The motive which prompted the

[16] *Epistola ad Innocentium*: "Quia et sanctissimus Christi Sanguis, sicut in tali tumultu continget, in praedictorum militum vestes effusus est."—*MPF*, LI, 533.

[17] C. 1, X, *de celebratione missae*, III, 41.

[18] *Commentaria Perpetua in Singulos Textus quinque Librorum Decretalium Gregorii IX* (5 toms., Lugduni, 1673), Tom. III, lib. III, tit. 44 *de custodia Eucharistiae*, cap. I, n. 7.

[19] St. Basil (330-379), *Epistola ad Caesarian Patriciam*, n. XCIII —*MPG*, XXXII, 483; St. Cyprian (200-258), *De Lapsis*, n. 26—*MPL*, IV, 486; *Corpus Scriptorum Ecclesiasticorum Latinorum* (Vindobonae: F. Tempsky, 1866-), III, pars I, 256 (hereafter cited *CSEL*); Tertullian (ca. 160-ca. 240), *Ad uxorem*, Lib. II, cap. 5—*MPL*, I, 1296. Cf. Many, *Praelectiones de Missa cum Appendice de Sanctissimo Sac-*

approval of such a practice was, no doubt, inspired by the keen desire felt by the early Christians to receive the Eucharist in danger of death, a desire which in many cases would not have been satisfied apart from such a permission. The character of the times in the days of the persecutions was such that at any moment a Christian might be dragged from his home and put to death, thus precluding the possibility of the priest's administering Holy Viaticum.

From the fourth century onward, however, various councils began to legislate against the practice. With the cessation of the persecutions and the restoration of a more normal manner of life, there was no longer the same need for it. The first instance of such prohibitive legislation is to be found in the Council of Saragossa in the year 380. In it there was enacted a condemnation of anyone who, upon receiving the Eucharist into his hands, did not immediately consume It but carried It off to his home.[20] In the year 400 the I Council of Toledo issued a similar condemnation of the practice.[21]

Even though the practice of reserving the Eucharist for the sick and the dying must have been of early origin, it was only in later centuries that any definite legislation governed it. That it came to be regarded as an obligation of increasing importance may be gathered from the many official prescriptions regarding it. In substance, those various decrees enacted that the Eucharist was always to be on hand lest anyone die without It.[22]

---

ramento Eucharistiae (Parisiis, 1903), p. 330 (hereafter cited *De Missa*).

[20] Can. 3—Mansi, III, 634.

[21] Can. 14—Mansi, III, 1000. This canon of the Council of Toledo is later found in the writings of Hincmar of Rheims, *De Synodalibus Causis*, cap. IX—Mansi, XV, 480; in those of Regino, Abbot of Prüm, *De Ecclesiae Disciplina*, Lib. I, can. 120—*MPL*, CXXXII, 215; in those of Burchard, Bishop of Worms, *Decretum*, Lib. V, cap. 68—Mansi, X, 601; and in the *Decree* of Gratiam, c. 93, D. II, *de cons.*

[22] *Capitula Radulfi* (840), VI—*MPL*, CXIX, 706; *Capitula Walteri* (871), cap. VII—*MPL*, CXIX, 734; Regino of Prüm (ca. 906), *De Ecclesiae Disciplina*, I, 69-70—*MPL*, CXXXII, 205; *Decretum* Burchardi

Finally, the same legislation was incorporated into the Decree of Gratian (ca. 1140).[23] After the time of Gratian, the practice of reserving the Eucharist in parochial churches for the purpose of administering It to the dying became universal. This is borne out by the fact that the IV General Council of the Lateran (1215) laid stress upon the safekeeping of the Eucharist rather than upon the necessity of Its reservation.[24]

Article 2. Special Legislation Concerning Dying Penitents

It must be noted that the conditions which existed in the early Church were such as to call for special legislation and disciplinary measures. During the stormy years of the persecutions the Church at times maintained a rather severe attitude and meted out long and rigorous penances upon certain classes of sinners. Foremost among these were apostates, adulterers and homicides. Here the question may be explored whether the Church extended its severity to the extent of excluding such dying sinners from the reception of Holy Viaticum after they had evidenced a repentant spirit.

While there are many and varied opinions on this question, they can be reduced to two main schools of thought. On the one side there are those who adopt the rigoristic at-

---

(ca. 1012), Lib. V, can. 9—*MPL,* CXL, 754; Ivo Carnotensis (†1117), *Decretum,* pars II, cap. 20—*MPL,* CLXI, 165; *Panormia* (ca. 1095), lib. I, can. 147—*MPL,* CLXI, 1097.

[23] C. 93, D. II, *de cons.*: "Presbyter eucharistiam semper habeat paratam, ut, quando quis infirmatus (aut parvulus infirmatus) fuerit, statim eum communicet, ne sine communione moriatur." This canon of Gratian was taken from the Capitularium of Ingelheim (809), c. 16. The *Glossa Ordinaria* to this canon, s. v. *Eucharistiam,* mentions that it was not of obligation to reserve the Precious Blood because of the danger of spilling It and the difficulty of guarding It.

[24] Can. 20—Mansi, XXII, 1007. This canon is also contained in the Decretals of Gregory IX (1227-1241)—c. 1, X, *de custodia Eucharisitiae, chrismatis, et aliorum sacramentorum,* III, 44.

titude and maintain that such penitents were neither reconciled nor admitted to Holy Viaticum when in danger of death. On the other hand, there are those who follow the milder view and maintain that, while there were undoubtedly cases of extreme rigorism, it cannot be concluded that the Church at any time adopted a policy of total exclusion. The number of isolated examples are not sufficient to warrant the formulation of such a general policy.[25]

The story of Serapion, as narrated above,[26] is a case in point. He undoubtedly had been an apostate. As he lay dying, his request that he might receive the last sacraments was granted. Dionysius of Alexandria (†264/5), in commenting upon this remarked that it was done on his orders lest any such penitent die without the help and comfort of the sacraments, especially those who had already asked for them.[27]

In Carthage, St. Cyprian (†258) maintained a somewhat similar attitude towards dying penitents. He, however, required that such penitents present a *libellus* from a martyr in testimony of their good will.[28] Both Dionysius and Cyprian were wont to refuse reconciliation and Holy Viaticum to those who deferred their repentance until the moment of death, for they feared that it was not repentance for sin but the fear of death that prompted such sinners to request the sacraments.[29] Pope Siricius (384-398) decreed that apostates were not to be given the Body and Blood of

[25] Cf. Schroeder, *Disciplinary Decrees of the General Councils*, pp. 42-44; J. King, *The Administration of the Sacraments to Dying non-Catholics*, The Catholic University of America Canon Law Studies, n. 23 (Washington, D. C.: The Catholic University of America, 1924), pp. 93-100.

[26] Cf. *Supra*, p. 9.

[27] Eusebius, *Historia Ecclesiastica*, Lib. VI, cap. 44—*GCS*, II, Pars 2, 625; *MPG*, XX, 630.

[28] *Epistola XII*—MPL, IV, 259; Prudentius Maran, *Vita Sancti Cypriani*—*MPL*, IV, 105.

[29] S. Cyprianus, *Epistola IV*, 23—*CSEL*, III, pars 2, 641. Cf. Schroeder, *op. cit.*, p. 43; King, *loc. cit.*

the Lord, but Holy Communion was not to be denied them at the time of death if they had repented.[30]

The earliest conciliar legislation treating of the question is to be found in the Council of Elvira (ca. 305) in Spain. In it were enacted several canons forbidding the administration of Holy Viaticum to certain classes of sinners, namely idolaters, adulterers and homicides.[31]

Further relevant legislation is to be found in subsequent Councils.[32] Its general tone was one of comparative mildness. Penances that were theretofore harsh were mitigated, and Viaticum was not to be refused.

In keeping with this milder attitude, the Fathers of the I General Council of Nicaea (325) decreed that penitents who had become dangerously ill before the prescribed term of penance had elapsed were to be given Viaticum, and in general each case of an excommunicate was to be left to the discretion of the bishop.[33] It has been disputed whether this canon of the Council of Nicaea was meant to put an end to the rigorism and harshness of the preceding councils. Schroeder (1875-1942) was of the opinion that such was its purpose. This same opinion had been held by Watkins (1847-1925), who regarded the canon as the final summation of the conflict. "Never again," he stated, "will the Church retire from this position. . . . only eighty years before it would have been hard to find a church in Christendom which had place for a penitent apostate this side of the waters of death."[34]

[30] *Epistolae et Decreta,* Cap. III—*MPL,* XIII, 1136.

[31] Cans. 1, 2, 6, 8 and 66—Mansi, II, 6 and 16. In all of these canous the phrase "nec in finem dandam (impertiendam) esse communionem" occurs. In answer to the question whether the word "*communio*" as used in the context is to be taken to mean sacramental communion, Hefele-Lechlercq stated that sacramental Communion was not to be excluded.—*Histoire des Conciles,* I, 221.

[32] Council of Arles (314), can. 22—Mansi, II, 473; Council of Ancyra (314), 16—Mansi, II, 532.

[33] Can. 13—Mansi, II, 681.

[34] *History of Penance for the whole Church to A. D. 450, and for the Western Church from A. D. 450 to A. D. 1215* (2 vols., London and New York: Longmans Green and Co., 1920), I, 291.

In the fifth century the position of the Church with regard to this question became more crystallized. In 405 Innocent I (401-417), in a letter to Exsuperius, Bishop of Toulouse, who had asked what should be done in the case of those who after baptism had led a licentious life and who at the moment of death had asked to be reconciled and admitted to Holy Communion, replied that in former times the practice had been more severe, but that now the attitude had become more lenient. He pointed out that the prior practice was to allow penance but to refuse Communion. During the persecutions the reception of Holy Communion was made difficult to the end that men might be regained from the apostasy into which they had lapsed. With the cessation of the persecutions and the restoration of peace to the Church, it seemed feasible for Communion to be given to those who were in danger of death.[35]

Subsequent to this reply of Pope Innocent I, it appears that there still existed vestiges of the old rigorism to such an extent as to have occasioned a similar reply from Pope Celestine I (422-432) to the bishops of the provinces of Vienne and Narbonne in the year 428. In this letter the pope recalled to mind the great mercy of God for sinners, and deplored the fact that penance was being denied to some.[36] In 487 Pope Felix III (483-492) ordered that those clerics who presented themselves for re-baptism, a practice which was regarded as heretical, be admitted to Holy Communion in danger of death. Neither the lower clergy nor the laity were to be refused Viaticum, but if they recovered from the danger of death they were to complete their pen-

[35] Ep. *Consulenti tibi* (ad Exsuperium), 20 febr. 405: "... iam depulso terrore communionem dare abeuntibus placuit, et propter Domini misericordiam quasi viaticum profecturis."—*MPL*, XX, 498-499. Denzinger, n. 95; Jaffé, *Regesta Pontificum Romanorum ab condita Ecclesia ad annum post Christum natum MCXCVIII* (2 ed., cura G. Wattenbach, F. Kaltenbrunner [ad annum 590], P. Ewald [anno 590-882], S. Löwenfeld [anno 882-1198], 2 vols. in 1, Lipsiae, 1885-1888), n. 293 (hereafter cited Jaffé).

[36] Ep. 4, *Cuperemus quidem*, 26 iul. 428—Denzinger, n. 111; Jaffé, n. 369.

ance as members of the third or highest class of penitents.[37]

In the sixth century the question evidently presented itself in other parts of the Christian world. First, there was the Council of Agde (506) in the south of Gaul, which found it necessary to decree that Viaticum was not to be denied to anyone at death.[38] Secondly, there was the Council of Epâon (517) in Burgundy, which decreed that no sinner who repented and amended was to be denied the hope of being received back into the Church. If he was sick, then the time of his penance was to be shortened, but in the event that he recovered after the reception of Holy Viaticum it was necessary for him to complete the appointed time of penance.[39]

Finally, this same legislation was in substance later incorporated into the *Decree* of Gratian and there was accorded a new status of universality and permanency.[40]

An incidental question now merits consideration. It is

[37] Cf. Jaffé, Vol. I, p. 82. By way of explanation it may be pointed out that there were at this time three classes of penitents. The first were known as the *audientes*, who were forced to remain in the vestibule of the church, and that only for the Mass of the Catechumens. The second class were known as the *substrati* or *genuflectentes*, who were allowed into the nave of the church, but had to remain kneeling or prostrate until they were ordered to leave with the Catechumens. The third class were known as the *consistentes*, who were allowed to partake of the Eucharist.

[38] Can. 15: "... viaticum tamen omnibus in morte positis non est negandum."—Bruns, II, 149.

[39] Can. 36—Bruns, II, 172.

[40] CC. 6, 7 and 8, C. XXVI, q. VI. Canon 6 reads: "Si quis de corpore exiens novissimum et necessarium communionis viaticum expetit, non ei denegetur. Quod si in desperatione positus post acceptum communionem iterum sanus fuerit factus, tantum oratione particeps sit, sacramentum vero non accipiat donec institutum penitentiae impleat tempus. Qui ergo in exitu mortis sunt, et desiderant accipere sacramentum, cum consideratione et probatione episcopi accipere debent." The *Glossa Ordinaria* s. v. *necessariam* explained that Viaticum was necessary for the reason that It cancelled venial sin. Cf. c. 1, C. XXVI, q. VII: "... ne illis ianua pietatis clausa videatur, orationibus et consolationibus ecclesiasticis, sacra unctione olei inuncti, secundum statuta sanctorum patrum communione viatici reficiantur."

the common teaching of theologians that the reception of Holy Viaticum is of divine obligation. How then is the ancient practice of refusing It to dying penitents to be reconciled with this doctrine? In an effort to provide an answer, Gaspari (1852-1934) pointed out that the councils which forbade the reception of Holy Viaticum on the part of dying penitents were merely local councils, and that the command of Christ was conditional, namely, that one is to receive Holy Communion provided the Church allowed him to do so.[41]

By way of further investigation of the problem, one may well point out that before a law, either divine or ecclesiastical, becomes binding it must be promulgated.[42] The authors are divided on the question as to when the divine precepts of Christ began to bind. Some maintain that objectively the law of Christ obtained its binding force at the death of Christ or at least after the first Pentecost. Others hold that it began to bind only when it was sufficiently divulged throughout the entire world, and in consequence did not become binding until after the death of the last apostle. Subjectively, however, individuals were not bound until they received knowledge of the particular precept. The question therefore resolves itself to this: did the bishops of the early Church advert to the fact that the reception of Holy Viaticum was of divine precept? In the light of so much subsequent discussion relative to the existence of such a precept, one might readily surmise that the awareness of it escaped the attention of the theological and canonical mind of the early Church.

Another avenue of escape from the apparent conflict is provided through the realization of the fact that, even though men are bound to receive Holy Viaticum in virtue of a divine command, there exists a similar divine precept to

[41] *Tractatus Canonicus de Eucharistia* (2 vols., Parisiis, 1897), II, n. 1149 (hereafter cited *De Eucharistia*).

[42] M. Lohmuller, *The Promulgation of Law,* The Catholic University of America Canon Law Studies, n. 241 (Washington, D. C.: The Catholic University of America Press, 1947), p. 23.

the effect that Holy Communion is to be denied to the unworthy. With the passage of time, the popes and councils took cognizance of the divine precept enjoining the reception of Holy Viaticum with the effect of reversing the rigorous practices of the earlier times.[43]

Article 3. The Beginnings of Current General Legislation

It may be said that the formative years of the body of general canonical legislation centered around the period which witnessed the compilation of the *Decree* of Gratian (ca. 1140) and the collections of the Decretals. The various collections of laws which made their appearance at that time had a crystallizing effect on the preceding legislation and served as a basis for subsequent legislation.

Relative to the laws and legislative prescriptions touching on Holy Viaticum, there is evidence of their having undergone that same stabilizing and generalizing effect. This will be borne out particularly with regard to the minister of Holy Viaticum, his obligation and his rights; and with regard to the manner in which Holy Viaticum was administered, the manner of bringing It to the sick, the actual method of administration and the relaxation of the law of the Eucharistic fast.

Concerning the minister of Holy Viaticum, the testimony of some of the early Fathers affords a basis for the conclusion that at least under extraordinary circumstances the laity administered the Eucharist to themselves and to others.[44] When the Eucharist was received from the hands of the laity this kind of reception generally occurred after the manner of Holy Viaticum, that is to say, when the recipients were in danger of death. This practice in common with that of the private reservation undoubtedly had its

[43] Cf. *infra*, pp. 40-45.

[44] Cf. *supra*, p. 13, where evidence of the practice of private reservation of the Eucharist is given, a practice which in itself leads to the assumption that lay administration was employed.

origin during the stormy years of the persecutions. It continued after that period but only in the form of an abuse. Conciliar legislation prior to the *Decree* of Gratian as also the *Decree* itself forbade priests to allow the laity, men or women, to carry the Blessed Sacrament to the sick, and imposed the penalty of degredation on any priest who violated that law.[45]

But even this legislation relative to the administration of Holy Viaticum from the hands of the laity insinuates that under ordinary circumstances the priest was the minister of the sacrament. This is borne out by much of the conciliar legislation of the early centuries. The *Statuta Ecclesiae Antiqua* (early fifth century) mentioned the *sacerdos* as the minister of penance and communion for those who were thought to be near death.[46]

The Council of Mainz (847) decreed that the sick be refreshed with the Communion of Viaticum *per presbyteros*.[47] In a similar manner the Council of Pavia (850) ordered that penance, extreme unction and the Holy Eucharist be administered by the priest of the place, by a neighbouring priest, or by the bishop.[48] Finally the Council of Anse (990), near Lyons, permitted no one except the priest (and the bishop) to administer Holy Viaticum.[49]

[45] Council of Rouen (650), Cap. 2, can. 7—Bruns, II, 268; c. 29, D. II, *de cons.*: "Pervenit ad notitiam nostram quod quidem presbyteri in tantum parvipendunt divina mysteria ut laico aut foeminae Sacrum Corpus Domini tradant ad deferendum infirmis.... Igitur interdicit per omnia synodus ne talis temeraria praesumptio ulterius fiat; sed omnimodo presbyter per semetipsum infirmum communicet. Quod si aliter fecerit, gradus sui periculo subiacebit."

[46] Can. 76—Bruns, I, 148; Mansi, III, 957. In the fifth century, however, the term *sacerdos* could mean either a priest or a bishop. It was only from the sixth century that the word became more restricted in meaning so as to apply only to a priest. In the early Church the bishop alone was regarded as the ordinary minister of all of the sacraments and the only true pastor.

[47] Can. 26—Mansi, XIV, 910; Hardouin, V, 13.

[48] Can. 8—Mansi,XIV, 932-933.

[49] Can. 1: "Ac vetaverunt a nullo homine Corpus et Sanguinem [praes]tare[i] ad infirmum nisi sacerdo[te]s sol]e[ius."—Mansi, XIX, 101.

The tendency of this conciliar legislation was to designate the priest as the ordinary minister of Holy Viaticum. In keeping with that tendency, the *Decree* of Gratian further emphasized the designation of the priest as the ordinary minister of the sacrament of the Eucharist in general and of Holy Viaticum in particular.[50]

Hostiensis (Henricus de Sugusio, †1271), in commenting upon canon 20 of the IV General Council of the Lateran (1215),[51] charged with the ministry of the Blessed Sacrament that priest who through his appointment was held to residence in his parish and in consequence had the obligation of administering to the needs of the people. It was he who was to carry the Eucharist to the sick with all due reverence, and it was upon him that rested the obligation of providing Holy Viaticum for all those who were committed to his care.[52]

Panormitanus (Nicolaus de Tudeschis, 1386-1453) in his commentary on the Decretals of Gregory IX reflected the interpretation of the law of his day by stating that it was the right and duty of the parish priest to care for the sick. He referred to this priest as the *sacerdos parochialis*, upon whom rested the obligation not to leave his parish until he had first made sure that no one was in danger of dying without Holy Viaticum.[53]

[50] C. 93, D. II *de cons.*, taken from the Capitularium of Ingelheim (809), cap. 16; c. 18, D. XCIII, taken from the *Statuta Ecclesiae Antiqua*, can. 38; c. 29, D. II, *de cons.*—Rufinus, when commenting upon this canon which stated that the priest was to communicate the sick *per semetipsum*, taught that if the priest was sick and there existed an urgent necessity for the dispensing of the sacrament, he could do so *per puerum.*—*Summa Decretorum* (ed. Heinrich Singer, Paderborn, 1902), p. 554; c. 8, C. XXVI, q. 6.

[51] C. 1, X, *de custodia eucharistiae, christmatis, et aliorum sacramentorum*, III, 44.

[52] *Commentaria in Quinque Libros Decretalium* (3 vols., Venetiis, 1581), Lib. III, tit. 41, c. 10; lib. III, tit. 44, c, 1 (hereafter cited *Commentaria*).

[53] *Commentaria in quinque Decretalium Libros* (5 vols., Venetiis, 1589), Lib. III, tit. 41, c. 1.

The concept of "pastor" seems to have been fairly well defined in the thirteenth century. The Council of Tarragona (1229) prescribed that the "proper pastor" was to administer the sacraments to only those who belonged to the territory over which he was placed. The Council, however, made an exception in the case of baptism and penance in the time of necessity, for then any priest could administer them. Though the Council did not mention Holy Viaticum, it is reasonable to suppose that It too was included in the exceptions allowed. At any rate, normally Viaticum was according to the Council to be administered by the "proper priest."[54]

From the thirteenth to the sixteenth century there existed a problem with regard to the minister of Holy Viaticum. On the one hand, the rights of the "parochial" or "proper" priest came to be more clearly defined. At least in theory he was given the exclusive right to administer Holy Viaticum to all within the territory assigned to him. On the other hand, due to the granting of many privileges to religious and to individuals, this right of the "proper priest" came to be diminished.[55] As a result, many disputes arose between the religious and the parochial priests, disputes which oftentimes became a source of scandal to the faithful.

Religious priests often assumed parochial functions inclusive of the act of administering at the beside of the dying.[56] Gratian, however, pointed to a restriction of right on the part of the monks to administer Holy Viaticum. He did not in this connection explicitly mention Viaticum, but spoke rather, in more general terms, of all parochial duties inclusive of the administration of Holy Viaticum. These duties the monks were not allowed to perform even in a case

[54] Can. 6—Mansi, XXIV, 1108.

[55] Cf. Gasparri, *De Eucharistia,* II, n. 1078.

[56] Cf. R. Shuhler, *Privileges of Religious to Absolve and to Dispense,* The Catholic University of America Canon Law Studies, n. 186 (Washington, D. C.: The Catholic University of America Press, 1943), p. 16.

of necessity, unless they had the permission of the bishop and the consent of the abbot.[57]

Clement V (1305-1314), in the Council of Vienna (1311-1312), tried to bring about a settlement of the contention between the parochial priests and the priests of the Religious Orders. In so doing he decreed that any priest religious who dared to administer Holy Communion, whether of devotion or as Viaticum, or who assisted at marriages without the permission of the "proper priest," would thereby incur an excommunication reserved to the Holy See. The religious, however, retained the right as priests to administer Holy Viaticum to their own domestic servants and to the poor living in their houses.[58]

This measure, while emphatically vindicating the right of the proper pastor to administer the sacraments in his own parish, and penalizing those who infringed upon this right, nevertheless conceded to religious a similar right relative to the administration of the last sacraments within their own houses.[59] In imposing the penalty and in upholding the right of the priest religious with respect to his own subjects, the measure departed from the older legislation.

In 1516 Leo X (1513-1521) forbade Regulars to administer to the sick and dying even after the pastor had denied them his services. This he did, he stated, to preserve mutual charity and tranquility between the bishops and religious superiors, to safeguard the peace and harmony of the universal Church, and to remove the cause of scandal. They could administer the sacrament only through the intervention of a just cause, the justness of which was sworn to under the seal of a notary or in the presence of two witnesses. He further decreed that the administration of the sacraments to the laity serving in the monastery was to be

[57] Cc. 1-19 and 41, C. XVI, q. 1.
[58] C. 1, *de privilegiis et excessibus privilegiatorum,* V, 7.
[59] *Loc. cit.*

restircted to the time when they were actually subject to the religious superior.[60]

Even the privileges that were accorded to religious give evidence of the prevailing practice of the times. By way of example one may point to the faculties granted to the Jesuits by Pope Paul III (1534-1549) in the year 1549. Despite the many permissions granted to them by virtue of those faculties, they were forbidden to administer the Eucharist to persons in danger of death, unless they had first received the permission of the proper priest or unless there was an urgent need for their so doing.[61]

About this same time there were granted to chaplains of hospitals many privileges inclusive of the right to hear the confessions of the patients and to administer to them Holy Communion and Holy Viaticum. After the middle of the thirteenth century, many bishops granted this privilege to the priests who cared for the spiritual needs of the sick in the hospitals within their diocese. In 1274 the bishop of Bremen granted such a privilege to the hospital at Kiel, and in 1215 the bishop of Utrecht granted a similar privilege to the hospital at Delft.[62]

About this time also there began to be formulated the distinction between the ordinary and extraordinary minister of the sacrament of the Eucharist. While such a distinction did not exist in the terminology that was current at the time of the compilation of the *Decree* of Gratian, yet it did exist in practice, for while the priest was regarded as the ordinary minister, the deacon was allowed to act in a case of urgent necessity.[63]

[60] Const. *Dum intra*, 19 dec. 1516—*Fontes*, n. 72.

[61] Const. *Licet debitum*, 18 oct. 1549, 29—*Bullarum Diplomatum et Privilegiorum Sanctorum Pontificum Taurinensis Editio* (24 vols. et Appendix, Augustae Taurinorum, 1857-1872), VI, 389 (hereafter cited *Bull. Rom. Taur.*).

[62] Cf. P. Browe, "Die Kommunion in der Pfarrkirche," *Zeitschrift für katholische Theologie* (Innsbruck, 1877-), LIII (1929), 488.

[63] C. 18, D. XCIII: "... praesente presbytero, diaconus Eucharistiam Corporis Christi populo, si necessitas cogit, iussus eroget." This law was originally contained in the *Statuta Ecclesiae Antiqua*, can. 38—Bruns, I, 145.

Further recognition of the deacon's rōle as extraordinary minister of the Eucharist was given by Hostiensis. He allowed the deacon to act in a case of necessity or with the permission of the priest or of the bishop.[64] To his vindication of the deacon's right to act as extraordinary minister of the Eucharist there may be added that of contemporary synodal legislation.[65] The more specific enactments of the latter are to be found in the Synod of Nīmes (1283). It allowed the deacon to act in two cases: 1). In the absence of a priest, and 2) in a case of urgent necessity, in which he did not have to seek the permission of the priest.[66]

In view of the importance which the early Church attached to the oral reception of the Eucharist before death, and in view also of the fact that the issues of eternity were often considered to rest upon the sick person's reception of the "food for the journey," considerable stress was laid upon the obligation of the priest to provide for Its timely administration.[67]

In evidence of this one may point to the Council of Aixla-Chapelle (836), which in describing the pastoral functions of priests charged with the care of souls emphasized especially their duty of sedulously guarding the faithful committed to their care, and of seeing to it that none died without the last sacraments.[68] In both the *Decree* of Gratian and in the Decretals of Gregory IX this same obligation of

[64] *Commentaria*, Lib. III, tit. 41, c. 10; lib. III, tit. 44, c. 1.

[65] Council of York (1195), can. 6—Mansi, XXII, 653; Odo, Bishop of Paris (1196-1208), *Synodicae Constitutiones*, Cap. V, n. 5—*MPL*, CCXII, 60; Synod of Nîmes (1283), *De sacramento Eucharistiae, et extrema unctione*—Hardouin, VII, 914.

[66] *Loc. cit.*

[67] Cf. P. Schaff-H. Wace, *The Nicene and Post-Nicene Fathers of the Church* (second series, 14 vols., New York: Scribners, 1900), XIV, 29-31, where, in their commentary on canon 13 of the I General Council of Nicaea, the authors give an excursus on Communion of the sick.

[68] *De Vita et Doctrina Inferiorum Ordinum*, canon 5—*Monumenta Germaniae Historica* (*MGH*) (188 vols. incomplete, Hannoverae, 1826-) *Leges in 4*, Sectio III (*Concilia*), Tomus II, pars II (ed. A. Werminghoff, 1908), 711-712.

caring for the sick and of ministering to their needs is set down as a duty not to be lightly regarded, the penalty of degredation being in store for any priest who neglectfully failed to fulfill it.[69] And so great was the desire of the Church that none should die without first having received Holy Viaticum, that Its administration was allowed even during the time of a general interdict, although it was not held as permissible to administer the sacrament of extreme unction.[70]

Relative to the actual administration of Holy Viaticum the sources are productive of much material. But inasmuch as no specific mention is made of the fact that Holy Viaticum was brought to the sick in a private manner, the use of such a method in early times is entirely a matter of conjecture. One feels, however, that such a method must have been in use especially during the period of the persecutions, when the public bringing of the sacrament to the sick might well have occasioned a further outburst of persecution and even a profanation of the Sacred Species. Outside of those abnormal and trying conditions, the sources reveal that it was customary to bring the Eucharist to the sick publicly.

The various enactments touching on his public function were such as to demand a proper respect and reverence for so holy a sacrament. Detailed instructions regulating the conduct of both the priest who carried the Blessed Sacrament and the laity who happened to come into contact with the procession were enacted. The vestments that were to be worn, the prayers that were to be said, and the special rubrics that were to be followed were all determined by the law of the Church. In the Council of York (1195) it was recommended that the laity be instructed to kneel and recite prayers while the procession passed.[71] Similar instructions were issued by the Council of Oxford (1222), and in addi-

[69] C. 93, D. II *de cons.*; c. 29, D. II, *de cons.;* c. 63, D. L.

[70] C. 11, X, *de poenitentiis et remissionibus*, V, 38.

[71] Can. 1—Mansi, XXII, 653.

tion it was indicated that, if circumstances so warranted, the Eucharist could be brought privately.[72]

About the same time, in a letter of Pope Honorius III (1216-1227) addressed to archbishops, bishops and other ecclesiastical prelates, it was demanded that the Blessed Sacrament be brought to the sick in a fitting manner. The priest was to carry the Host on his breast in a vessel covered with a veil. The faithful were to be taught to genuflect as a mark of reverence whenever they came in contact with the procession, and all who failed to observe these prescriptions were subject to ecclesiastical penalty.[73] In addition to these requirements, Hostiensis (†1271) made mention of further regulations to the effect that a bell was to be rung and that the priest who carried the Blessed Sacrament was to wear a surplice and a stole.[74]

In order that Holy Viaticum might be brought to the sick in a safe and becoming manner, each church was required to have a suitable pyx in which to place It. To this end, Hincmar, Archbishop of Reims, in 858 demanded an annual report from the churches of his docese concerning the pyx used for the reservation of the Blessed Sacrament and the bringing of It to the sick.[75] Similar demands were later reflected by Regino, Abbot of Prüm (†915),[76] and by Ivo, Bishop of Chartres (1090-1117).[77]

Yet despite these decrees there does not seem to have been any uniformity regarding the kind of vessel that was to be used. During the middle ages and even up to the

[72] De Sacramento Altaris; "... Eucharistia tam calice quam lucerna praecedente, ad aegrotos per sacerdotem, aut in summa necessitate per diaconum cum solemnitate et reverentia defrtaur, nisi forte remisso loci aut temporis inaequalitas interdicat...."—Mansi, XXII, 1175.

[73] C. 10, X, *de celebratione missarum, et sacramento eucharistiae et divinis officiis*, III, 41; A. Potthast, *Regesta Pontificum Romanorum inde ab anno post Christum natum MCXCVIII ad annum MCCCIV* (2 vols., Berolini, 1874-1875), n. 6166 (hereafter cited Potthast).

[74] *Commentaria*, Lib. III, tit. 41, c. 2.

[75] *Capitula*, VIII—*MPL*, CXXV, 779.

[76] *De Ecclesiae Disciplina*, I, 69—*MPL*, CXXXII, 205.

[77] *Decretum*, cap. 19—*MPL*, CLXI, 165.

eighteenth century various methods were employed. Sometimes Viaticum was carried in the chalice, sometimes in a small square linen cloth like a corporal. At other times It was placed in a burse which was suspended from a cord fastened around the neck. In the Syrian Church It was carried wrapped in paper or between the leaves of trees.[78]

Various materials were used in the construction of the pyx: alabaster, crystal, glass, tin, copper, wood, ivory, marble, silver and gold were among the most common.[79] In nearly all cases, however, the interior was of gold. In the year 1227, the Council of Münster decreed that the pyx should be of ivory, silver or gold, and should always be placed in a clean white linen cloth.[80]

Relative to the actual administration of the sacrament of the Eucharist there is sufficient evidence to show that it was the ordinary rule of the early Church for the faithful, as well as the celebrating priest, to receive Holy Communion under both species.[81] On occasion, however, when convenience or necessity required it, the faithful partook of only one species. Tertullian (ca. 160-ca. 240) was witness to the custom of receiving the Eucharist at home under the species of bread alone.[82] Dionysius of Alexandria, in relating the

[78] Cf. J. Corblet, *Histoire Dogmatique, Liturgique et Archéologique du Sacrement de l'Eucharistie* (2 vols., Parisiis, 1885-1886), I, 379 and 390. As evidences of these usages the author refers to the statutes of Odo (1196), Bishop of Paris (1196-1208), to the Council of Westminster (1200), and to the *Resolutiones Canonicae* of St. James of Edessa (687).

[79] Cf. W. T. Cavanaugh, *The Reservation of the Blessed Sacrament,* The Catholic University of America Canon Law Studies, n. 40 (Washington, D. C.: The Catholic University of America, 1927), p. 67.

[80] Can. XI—Mansi, XXIV, 315.

[81] Cf. Origen (185/6-254), *Commentarium in Evangelium secundum Joannem,* Lib. XXVIII, cap. 4—*MPG,* XIV, 687; St. Cyprian, *De* Lapsis, cap. 25—*MPL,* IV, 485; St. Cyril of Jerusalem (†386), *Catechesis XXIII, Mystagogica,* V—*MPG,* XXXIII, 1125; St. Ambrose, *De Mysteriis,* Lib. I, n. 48—*MPL,* XVI, 405; St. Augustine, *Ep. CCXVII,* cap. 5, n. 16—*MPL,* XXXIII, 984.

[82] *Ad Uxorem,* Lib. II, cap. 5—*MPL,* I, 1296.

incident of Serapion,[83] indicated that he received Holy Viaticum under the form of bread.

Cardinal Bona (1609-1674) stated that outside of Mass and outside of the church Communion was administered under the form of bread alone. He alluded to the practice of the faithful who brought the Eucharist to their homes and on journeys whenever they could not be present in church to receive It under both species and in the usual manner. He further remarked that the Greeks administered Holy Communion to their sick under the form of bread, which they sometimes dipped in wine.[84]

On the other hand, the XI Council of Toledo (675) allowed the reception of Holy Viaticum under the species of wine alone, but this was by way of exception, when on account of the dryness of the mouth the sick person was unable to receive the Eucharist under the form of bread.[85]

During the first twelve centuries, however, there were indications that Viaticum was also administered under the double form. Ménard (1585-1644), in his *Notes of the Gregorian Sacramentary,* listed several formulas which were in use in the time of Gregory the Great (590-604), some of which implied the use of the double form in the administration of Holy Communion to those in danger of death.[86] It seems likely also that It would have been administered under both species whenever Mass was celebrated in the house of the sick person, a practice which had become common in the eighth century.[87]

From what has been said it can be readily seen that neither the administration of Holy Viaticum under both

[83] Cf. *cupra,* p. 9.

[84] *Rerum Liturgicarum Libri Duo* (Romae, 1671), Lib. II, cap. 28.

[85] Can. 11: "... solet enim humanae naturae infirmitas in ipso mortis exitu praegravata tanto siccitatis pondere deprimi, ut nullus ciborum illationibus refici, sed vix tantumdem illati delectetur poculi gratia sustentari.... "—Bruns, I, 314.

[86] —*MPL,* LXXVIII, 528-565.

[87] Cf. Many, *De Missa,* p. 55. The author stated that many ancient sacramentaries testified to this, and that some contained a special "Missa pro Infirmo."

species nor Its administration under one species was the universal practice of the Church up to the fifteenth century. Its distribution under one or both species does not belong to the essence of the sacrament nor was it a precept given by Christ. Rather it was the prerogative of the Church to determine the manner in which Holy Communion was to be received, and this the Church did in the Council of Constance (1414-1418) in 1415. From that time onward the universal law of the Western Church restricted the reception of Holy Communion under both species to the celebrating priest, while the Eastern Church retained the old practice of administering Holy Communion under the double form.[88]

Even though the Council legislated nothing specifically concerning the administration of Holy Viaticum, it is beyond doubt that the manner of Its administration likewise fell under the general enactment of the council, so that thereafter It could no longer be administered under both species. Any departure from this general rule could obtain only by reason of a special privilege granted by the Holy See. Benedict XIV (1675-1758) mentioned that at one time the kings of France enjoyed such a privilege both on the day of their coronation and in danger of death.[89]

Relative to the order in which the last sacraments were to be administered, there seems to have been more than one change over the course of the centuries. The earliest extant

[88] Sessio XIII, 15 iun. 1415: "... Et sicut haec consuetudo ad evitandum aliqua pericula et scandala est rationabiliter introducta: quod licet in primitiva ecclesia huiusmodi sacramentum reciperetur a fidelibus sub utraque specie, tamen postea a conficientibus sub utraque specie et a laicis tantummado sub specie panis suscipiatur, cum firmissime credendum sit et nullatenus dubitandum, integrum Christi corpus et sanguinem tam sub specie panis, quam sub specie vini veractiter contineri...."—Mansi, XXVII, 7270; Hardouin, VIII, 381B; Denzinger, n. 626. In condemning the errors of the Hussites and Wyclifites, the Council showed that the practice of the Western Church had already prevailingly become that of Communion under one species.

[89] *De Sacrosancto Missae Sacrificio Libri Tres* (2. ed., Romae, 1748), Lib. II, cap. 22, n. 32.

reference seems to place Holy Viaticum prior to extreme unction. Pope Leo IV (847-855), speaking of the sacrament of extreme unction in the Council of Pavia (850), gave his approval of this order. Later, however, the reverse seems to have been the case. Then Viaticum was to be administered last in keeping with the idea that It constituted the food for the journey, and as such should be the last sacrament received by the dying person.[90]

Suarez (1548-1617), in referring to this question, stated that it was an ancient custom to administer Viaticum lastly, a practice which was evident from many of the lives of the saints. He added, however, that there was no definite precept governing the order to be followed in the administration of the last sacraments, and that one could be administered without the other apart from the intervention of any grave cause.[91] Among certain Religious Orders it is still the practice to administer the sacrament of extreme unction prior to that of Holy Viaticum.[92]

Later, however, there was a general reversion to the older order, which order obtains at the present day. From what has been said it readily appears that during the period under discussion there was no definite rule of law regulating the order in which the last sacraments were to be administered; the actual practice rather depended on various local customs.

As early as the second century it had become the almost universal practice to observe a strict natural fast prior to the reception of Holy Communion.[93] Yet while this was the

[90] Cf. Denzinger, n. 315; Regino, Abbot of Prüm, *De Ecclesiae Disciplina*, Cap. CXIX—*MPL*, CXXXII, 215.

[91] *De Extrema Unctione*, q. 90, art. IV, disp. 44, sect. 1, n. 8—*Opera Omnia* (28 vols., ed. nova, Parisiis: L. Vivès, 1856-1861), XXII, 865.

[92] Cf. Felix M. Cappello, *Tractatus Canonico-Moralis de Sacramentis* (5 vols., Vol. I, 4. ed., 1945; Vol. II, 4. ed., 1944; Vol. III, 2. ed., 1942; Vol. IV, 2. ed., 1947; Vol. V, 5. ed., 1947, Romae-Taureni: Marietti), III, n. 88 (heerafter cited *De Sacramentis*).

[93] Cf. Tertullian, *Ad Uxorem*, Lib. II, c. 5—*MPL*, I, 1296; Canons of Hippolytus (217-235), n. 205—Duchesne, *Christian Worship*, Appendix; St. Basil, *De Ieiunio*, *Homilia I*, n. 6—*MPG*, XXXI, 171; St.

general law in both the Eastern and the Western Church, an exception was allowed in favor of those who were sick and in the danger of death. When one was sick but not in the danger of death, the law was still binding in its universal obligatory force.[94]

In the Western Church the *Decree* of Burchard pointed to a relaxation of the law of the Eucharistic fast in favor of those who were about to receive Holy Viaticum, and attributed the ruling to Pope Eutychianus, who ruled the Church in the years 275-283.[95]

In the Eastern Church a similar relaxation was referred to in the Canons of Timothy, Bishop of Alexandria (381-385),[96] and likewise in those of St. James of Edessa (687).[97]

In the fifteenth century the relaxation of the law of the Eucharistic fast in favor of the recipient of Holy Viaticum underwent a more stablizing and generalizing effect. The Council of Constance (1414-1418), in its thirteenth session confirmed the universal Latin practice that the laity were to receive Holy Communion under the form of bread alone, and that they were to receive It while they were fasting, except in case of sickness or in any other necessity approved

---

Gregory Nazienzen, *Oratio XL—MPG,* XXXVI, 402; c. 54, D. III. *de cons.*

[94] Cf. T. Anglin, *The Eucharistic Fast,* The Catholic University of America Canon Law Studies, n. 124 (Washington, D. C.: The Catholic University of America Press, 1941), p. 35.

[95] Lib. V, cap. 35: "Qui acceperit sacrificium post cibum ... nisi pro viatico ... poeniteat."—*MPL,* CXL, 759. The quotation is headed "Ex decreto Eutychii Papae," but its authenticity seems altogether unacceptable.

[96] *Resolutiones Canonicae Timothei Alexandrini*: "Nisi necessitas urgeat, non licet edere quidquam aut bibere ... nisi ex causa gravissima infirmitatis, cum vitae periculo."—Many, *De Missa,* p. 326.

[97] *Resolutiones Canonicae Jacobi Edessini*: "Nemini licet cibum aliquem aut panem quemcumque capere ante sacramentorum sumptionem, nisi urgente morbi necessitate, aut in mortis periculo."—T. Lamy (1827-1907), *Dissertatio de Syrorum Fide et Disciplina in Re Eucharistica* (Lovanii: Universitatis Catholica Lovaniensis, 1859), p. 183.

by the Church as not requiring the observance of the law of the Eucharistic fast.[98] This legislation of the thirteenth session later received the approval of Pope Martin V (1417-1431), who presided at the last session of the Council in 1418.[99]

[98] Sessio XIII, 15 iun. 1415: "... neque a fidelibus recipi non ieiunis, nisi in casu infirmitatis aut alterius necessitatis a iure vel Ecclesia concesso vel admisso...."—Denzinger, n. 626; Mansi, XXVII, 727C; Hardouin, VIII, 381B.

[99] Const. *In eminentis*, 22 febr. 1418—*Fontes*, n. 44.

CHAPTER III

HOLY VIATICUM FROM THE COUNCIL OF TRENT (1545-1563) TO THE CODE OF CANON LAW (1918)

Article 1. The Legislation and Cetechism of the Council of Trent

Section 1. The Legislation of the Council of Trent

The Council of Trent, convoked by Pope Paul III (1534-1549) on May 22, 1542, held its first session on December 13, 1545. In the list of general councils it holds first place, not only because of its restatement of Catholic doctrine and its initiation of a genuine reform, but also because of its extraordinary influence both within and outside of the Church. Its purpose was twofold: to define the doctrines of the Church that had been subjected to heretical attack, and to bring about a thorough reform of the interior Christian life.

With regard to Holy Viaticum, the Council does not contain much specific legislation, a fact which perhaps can be attributed to the absence of abuses relating to the particular sphere of Eucharistic belief and practice. The Council did state, however, that the practice of taking the Eucharist to the sick and of reserving It carefully for that purpose in churches, besides being exceedingly reasonable and appropriate, was also enjoined by numerous councils and was a very ancient observance of the Church. Accordingly the Council decreed that this salutary and necessary custom was by all means to be retained, and declared anathema anyone who denied that it was lawful to reserve the Eucharist and to carry It with honor to the sick.[1]

[1] Conc. Trident., sess. XIII, *Decretum de Sanctissimo Eucharistiae Sacramento,* c. 6 and can. 7: "Si quis dixerit, non licere sacram Eucharistiam in sacraria reservari, sed statim post consecrationem abstantibus necessaria distribuendam; aut non licere, ut illa ad infirmos

In its twenty-first session the Council declared that laymen, and also clerics when not offering the sacrifice of the Mass, were not bound by the divine law to receive the Holy Eucharist under both species. The Church, therefore, cognizant of its authority in disciplinary matters, legislated that laymen should communicate under the one form of bread.[2] The further question proposed for discussion, namely, whether the reasons for so legislating were such that under no conditions was the use of the chalice to be permitted to anyone, and whether in a particular case and under specific conditions its use was to be conceded to any nation and under what conditions, were to be referred to the pope, who would judge each petition according to his own prudence.[3] Thus the Fathers of Council of Trent saw fit to re-enact the earlier legislation of the Council of Constance,[4] and to reaffirm its stand on the question of administering the sacrament of the Eucharist under the species of bread alone.

With regard to children as the recipients of Holy Viaticum, a question which will be discussed more fully later in this chapter, the Council legislated that it was not necessary for infants who lacked the use of reason—*parvuli*—to receive sacramamental Communion, but at the same time those who practised this custom in the early days of the Church were not to be condemned.[5] In the light of this teaching, the reception of Holy Viaticum was not to be regarded as necessary for such children.

One further question of importance to the present work, namely, whether the reception of Holy Viaticum is of divine

---

honorifice deferatur: anathema sit."—H. J. Schroeder, *Canons and Decrees of the Council of Trent* (St. Louis: Herder, 1941), pp. 353 and 356.

[2] Sess. XXI, *Doctrina de communione sub utraque specie et parvulorum*, c. 1 and can. 2—Schroeder, *op. cit.*, pp. 406 and 409.

[3] Conc. Trident., sess. XXII, de ref., *Decretum super petitione concessionis calicis*, following c. 11—Schroeder, *op. cit.*, p. 431.

[4] Cf. *supra*, p. 31.

[5] Sess. XIII, *Doctrina de communione sub utraque specie et parvulorum*, c. 4 and can. 4—Schroeder, *op. cit.*, pp. 408-409.

or of ecclesiastical precept, was touched upon by the Council. And while it did not definitely decide the issue, it at least afforded a basis for the argument in favor of its being of divine precept. It stated that Christ wished this sacrament to be received as the spiritual food of souls, whereby they might be nourished and strengthened and preserved from mortal sin.[6] And if Christ so wished that the Eucharist be received, certainly He must have intended It to be received in danger of death, a time when spiritual strength and nourishment are most necessary.

Section 2. The Doctrine of the Catechism of the Council of Trent

The Catechism of the Council of Trent was issued by order of Pope St. Pius V (1566-1572) to the end that parish priests might have at their disposal, in brief and concise form, the various doctrines defined by the Council itself. Bearing, as it did, papal approval, it can readily be regarded as an authoritative statement of Catholic doctrine, and as a true indication of the ecclesiastical practice of the times.

Relative to the present subject, the Catechism stated that the Eucharist was also frequently called "Viaticum" by the sacred writers, both because It is the spiritual food by which men are sustained on their pilgrimage through life, and also because It paves the way to eternal glory and happiness. Therefore, according to the ancient usage of the Church, pastors were to see to it that none of the faithful were permitted to die without this sacrament.[7]

With regard to the minister of Holy Viaticum, the Catechism taught nothing specifically. It merely reiterated the general doctrine enunciated by the Council, namely that priests are the ordinary ministers of the sacrament of the

[6] Sess. XIII, *Decretum de Santissimo Eucharistiae Sacramento,* c. 2—Schroeder, *op. cit.,* p. 351.

[7] Callan and McHugh, *The Catechism of the Council of Trent for Parish Priests issued by order of Pope Pius V* (English translation, tenth printing, Wagner: New York, 1947), p. 215.

Eucharist both as to Its consecration and administration. In defining the position of the laity, the Catechism stated clearly that not only were they not allowed to touch the Sacred Host, but also it was forbidden them to touch the vessels and linens necessary for consecration, unless there was a grave reason for so doing.[8]

Concerning children as the recipients of the Eucharist, the Catechism stated that even though the law obliging the faithful to partake of the Eucharist was sanctioned by the authority of Christ and the Church, nevertheless there were to be excepted those who on account of their tender age had not yet attained the use of reason. The reasons advanced for this exception were to be found in the fact that such children were unable to discern the Eucharist from common bread and were incapable of sufficient piety and devotion. Accordingly the ancient practice of allowing such children to receive the Eucharist was thenceforth to be discontinued, and the right to determine the presence or absence of the necessary dispositions was to be left in the hands of the parents or the confessor.[9] Thus, in the administration of Holy Viaticum to children, pastors were afforded a norm of action by which they were to be guided, and in accordance with which they were to deny It to children who had not attained the necessary discretionary powers or devotional capability.

The Catechism, however, stated that it was lawful to administer Holy Viaticum to the insane, provided that prior to the state of insanity they had evidenced a devotion for the Eucharist, and provided that there was no danger of irreverence.[10]

In restating theounciliar law which forbade the administration of the Eucharist under the double form, the Catechism advanced the reasons for its introduction. Principally it was enacted with a view to obviating the danger of

[8] Callan and McHugh, *op. cit.*, pp. 253-254.
[9] Callan andMcHugh, *op. cit.*, p. 251.
[10] Callan and McHugh, *loc. cit.*

spilling the Precious Blood, and, since the Eucharist had to be reserved for the Communion of the sick, there was the further danger that, if the Holy Communion under the species of wine were reserved for a time, the consecrated wine would turn acid.[11]

Finally, with regard to the effects of Holy Viaticum, the Catechism declared:

> When the hour of departing from this world shall have arrived, like Elias, who in the strength of the bread baked upon the hearth, walked to Horeb, the Mount of God, men too, invigorated by the strengthening influence of this heavenly bread, will ascend to unending glory and bliss.[12]

ARTICLE 2. LEGISLATION AFTER THE COUNCIL OF TRENT

Before all further exploration of the historical development of the law as it touches on Holy Viaticum, it is proper to pause in order to assess briefly the importance of the post-Tridentine period. The centuries that immediately followed the Council of Trent have been rightly termed "the golden age of canonical science."[13] To it belongs a galaxy of authors who, in regard to Canon Law, were of the highest merit. Even today, after the promulgation of the Code of Canon Law, the opinion of the majority of canonists of that period is in almost daily use. For today the disposition of the present law, in so far as it agrees either in whole or in part with the former law, is to be interpreted in the light of the majority opinion of those approved authors and canonists.[14] Furthermore, the common and constant opinion

[11] Callan and McHugh, *op. cit.*, p. 252.

[12] Callan and McHugh, *op. cit.*, p. 244.

[13] Cf. A. Van Hove, *Prolegomena ad Codicem Iuris Canonici* (ed. altera, auctior et emendatior, Mechliniae-Romae: H. Dessian, 1945), p. 533.

[14] Cf. *Codex Iuris Canonici Pii X Pontificis Maximi iussu digestus Benedicti Papae XV auctoritate Promulagatus* (Romae: Typis Polyglottis Vaticanis, 1917), can. 6, n. 2 (hereafter simply the canon is cited).

of approved authors affords a guiding norm in cases wherein the law itself is silent.[15]

But the remarkable post-Tridentine development of canonical science is to be attributed not solely to canonists. The many theologians of that period, rather than wholly confining themselves to the field of theology proper, often digressed into the field of canon law. Many of these theologians will be cited in this article.

Section 1. The Obligation to Receive Holy Viaticum

A. The nature of the obligation

The determination of the precise nature of the obligation which binds one when in danger of death to receive Holy Communion was a problem which loomed large in the theological and canonical minds of the period. Whether there existed any particular obligation in the matter, and, if so, whether that obligation derived its binding force from the divine or from the ecclesiastical law, were questions which presented themselves. So few, indeed, were those who denied the existence of any specific obligation that their opinion can be ignored as not being tenable at any time.

With regard to the remaining question, namely, whether the obligation derives from the divine or from the ecclesiastical law, the authors seem to have been divided into two main schools of thought, one holding that it was merely an ecclesiastical precept, while the other held that it was divine.

First, there were those who, while admitting that there was a divine precept to receive Holy Communion during one's lifetime, inferred from that that one who had already fulfilled that precept was no longer bound by it, not even in danger of death. A positive precept, they held, was sufficiently satisfied by one act. Among the proponents of this

[15] Cf. can. 20.

view were such men as Paludanus (1280-1342), Cajetan (1469-1534) and P. Ledesma (†1616).[16]

Secondly, and in line with the foregoing theory, there were those who held that there was no special obligation deriving from a divine precept binding one to a reception of the Eucharist while one was in danger of death. At most there was only an ecclesiastical precept, or a custom which had obtained the force of a precept. Among the advocates of this view were Bonaventure (1221-1274), Silvester Prieras (1456-1523) and Bartholomaeus Fumus (†1545).[17] In defending their view, they followed the general line of argument that a divine precept once fulfilled no longer binds. The words of Christ: "Unless you eat of the flesh of the Son of Man, and drink his blood, you shall not have life in you,"[18] imposed an obligation which could be satisfied by one reception, just as His words: "Unless a man be born again of water and the Holy Ghost, he cannot enter into the kingdom of heaven,"[19] which likewise imposed an obligation, saw their fulfillment through a single reception of the sacrament of baptism. At most, the obligation to receive Holy Viaticum was by nature ecclesiastical.

Suarez (1548-1617) was among the first to doubt the correctness of this opinion. He was not prepared, however, to depart any further from the haven of common opinion than to state that the theory which supported the divine nature of the precept to receive Holy Viaticum was at least on the side of probability. In support of that theory he himself relied upon the constant practice of the Church, which, he said, had always recognized a special gravity in the obligation to receive Holy Communion in danger of death.[20]

[16] Cf. De Lugo, *De Sacramento Eucharistiae,* disp. XVI, sect. 2, n. 25—*Disputationes Scholasticae et Morales* (ed. nova, 8 vols., Parisiis: L. Vivès, 1868-1869), IV, 140.

[17] Cf. De Lugo, *De Sacramento Eucharistiae,* disp. XVI, sect. 2, n. 26—*op. cit.,* IV, 140.

[18] John, VI: 54.

[19] John, III: 5.

[20] *De Eucharistia,* q. 71, disp. 69, sect. 3, n. 2—*Opera Omnia,* XXI, 533.

From that time onward, a shifting of opinion among theologians and canonists become more pronounced. Vasquez (1549-1604), a contemporary of Suarez, was the first to depart from the hitherto common opinion and to maintain that the obligation to receive Holy Communion while one was in danger of death was of divine origin. In order to justify his stand, he too pointed to the practice of the Church and stressed the nature of the sacrament.[21]

Vasquez was closely followed by De Lugo (1583-1660). According to the latter's view there derived from the divine law an obligation to receive the Eucharist a certain number of times during life, and there was also a special obligation to receive It in danger of death. His use of the phrase "a special obligation" might lead one to suspect that he was evading the issue as to the precise nature of this obligation. He himself, however, interpreted it to mean an obligation that derived its binding force from the divine law.[22] Moreover the nature of the sacrament was such as to give rise to a special obligation demanding its reception whenever there arose a special need for its help. But never could there be a greater need for this divine food than when one was in danger of death.[23]

St. Alphonsus Liguori (1696-1787) taught that there existed a divine precept to receive Holy Viaticum, and that consequently anyone in danger of death or anyone who foresaw that he would be, for example, because of impending battle, was bound under pain of mortal sin to receive It.[24]

The canonists of the period who discussed the question were almost unanimous in their support of the view that the obligation to receive Holy Viaticum was of divine origin.

[21] *Libri Commentariorum in Tertiam Partem S. Thomae* (4 toms. in 3 vols., Lugduni: Sumptibus Jacobi Cardon, 1630-1631), Tom. III, disp. 214, cap. 2, nn. 6-10 (hereafter cited *Libri Commentariorum*).

[22] *De Sacramento Eucharistiae*, disp. XVI, sect. 2, nn. 27 and 33—*op. cit.*, IV, 140 and 142.

[23] *De Sacramento Eucharistiae*, disp. XVI, sect. 2, n. 35—*loc. cit.*

[24] *Theologia Moralis* (4 vols., Taurini: Matietti, 1872), Lib. VI, *De Eucharistia*, n. 290.

Eminent among these were Barbosa (1589-1649)[25] and Pope Benedict XIV (Prosper Lambertini, 1675-1758),[26] both of whom stated that in virtue of the words of Christ: "Unless you eat of the flesh of the Son of Man and drink his blood, you shall not have life in you," there existed a divine precept binding on all of the faithful to receive the sacrament of the Eucharist, not only during one's lifetime but also in danger of death. They concluded by declaring that it could hardly be possible for anyone to hold the contrary opinion and not be branded as temerarious.

Posited the existence of a general divine command to partake of the Eucharist, it is the right and duty of the Church to determine specifically such a general precept. Even though Christ Himself at no time explicitly stated that one in danger of death was to receive the Eucharist, nevertheless it is wholly within the competence of the Church, the divinely appointed interpreter of the revealed truth and the custodian of the sacraments, to interpret the general command of Christ as applying at a certain time, as in danger of death.

Apart from any positive teaching of the Church, it is possible through reasoning from the very nature of the sacrament to derive from the general divine command the special necessity of a reception of the Eucharist in danger of death. The purpose of the command in the mind of the legislator—Christ—was that man should supply a definite spiritual need in partaking of the Eucharist. Whenever that special need is present, as it is in the danger of death, then it is not unreasonable to expect that that command, general in its form, would become specific when such need became operative in its demands.

To further establish the nature of the precept to receive Holy Viaticum, one may examine the decrees of the many

[25] Lib. I, tit. XXXVI, *de transactionibus*, cap. 8, n. 10—*Collectanea Doctorum tam Veterum quam Recentiorum in Jus Pontificium Universum* (5 vols., Lugduni, 1641), I, 307.

[26] *De Synodo Dioecesana* (4 vols., Mechliniae, 1842), Lib. VII, cap. XI, n. 2.

local councils of the period which are certainly indicative of the mind of the Church, both because of their number and because of their being representative of the universal Church. In France the provincial council of Aix (1850) expressly decreed that all persons who had reached the use of reason were obliged in virtue of a divine precept to receive Holy Viaticum when in danger of death.[27] In Italy, the provincial council of Ravenna (1855) in like manner declared the reception of Holy Viaticum to be of divine precept.[28] The Council of the Port of Spain (West Indies), which was held in 1854 in the interest of the colonies of England, Holland and Denmark, warned pastors that they were not to allow the faithful to die without Viaticum, which by divine precept they were bound to receive.[29] In similar fashion, the Synod of Suchow (1803), a vicariate in China, exhorted missionaries to be mindful of the divine precept that binds those who are in danger of death to receive Holy Viaticum.[30]

In America, the II Plenary Council of Baltimore (1866), while not explicitly declaring the reception of Holy Viaticum to be of divine precept, at least implicitly insinuated it by declaring that those in danger of death were bound *"sub gravissima obligatione"* to receive It. Any pastor who through his own negligence allowed even one soul committed to his care to die without having received Holy Viaticum was to be accounted guilty of grave sin.[30a]

Thus it was that the period from the Council of Trent

[27] Tit. VII, cap. V, n. 6—*Acta et Decreta Conciliorum Recentiorum, Collectio Lacensis* (Auctoribus Presbyteris S. J. e domo B. V. M. sine Labe Conceptae ad Lacum, 7 vols., Friburgi Brisgoviae, 1870-1892), IV, 991 (hereafter cited *Coll. Lac.*)

[28] Pars II, cap. IV, n. 6—*Coll. Lac.*, IV, 155.

[29] Art. III: "... ad quod suscipiendum ex praecepto divino (fideles) tenentur."—*Coll. Lav.*, III, 1098. The decrees of this council later received the approval of the Sacred Congregation for the Propagation of the Faith.

[30] Cap. IV, n. 9—*Coll. Lac.*, VI, 602.

[30a] *Concilii Plenarii Baltimonensis II Acta et Decreta* (Baltimorae: John Murphy, 1868), n. 262 (hereafter cited *Acta et Decreta*).

(1545-1563) to the promulgation of the Code of Canon Law (1918) witnessed a new alignment of the authors in support of the doctrine that the precept obliging the faithful when in danger of death to receive Holy Communion was by nature a divine precept. But from this alignment there did not result a conclusive definition of the question so as to put it beyond all further discussion. For that reason the question will be discussed again in the light of the teaching of modern commentators.[31]

B. The temporal element in the obligation

In order to explore fully the obligation that binds one to receive Holy Viaticum, it is hardly enough to determine its nature. One must go further and determine the precise time in which or during which the obligation becomes operative. The theologians and canonists commonly taught that it bound only *in periculo mortis,* a phrase which they interpreted to mean any proximate danger of death, whether from an intrinsic or from an extrinsic cause. Thus St. Alphonsus taught that in any serious danger of death which one foresaw, or with good reason feared, there was a grave obligation to receive.[32] Gasparri asserted that it was a matter of indifference whether the danger arose from an intrinsic or from an extrinsic cause, such as capital punishment.[33] Their assertions are in accord with the comprehensive definition of the phrase *periculum mortis,* as given by D'Annibale (1815-1892):

> ... illud rerum discrimen, in quo quis constitutus est, ipsum, et superesse, et occumbere posse, utrumque est vere graviterque probabile; sive periculum immineat *ab intrinsico,* ut puta ex morbo, vulnere inflicto, partu difficili, extrema senectute; sive *ab extrinsico* imineat, velut ex bello, navigatione periculosa, etc. Hoc amplius: si quis versetur in periculo incidendi in perpe-

[31] Cf. *infra,* pp. 76-84.

[32] *Theologia Moralis,* Lib. VI, *De Eucharistia,* n. 291.

[33] *De Eucharistia,* II, n. 1147.

tuam amentiam, perinde habetur ac si versaretur in periculo mortis.[34]

Two responses of the Sacred Congregation for the Propagation of the Faith confirm the fact that the danger of death which imposes an obligation to receive Holy Viaticum may derive either from an intrinsic or from an extrinsic cause. The first, dated February 20, 1801, was an affirmative answer to the question whether missioners in China could administer Holy Viaticum to persons suffering from tuberculosis or kindred diseases, when it was foreseen that they would linger on for many months, but when it was likewise foreseen that they would die within the year or at a time when perhaps missioners would not be at hand to administer It to them.[35]

The second reply dealt with prisoners condemned to death. It was asked whether Holy Communion could be brought to priests and the laity condemned to death for the faith, on the day of or on the day preceding their execution. The answer given was: "In the affirmative, and by way of Viaticum."[36]

From these responses of the Sacred Congregation for the Propagation of the Faith and from the teaching of the authors the general rule can be formulated that the precept to receive Holy Viaticum binds in danger of death irrespective of whether that danger arises from an intrinsic or from an extrinsic cause. In this Viaticum differs from extreme unction, which can be administered only in a danger of death that arises from an intrinsic cause—sickness or old age.

Gasparri taught that the precept to receive Holy Viaticum began to bind at the emerging of the danger of death and ceased to bind only when the danger of death had passed.

[34] *Summula Theologiae Moralis* (5. ed., 3 vols., Romae: Ex Typographia Polyglotta, 1908-1909), I, n. 38.

[35] *Fontes*, n. 4662; *Collectanea S. Congregationis de Propaganda Fide* (2 vols., Romae: Typographia Polyglotta S. C. de Propaganda Fide, 1907), n. 651 (hereafter cietd *Collect.*).

[36] S. C. de Prop. Fide (C. P. pro Sin.—Tunkin Occident.), 21 iul. 1841, ad 1—*Fontes*, n. 4789; *Collect.*, n. 928.

During that period the obligation was satisfied through any reception of Holy Communion, even though one was ignorant of the danger of death or had not formed any positive intention of fulfilling the precept by means of that reception of the Eucharist. Hence he concluded that it was necessary, but at the same time sufficient, for the satisfying of the precept that the recipient be in actual danger of death at the time of his reception of the sacrament.[37] Vasquez stated that the recipient did not have to advert consciously to the reception as an act of receiving Holy Viaticum.[38]

On the other hand, Gasparri held that if one could not fulfill the precept during the actual danger of death, as in the case of those going into battle or of those about to undertake a dangerous journey, the precept began to bind at a point of time prior to the commencement of the actual danger.[39] This teaching of Gasparri was in accord with the two responses of the Sacred Congregation for the Propagation of the Faith already cited. It was confirmed by a later response of the Sacred Penitentiary, given on May 29, 1915, which declared that every soldier who was in a state of warlike assembly, or "mobilization" as it is called, could by that very fact be regarded as in a danger of death, so that he could be absolved by any priest.[40]

Conciliar legislation had taken cognizance of the teaching as it was later proposed by Gasparri inasmuch as it ordered that Holy Viaticum was to be administered to persons in a probable and proximate danger of death; it was not pastulated that they be in some actual danger of death.[41]

[37] *De Eucharistia,* II, n. 1150.

[38] *Libri Commentariorum,* Tom. III, disp. 214, cap. 2, n. 17.

[39] *Loc, cit.*

[40] *Acta Apostolicae Sedis, Commentarium Officiale* (*AAS*) (Romae, 1909-1929; Civitate Vaticana, 1929-), VII (1915), 282.

[41] Cf. II Provincial Council of Quebec (1854), decret. X, sect. 7: "Infirmo qui in mortis periculo probabili et proximo, quamvis non actuali et imminente, versatur, Viaticum Corporis Domini Nostri Jesu Christi, summo studio ac dilegentia, opportuno tempore, deferendum est. . . . "—*Coll. Lac.,* III, 642; Provincial Council of Rheims (1849), Tit. VII, cap. 3—*Coll. Lac.,* IV, 117.

From these sources it was possible to formulate a second general rule, namely that Holy Viaticum should be administered outside of the actual danger of death whenever it was probable that the prospective recipient will not be afforded a further opportunity for Its reception.

A third question, namely, whether a devotional reception of the Eucharist that took place a short time prior to the emerging of the danger of death sufficed in and of itself to satisfy one's obligation to receive the Eucharist while in the actual danger of death, was much discussed by the authors. Vasquez was of the opinion that such was not possible. The precept to receive Holy Viaticum bound only in danger of death, so that outside of that time it could not be satisfied, just as the precept to hear Mass could not be satisfied on a day other than the feast day for which the obligation existed.[42]

Suarez, on the contrary, denied the opinion of Vasquez. He maintained that the precept to receive Holy Communion in danger of death was substancially fulfiled by means of a prior reception of Holy Communion of devotion, even after a lapse of eight days. In support of his stand he stated that one was to be regarded as having a virtual intention of fulfilling each and every obligation that one was able, when called upon, to fulfill. In the present case, even though one was unaware of the obligation, still one could be regarded as having the virtual intention of receiving Holy Viaticum.[43]

This opinion of Suarez was adopted by De Lugo and Laymann (1574-1635). The former added that if through a revelation one knew of one's impending death as unaccompanied with the reception of the last sacraments, one would be obliged to receive them at a time when an actual danger of death did not exist. The Communion received within an eight-day period prior to the emerging of the danger

[42] *Libri Commentariorum,* disp. 214, cap. 2, n. 13.

[43] *De Eucharistia,* q. 80, art. XI, disp. 69, sect. 3, n. 3—*Opera Omnia,* XXI, 534.

could be regarded as received within a period in which the precept of Holy Viaticum was binding.[44] The latter declared that after a lapse of one, two, three or even eight days, there was no obligation to receive again, as it had already been substancially fulfilled.[45]

Verano (1648-1713), while not specifically defining any time limit within which it was possible to anticipate the obligation, stated the general principle that the obligation could be anticipated. If it was feared that later the condition of the person would be such as to prevent his reception of the Eucharist, then it became possible to administer Holy Viaticum, notwithstanding the absence of an actual danger of death. The obligation to receive It was binding *pro ultimo tempore vitae* in so far as this could be known. In the present case one could regard the occasion as the last time in life in which the reception was not only possible but also obligatory.[46]

Gasparri inclined to this opinion also. He contended that morally one who received the Eucharist eight days prior to the actual danger of death could be regarded as having received It in danger of death.[47] In the light of this teaching the formulation of a third general rule seemed possible, namely, in circumstances wherein the danger of death was not foreseen, a devotional reception of the Eucharist by as much as eight days prior to the emerging danger substantially fulfilled the obligation of receiving It in the actual danger.

A further question, namely, if one received Holy Communion of devotion in the morning, was one bound to receive again within the same day by way of Viaticum, was

[44] *De Sacramento Eucharistiae*, disp. XVI, sect. 2, n. 41—*Resolutiones Scholasticae et Morales*, IV, 144.

[45] *Theologia Moralis in Quinque Libros Distributa* (ed. nova, Venetiis, 1630), Lib. V. tract. IV, cap. V, n. 4 (hereafter cited *Theologia Moralis*).

[46] *Iuris Canonici Universi Commentarius Paratitlaris* (5 vols., Monachii, 1703-1708), Vol. III, lib. III, tit. 44, n. 16.

[47] *De Eucharistia*, II, n. 1151.

also discussed by the authors of this period. Their answers afforded a basis for three distinct opinions. The first opinion held that one was bound, because only by so doing could one fulfill the precept to receive Holy Viaticum. The second maintained that one was not bound, but that one remained free to do so, while the third stated that neither was one bound nor was it allowable for one to do so. All three opinions were regarded by Benedict XIV as offering a probability of correctness.[48]

The better solution for the question seemed to be that of St. Alphonsus and De Lugo. They distinguished between a case in which one in perfect health received out of devotion in the morning but later on the same day was exposed to the danger of death, and the case in which one who was ill, but not seriously so, received out of devotion in the morning and later on the same day fell seriously ill. In the former case the person not only could receive again but was obliged to do so, while in the latter there was no such obligation to receive again within the course of the same day.[49]

Relative to the repeated reception of Holy Viaticum during the same danger of death, the authors agreed that such a repeated reception was possible even though the recipient had not observed the law of the Eucharist fast. There was, however, some difference of opinion with regard to the length of time that should elapse between one reception and the next. Some thought that a period of eight days should elapse, but it was more commonly held that the reception of Viaticum could be repeated each day as long as the danger of death lasted.[50]

[48] *De Synodo Dioecesana*, Lib. VII, cap. XI, n. 2.

[49] St. Alphonsus, *Theologia Moralis*, Lib. VI, *De Eucharistia*, n. 285; De Lugo, *De Sacramento Eucharistiae*, disp. XVI, sect. 3, nn. 53-54—*Resolutiones Scholasticae et Morales*, IV, 147.

[50] Cf. St. Alphonsus, *Theologia Moralis*, *loc. cit.*

Section 2. The Proper Minister of Holy Viaticum and the Manner of Administration

A. The proper minister

By a positive disposition of law and in virtue of his power of Orders the priest is constituted the ordinary minister of the sacrament of the Eucharist.[51] Only in a case of necessity and in the absence of a priest could a deacon administer It.[52] Such a case of necessity was considered to be present in the event that one was in danger of dying without the reception of Holy Viaticum. In the act of administering the Eucharist the deacon was regarded as being merely the agent of the priest; he did not act in virtue of any innate right of his own. In this sense a subdeacon or even a lay person could validly administer Holy Viaticum.[53]

But while any priest could validly administer Holy Viaticum, its licit administration called for the fulfillment of two conditions. The priest had to possess jurisdiction over the recipient and at the same time had to be free of any impediment imposed by the Church through suspension or excommunication. A priest who lacked such jurisdiction had to obtain the delegated faculty from the proper pastor, while one who proceeded without it acted indeed validly, but illicitly, and sinned gravely in infringing upon the rights of aonther.[54]

In this section, consideration will be given to those priests to whom belonged by law the right to administer Holy Viati-

[51] Conc. Trident., sess. XIII, *decretum de Sanctissimo Eucharistiae Sacramento*, c. 8; sess. XXIII, *Doctrina de Sacramento Ordinis*, can. 1—Schroeder, *Canons and Decrees of the Council of Trent*, pp. 354 and 435.

[52] Barbosa, *De Officio et Potestate Parochi Descriptio* (ed. U. Giraldi a S. Cajetano, Romae, 1774), Pars II, cap. 20, n. 3; Cf. S. R. C., *Tonkini Occidentalis*, 14 aug. 1858—*Fontes*, n. 5990; De Lugo, *De Sacramento Eucharistiae*, disp. XVIII, sect. I, n. 1,—*Resolutiones Scolasticae et Morales*, IV, 167.

[53] Cf. De Lugo, *ibid.*, nn. 21-23—*Op. cit.*, IV, 172-173; Laymann, *Theologia Moralis*, Lib. V, tract. IV, cap. VII, n. 2.

[54] Barbosa, *op. cit.*, Pars II, cap. 22, n. 2.

cum. The writer has found it convenient to treat the matter under four distinct headings: the parish priest, the hospital chaplain, the superior of clerical exempt religious, and the minister for the bishop and the pastor.

1. The Parish Priest

It was among the chief purposes of the Council of Trent to correct abuses, to restore discipline particularly in the realms of the pastoral office, and to assert the importance of ecclesaistical organization along parochial lines. To achieve these purposes it ordered that parishes have definite boundaries, and made it unlawful for the respective parishioner to receive the sacraments from any priest other than their own parish priest.[55]

Consequent upon this Tridentine legislation, the general trend as indicated by the papal encyclicals, and the decrees and decisions of the Roman Curia, developed in favor of the right of the pastor to administer the sacraments to his own subjects.[56] Among the theologians and canonists there was

[55] Sess. XXIV, *de ref.*, c. 13: "In iis quoque civitatibus ac locis ubi parochiales ecclesiae certos non habent fines, nec earum rectores proprium populum, quem regant, sed promiscue petentibus sacramenta administrant, mandat sancta Synodus episcopis, pro tutiori animarum eis commissarum salute, ut, distincto populo in certas propriasque parochias, unicuique suum perpetuum peculiaremque parochum assignent, qui eas cognoscere valeat, et a quo solo licite sacramenta suscipiant. . . . ."—Schroeder, *Canons and Decrees of the Council of Trent*, p. 473.

[56] Cf. Benedictus XIV, ep. encycl. *Inter omnigenas*, 2 febr. 1744—*Fontes*, n. 339; Innocentius X, const. *Cum sicut*, 14 maii, 1648 (1653)—*Fontes*, n. 232. Pius IX (1846-1878), in the Constitution *Apostolicae Sedis*, on October 12, 1869, declared that an *ipso facto* incurred excommunication reserved to the Holy See was contracted by all religious who presumed to administer the sacraments of extreme unction and Holy Viaticum to clerics or to lay people without the permission of the pastor.—*Fontes*, n. 552. Cf. also S. C. de Prop. Fide, 13 iun. 1633—*Fontes*, n. 4450; S. C. C., *in Ripana*, 3 febr. 1652—Pallottini, *Collectio omnium Conclusionum et Resolutionum quae in causis propositis apud Sacram Congregationem Cardinalium S. Concilii Tridentini Interpretum prodierunt ab eius institutione anno MDLXIV ad annum MDCCCLX, Distinctis Titulis Alphabetico ordine per Materias*

not to be found anyone who denied that right of the pastor; all were emphatic in upholding it.[57] Barbosa pointed out that an excommunicated pastor could not distribute the Eucharist in the church, and likewise could not carry It to the sick. A pastor who acted contrary to this norm sinned gravely and incurred an irregularity. He added, however, that an excommunicated pastor could administer Holy Viaticum when no other priest was available.[58]

This positive and authoritative teaching of the Church was reflected in much of the contemporary conciliar legislation. This legislation, even though of a local nature, lent further support to and vindication of the right of the pastor to administer Holy Viaticum to the dying members of his flock.[59]

It was both the duty and the right of the local pastor to administer Holy Viaticum to his own subjects domiciled within the limits of his parish. That right was further extended so as to include *peregrini*—those having a domicile

---

digesta (17 vols., Romae, 1868-1895), s. v. *Parochus,* XIV, II, n. 33 (hereafter cited Pallottini); S. C. C., *in Monopolitana* (*Iuris Sepeliendi*), 24 sept. 1670—*loc. cit.*

[57] Cf. Barbosa, *De Officio et Potestate Parochi Descriptio,* Pars II, cap. 22, n. 2; Laymann, *Theologia Moralis,* Lib. V, tract. 8, cap. 6, n. 2; Pirhing, *Jus Canonicum nova Methodo Explicatum* (4 vols., ed. novissima, Dilingae, 1722), Lib. I, tit. 31, nn. 143 and 152 (hereafter cited *Jus Canonicum*); Schmalzgrueber, (1663-1735), *Jus Ecclesiasticum Universum* (5 vols. in 12, Romae, 1843-1845), Lib. III, tit. 29, n. 10; De Lugo, *De Eucharistia,* disp. XVIII, sect. I, nn. 36-37—*Op. cit.* IV, 176; Wernz (1842-1914), *Ius Decretalium* (6 vols., Vol. II, 3. ed., Romae et Prati, 1915), II, pars II, tit. 39.

[58] *Op. cit.,* Pars II, cap. 22, n. 10.

[59] Cf. The Provincial Council of Prague (1678), Tit. IV, cap. VI: "... sacramentum Eucharistiae ministretur per modum Viatici, et quidem ordinarie a parocho eiusve vicario, ab alio autem sacerdote extra casum necessitatis nonnisi de parochi licentia."—*Coll. Lac.,* V, 504; The Provincial Council of Utrecht (1865), Tit. IV, cap. 7—*Coll. Lac.,* V, 824; The Provincial Council of Urbino (1865), Pars I, cap. IV, n. 6—*Coll. Lac.,* VI, 14. The II Plenary Council of Baltimore (1866) charged the pastor with the grave obligation of administering the Eucharist to the sick—*Acta et Decreta,* n. 262.

outside of the parish in which they happened to take sick while sojourning therein.[60]

It appears that there existed some conflict between the parochial church and the cathedral church concerning the right to administer the last sacraments to pilgrims, travellers, rulers, strangers, soldiers, officials and their agents, those in prison and those who had been condemned to death. The question was asked whether these were subject to the cathedral church or rather to the parochial church where they sojourned. The Sacred Congregation of the Council replied that the question should be decided in the light of local custom and agreements.[61]

2. Hospital Chaplains

In view of the regulations made by the Council of Trent,[62] the parish priest was accorded full parochial jurisdiction over all the faithful in his parish. These regulations, however, were in many cases modified in view of exemptions which obtained either by reason of the common law, through apostolic indult, or by reason of immemorial custom.[63]

Any exemption, total or partial, had to be proved. In the many litigations between the parish priest and the priests having charge of hospitals within the parish, Rome consistently upheld the more basic rights of the pastor. Not only did the latter's right extend to those of his parishioners

[60] S. C. C., *in Viterbien.*, 18 mart., 27 maii, 1645—Pallottini, s. v. *Sacramentum Eucharistiae*, XVI, I, n. 32. In this decision, reference was made to parishes situated in seaport towns. It was the right of the local pastor to administer Holy Viaticum to the sailors and others on board while the ship stayed in the port.

[61] S. C. C., *in Savonen.* (*Iurium Parochialium*), 12 nov., 13 dec., 1712, 17 iun. 1713—Pallottini, s.v. *Parochus*, XIV, III, n. 19.

[62] Cf. *supra*, p. 52.

[63] Cf. Bouix, *Tractatus de Parocho* (3. ed., Parisiis, 1880), p. 653; Drumm, *Hospital Chaplains*, The Catholic University of America Canon Law Studies, n. 178 (Washington, D. C.: The Catholic University of America Press, 1943), p. 21; S. C. Ep. et Reg., 21 iul. 1876—*Acta Sanctae Sedis* (41 vols., Romae, 1865-1908), X (1877), 405 (hereafter cited *ASS*).

who were confined to the hospital, but also to those inmates who did not belong to his parish. In the case of the latter, however, they did not cease to be subjects of their respective pastors.[64]

Pre-Code law accorded to hospitals the same canonical status as to non-exempt religious houses of men and women, to colleges, to orphanages, and to similar institutions.[65] Thus a general hospital operated by exempt religious as part of their house was not thereby withdrawn from the jurisdiction of the local pastor. Consequently to him belonged the right to administer the last sacraments to externs. But in the case of exempt religious who operated their own private infirmary, solely for the benefit of the community, the exemption enjoyed by the religious community itself extended to such an infirmary and to the priest deputed to look after the sick therein. As far as the law was concerned, it appears that an exemption was allowed only in regard to institutions that were of their nature exempt.

A more important source of exemption was the apostolic indult. Immediately following the Council of Trent, Pope Pius IV (1559-1565) confirmed all the privileges that had been granted to the various Religious Orders since the time of Pope Honorius II (1124-1130). These privileges included the right to administer the sacraments to all the faithful in their hospitals and asylums.[66]

A short time later, Pope Pius V (1566-1572), in approving the Congregation of the Brothers of St. John of God for hospital work, allowed them to attend to the spiritual needs of all the patients, but under the jurisdiction of the local

[64] De Luca, *Theatrum Veritatis et Iustitiae seu Decisivi Discursus ad Veritatem editi in Forensibus Controversiis Canonicis et Civilibus* (4 vols., Romae, 1706), *De Parocho*, disc. XXIII, n. 9.

[65] S. C. Ep. et Reg., 19 sept. 1862—*ASS*, I (1865), 613.

[66] Const. *Inter assidua Dominici*, 18 maii, 1565: "Ac omnibus et singulis christifidelibus et leprosis pauperibus infirmis, in dictis hospitalibus pro tempore degentibus, ecclesiastica sacramenta ministrare." —*Bull. Rom. Taur.*, VII, 365.

ordinary.[67] This privilege, in effect, entailed complete exemption from the jurisdiction of the local pastor, and the consequent exclusion of the latter's right to administer Holy Viaticum in such hospitals. Later it received confirmation from Popes Gregory XIII (1572-1585), Sixtus V (1585-1590), and Gregory XIV (1590-1591).[68]

The third source of exemption from parochial jurisdiction in the matter of administering Holy Viaticum was custom. The force of custom as giving rise to an exemption was first noted by the General Council of Vienne (1311-1312).[69] Its legality was later confirmed by the Sacred Congregation of Bishops and Regulars in spite of the fact that it derogated from the law of the Council of Trent.[70]

It must be noted, however, that only a centenary or immemorial custom was productive of such an effect. The mere fact that a pastor had not exercised his right of discharging parochial functions in a hospital that had been served for a period of years by its own chaplain did not thereby deprive him of that right.[71]

Custom gave rise sometimes to a total exemption, sometimes to only a partial exemption. A decision of the Sacred Congregation of the Council, given in a specific case, decided in favor of the right of the pastor upon request to administer to the spiritual needs of all the faithful, both staff and patients, in the hospital within the limits of his parish, though he remained without the absolute right to administer to them the last sacraments. Only on condition of his being called in by a patient could he exercise the right of administering to his needs.[72]

[67] Const. *Licet ex debito,* 4 ian. 1572—*Bull. Rom. Taur.,* VII, 960.

[68] Cf. S. C. Ep. et Reg., 1 apr. 1892—*ASS,* XXIV (1892), 615.

[69] C. 7—c. 2, *de religiosis domibus, ut sint episcopo subjectae,* III, 11, in Clem.

[70] S. C. Ep. etReg., 21 iul. 1876: "(Ex his colliges): parochilea ius huiusmodi ad pias domus extendi, nec cessare nisi ... ob speciale privilegium aut ob centenariam vel immemorabilem consuetudinem tale factum sit."—*ASS,* X (1876), 405.

[71] S. C. C., 14 aug. 1863—*Fontes,* n. 4195.

[72] S. C. C., *Lauden.,* 2 maii 1857—*Fontes,* n. 4154.

In general, it may be noted that the right of the hospital chaplain to administer Holy Viaticum depended primarily on the nature of the hospital, its privileges, and its established customs. In the absence of any of these factors the right of the pastor remained intact, and a chaplain, if there was one, acted merely as the vicar of the pastor or as an auxiliary priest assigned by the bishop to the care of large hospitals with the express or tacit agreement of the pastor.[73]

A similar condition obtained with regard to other institutions in the parish. Colleges, orphanges, prisons, and non-exempt houses of men and women were entirely subject to the pastor. In some few cases, however, the rendered decisons favored the right of the chaplain of such institutions in the matter of administering the last sacraments.[74]

3. The Superior of Clerical Exempt Religious

In virtue of a decree of the Council of Trent, certain clerical Religious Orders were withdrawn from episcopal jurisdiction.[75] Such Orders as received this privilege of exemption from the jurisdiction of the local ordinary were *a fortiori* exempt from the jurisdiction of the local pastor. Consequently these acquired certain rights in the matter of administering the sacraments in general, and Holy Viaticum in particular. These various rights will here be summarized.

The superior of each clerical exempt house had the right to administer Holy Viaticum to all the professed members, novices, and lay brothers. The licit exercise of the same function on the part of any other priest required the permis-

[73] Cf. Drumm, *Hospital Chaplains*, p. 29.

[74] S. C. C., *Mediolanen.* 28 iul. 1705—*Fontes*, n. 2996; S. C. C., *Romana*, 27 aug. 1667—*Fontes*, n. 2802; S. C. C., *in Asten.* (*Iurium Parochialium*), 27 nov. 1717—Pallottini, s.v. *Parochus*, XIV, II, n. 34; S. C. C., *in Praenestina* (*Administrationis Sacramentorum*), 22 mart. 1823—Pallottini, s.v. *Parochus*, XIV, II, n. 29; S. C. Ep. et Reg., 21 iul. 1848—*Fontes*, n. 1954; S. C. Ep. et Reg., *Parmen.*, 21 iul. 1848—*Collectanea in Usum Secretariae Sacrae Congregationis Episcoporum et Regularium*, cura A. Bizzarri, Secretarii (2. ed., Romae, 1885), p. 583.

[75] Sess. XXV, *de regularibus*, c. 11—Schroeder, *Canons and Decrees of the Council of Trent*, p. 492.

sion of the superior.[76] The pastor, however, retained the right to administer Holy Viaticum to all those who worked and resided within the monastery, such as the *familiares*—the household servants. At any time he could vindicate his right in their regard, which right the superior could not deny.[77] But on the verification of certain conditions the *familiares* also became the subjects of the religious superior in regard to the administration of the last sacraments. These conditions were: 1) They had to be employed in the actual service of the monastery; 2) they had to reside within the monastery grounds; 3) they had to live in the subjection of obedience to the religious superior.[78]

In the case of those who were attached to the monastery, in the sense that they worked there during the day but resided in their own homes outside the monastery grounds, ordinarily the administration of Holy Viaticum belonged to their own proper pastor.[79]

Finally, it was the right of the religious superior to administer Holy Viaticum to the nuns and domestics who resided in a building erected on the monastery grounds. Both before and after the Council of Trent, nuns enjoyed the same privileges of exemption as the regulars to whom they were subject.[80]

[76] Barbosa, *De Officio et Potestate Parochi Descriptio,* Pars II, cap. 22, n. 4; Zitelli (†1887), *Apparatus Iuris Ecclesiastici iuxta Recentissimos SS. Urbis Congregationum Resolutiones* (Romae, 1886), Lib. III, art. V, n. 374.

[77] Barbosa, *loc. cit.; Diana Coordinatus* (10 tomes in 5 vols., prepared by M. de Alcolea, Venetiis, 1728), Tom. II, tract. II, *de praecepto divina et ecclesiastico sacrae communionis,* resols. 18 and 20.

[78] Conc. Trident., sess. XXIV, *de ref.*, c. 11; Gregorius XIII (1572-1585), const. *Circumspecta,* 25 nov. 1580—*Bull. Rom. Taur.*, IV, 454-456.

[79] S. C. C., *in Vratislavien.* (*Iurium Parochialium*), 25 ian. 1783—*Thesaurus Resolutionum Sacrae Congregationis Concilii* (167 vols., Romae, 1718-1908), VIII, 17; *Diana Coordinatus* held that, if they fell ill while actually within the monastery grounds, the right to administer Viaticum belonged to the religious superior.—*loc. cit.*

[80] Cf. S. C. C., *Ulixbonen. Occident.*, 22 nov. 1721—*Fontes*, n. 3234; S. C. C., *in Ulixbonen. Occident.* 17 sept. 1722—*Fontes*, 3247; S. C. Ep. et Reg., *Caesenaten.*, mense maio 1788—*Fontes*, n. 1881.

4. The Minister for the Bishop and the Pastor

To whom belonged the right to administer Holy Viaticum to the bishop and to the pastor? In the case of the former it appears that the right belonged to the highest dignitary of the cathedral chapter, so that nowise was it the prerogative of the pastor.[81]

With regard to the latter, there was no definite prescription regarding the one to whom belonged the right to administer Holy Viaticum to him. Barbosa stated that the nearest neighboring pastor always had that right, but at the same time one was free to call any priest of one's choice.[82]

With regard to canons, it was the right of the local pastor to administer Holy Viaticum to them whenever they resided outside of the proper residence of the canons. If, however, they resided permanently in the proper residence of the canons but happened to take sick while outside of it, then it was the right of the cathedral priests to administer Holy Viaticum to them.[83] It appeared to be the more or less general rule that canons were to receive Holy Viaticum from the parochial church of domicile rather than from the collegiate church. There were allowed, however, some exceptions by reason of apostolic privilege or legitimate custom in favor of the right of the collegiate church.[84] In the ab-

[81] S. C. C., *in Firmana* (*Iurium Parochialium*), 4 aug. 1685—Pallottini, s. v. *Parochus*, XIV, II, n. 21; S. C. C., *in Faventina* (*Praeeminentiarum et Funerum*), 7 iun. 1760—Pallottini, s. v. *Parochus*, XIV, II, n. 22.

[82] *De Officio et Potestate Parochi Descriptio*, Pars II, cap. 22, n. 2.

[83] S. C. C., *Tiburtina*, 12 maii 1685—*Fontes*, n. 2886; S. C. C., *Tolentinaten.*, 11 sept. 1694—*Fontes*, n. 2944; S. C. C., *Novarien.*, 27 aug. 1695, ad 1—*Fontes*, n. 2950; S. C. C., *Narnien.*, 26 sept. 1699—*Fontes*, n. 2971; S. C. C., *in S. Miniatis* (*Iurium Parochialium*), 24 nov. 1821—Pallottini, s. v. *Parochus*, XIV, II, n. 12; S. C. C., *in Andrien.*, 24 ian., 19 sept. 1767—Pallottini, s. v. *Sacramentum Eucharistiae*, XVI, I, n. 26.

[84] S. C. C., *Derthonen*, 3 dec. 1718—*Fontes*, n. 3177; S. C. C., *Derthonen.*, 7 dec. 1720—*Fontes*, n. 3217.

sence of any contrary custom, all minor clerics received the last sacraments from the hands of the pastor.[85]

B. The manner of administration

In the period under consideration it was still customary to bring the Holy Eucharist to the sick in a public manner. Not only was such a method regarded as laudable, but it was also enjoined by the authority of the Roman Curia and the prescriptions of various local councils, in keeping with the former legislation.[86]

While it was the general law of the Church that Holy Viaticum be brought in a public manner, exceptions were certainly admitted whenever the presence of a just cause demanded that It be brought privately. In 1608 Pope Paul V (1605-1621) decreed that the Blessed Sacrament should be brought to the sick privately in those lands which were under the domination of Jews, Moors or Turks. The pope in allowing such a consession was motivated by the constant threat of irreverence that was involved in the public bringing of the Eucharist in such lands.[87]

A similiar concession was later granted by Pope Benedict XIV (1704-1758) in 1744. He exhorted adherence to the general law whenever that was possible, but at the same time laid down the following regulations: In those regions where Turks were prominent and where iniquity prevailed, the priest was to carry the Sacred Host in a pyx. The pyx was to be enclosed in a burse, which in turn was by means of a cord to be suspended from the neck, and carried under cover of the outer garments. Moreover, the priest was not

[85] S. C. C., *Eugubina* (*Iurium Parochialium*), 2 apr. 1729—Pallottini, s. v. *Parochus*, XIV, II, n. 17.

[86] S. C. C., decr., 12 febr. 1679—*Fontes*, n. 2848; the Provincial Council of Prague (1860), tit. IV, cap. 6—*Coll. Lac.*, V, 504; the Provincial Council of Kolocsa (Hungary) (1863), tit. III, cap. IV—*Coll. Lac.*, V, 647; the Provincial Council of Ravenna (1855), pars II, cap. IV, n. 9—*Coll. Lac.*, VI, 158.

[87] Const. *Ex omnibus Christianae*, 8 febr. 1608, nn. 6-7—*Bull. Rom. Taur.*, XI, 462.

to go alone, but in the company either of another priest or of a layman.[88]

In 1822 the Sacred Congregation for the Propagation of the Faith, in response to a question concerning the manner in which the Eucharist was to be brought and administered to the faithful living in pagan homes, replied to the effect that the faculty to bring It privately had already been granted by the pope and, furthermore, that missioners could under such circumstances administer It without the use of surplice, stole or lighted candle.[89]

In a similar manner, the Sacred Congregation of the Holy Office granted permission for the private bringing of the Holy Eucharist to prisons and to houses of infidels in which a member of the faithful happened to be, provided that there was no danger of irreverence or of contempt.[90]

It appears that at no time was there granted any general faculty to bring the Blessed Sacrament to the sick in a private manner. Each particular set of circumstances had to be examined on its own merits, and the reasons alleged for each case had to be weighed. Bishops could dispense from the general law only in virtue of a faculty granted by the Holy See.[91]

The II Plenary Council of Baltimore (1866) deplored the fact that the condition of the country was such as to prevent the public bringing of the Eucharist to the sick with full solemnity and ceremony according to the mind of the Church. Priests were exhorted to do their utmost to supply the lack of external devotion through their own internal dispositions of piety, and as far as possible they were to evidence that external reverence that was due to the real presence of Christ in the Eucharist. They were to abstain

[88] Ep. encycl. *Inter omnigenas*, 2 febr. 1744, n. 23—*Fontes*, n. 339; *Collect.*, n. 345.

[89] (C. P. pro Sin.), 26 iun. 1882—*Collect.*, n. 778.

[90] (Coreae), 5 iul. 1854—*Fontes*, n. 926.

[91] Provincial Council of Prague (1860), tit. IV, cap. VI—*Coll. Lac.*, V, 505; the Provincial Council of Kalocsa (1863), tit. III, cap. IV—*Coll. Lac.*, V, 647.

from all unnecessary conversation while carrying the Blessed Sacrament, and were to give themselves to pious contemplation and prayer. Furthermore, the Council reminded the priest of his grave obligation to carry the Sacred Host on his breast, and never, outside the case of extreme necessity, to handle It or the pyx containing It without wearing at least a stole. In taking the Blessed Sacrament from the tabernacle the priest was to wear both surplice and stole, and in administering It to the sick he was to observe, as far as possible, the prescriptions of the Roman Ritual.[92]

Further prescriptions regulating the actual administration of Holy Viaticum are to be found in the various replies of the Roman Curia and in the conciliar legislation of the period. In 1658, Pope Alexander VII (1655-1667), in his Constitution dealing with the spiritual rule of the faithful in Goa and the adjacent islands, warned that Holy Viaticum was to be administered to all who were in danger of death, no matter what their condition or the condition of their homes, since with God there was no acceptance of persons.[93]

In some places the pastor was exhorted to instruct the faithful in the manner of preparing the sick room.[94] If the home of the sick person was very poor, it was recommended that the pastor take with him all things necessary for the proper administration of the sacrament.[95]

In reply to questions concerning the celebration of Mass in the home of the sick person, the Sacred Congregation for the Propagation of the Faith stated that it was unlawful to do so as long as there remained the possibility of bringing the Eucharist, even secretly. In the absence of this possibility Mass could be celebrated in the patient's home or in some nearby and becoming place.[96] However, a missioner

[92] *Acta et Decreta,* n. 264.

[93] Const., *Sacrosancti,* 18 ian. 1658, n. 3—*Fontes,* n. 129.

[94] Synod of Mount Lebanon (1736), n. 25—*Coll. Lac.,* II, 210.

[95] I Provincial Council of Westminster (1852), decr. XVIII, n. 12—*Coll. Lac.,* III, 932.

[96] 14 dec. 1668—*Collect.,* n. 172.

who lived at a distance from a church or on oratory was allowed to reserve a number of consecrated particles for the purpose of administering Holy Viaticum.[97]

Barbosa taught that in time of pestilence the pastor was bound to administer Holy Viaticum with his hands, and was not allowed to do so by means of some instrument. He was bound by reason of the obligation imposed by his office to administer It to patients affected with contagious disease, but only when he could do so with due reverence and without any probable danger to his own life.[98] But the Sacred Congregation of the Holy Office, when asked whether it was possible to administer Holy Viaticum to persons infected with a contagious disease, not by hand but by means of a long rod to which was attached a silver plate which was purified by fire after each use, replied that such a method was allowable, but should be resorted to only in rare cases and always with the proper safeguarding of due reverence.[99]

During the post-Tridentine period certain abuses arose in the manner of administering Holy Viaticum to the sick. There were repeated condemnations of the practice of carrying the Eucharist to the sick who were unable to receive It, in order that they would be afforded the opportunity of at least adoring It.[100]

Another abuse of the post-Tridentine period, one which appears to have been widespread, was that of priests resorting to the practice of carrying the Eucharist about on

[97] S. R. C. (Daniae), 4 febr. 1871, ad 3—*Collect.* n. 1365.

[98] *De Officio et Potestate Parochi Descriptio,* pars II, cap. XX, n. 46; cf. Synod of Suchow (1803), Cap. IV, n. IX—*Coll. Lac.* VI, 602.

[99] 11 iul. 1754—*Collect.* n. 391. Cf. St. Alphonsus, *Theologia Moralis,* Lib. VI, n. 24; Benedict XIV, *De Synado Diocesana,* Lib. XIII, Cap. XIX, nn. 20-27.

[100] Synodal Constitutions of Benevento (1693), tit. XXXV, cap. XI —*Coll. Lac.,* I, 68; Barbosa, *op. cit.,* pars II, cap. XX, n. 44; Benedictus XIV, *De Sacrosancto Missae Sacrificio Libri Tres,* Lib. III, cap. XIX, n. 4; Engel, *Collegium Universi Iuris Canonici servato ordine Decretalium* (ed. nova, Beneventi, 1760), Pars III, cap. 3, n. 9; Fermosini (†1669), *De Officiis et Sacris Ecclesiae,* n. 91—*Opera Omnia* (2. ed., 14 vols., Coloniae Allobrogum, 1741), III, 512.

their person throughout the day in order that they might administer It immediately to anyone whom they found in danger of death. This practice, although perhaps prompted by a high motive, was condemned by the Church.[101] Likewise it was forbidden to priests to carry the Eucharist when they undertook long journeys or went to places which were the scenes of fires or floods.[102]

Since it appears to be a command of the divine law that the faithful receive Holy Viaticum when they are in danger of death, it was necessary for the Church to make an exception to its own positive law which prescribed that the faithful receive Holy Viaticum in their own rite. And this the Church has always done, permitting the reception of Holy Viaticum in any Catholic rite when it was impossible for one to receive in one's own rite.

The exception by which it was lawful to receive Holy Viaticum in another rite became operative in two cases: (1) when there was no priest of the prospective recipient's rite present, and (2) when a priest of the dying person's own rite was present, but when at the same time there was not available to him any Scared Host consecrated in his rite. A letter of the Sacred Congregation for the Propagation of the Faith made this clear when it forbade Latin missionaries to administer the sacraments to Catholics of an Oriental rite when there was a priest of their own rite present. But it was allowed them to administer Holy Viaticum in a case of necessity to dying Catholics of an Oriental rite, even under species that were consecrated according to the Latin rite.[103]

The Holy Office granted the Patriarch of Cilicia the faculty to dispense Armenian Catholics (who usually communicate in unleavened consecrated bread) living in the town of Diyarbekir, in order that, while they lacked priests of their own rite, they could communicate in consecrated leavened

[101] Cf. S. C.de Prop. Fide, instr., 25 febr. 1859—*Collect.* n. 1171.

[102] Cf. S. C. S. Off., 27 mart. 1665, notanda, n. 1—*Collect.* n. 1171; Provincial Council of Tarragona (1717), n. 16—*Coll. Lac.*, I, 765.

[103] Litt., 11 oct. 1780—*Fontes*, n. 4584.

bread at the hands of a priest of the Chaldean rite, and thus not be deprived of Holy Viaticum.[104] This faculty was later extended by the Sacred Congregation for the Propagation of the Faith to all Catholics who communicated in consecrated unleavened bread.[105]

Pope Leo XIII (1878-1903) regulated the quetsion of the parochial status and rights in relation to Orientals who had no priest or church of their own rite to the effect that these Catholics, since they had no pastor of their own rite, were to be cared for by the pastor of another rite in whose territory they lived.[106]

Finally, Pope Pius X (1903-1914) in his Constitution *Tradita ab antiquis* set down the law for the reception of Holy Viaticum:

> Sanctum Viaticum moribundis ritu proprio de manibus proprii parochi accipiendum est; sed, urgente necessitate, fas est a sacerdote quolibet illud accipere; qui tamen ritu suo ministrabit.[107]

This law of Pope Pius X was later made applicable to Oriental Catholics of the Ruthenian rite living in the United States,[108] and was ultimately incorporated into the Code of Canon Law.[109]

Section 3. The Recipient of Holy Viaticum

A. Recipients in general

In general, it may be stated that the dispositions required for the lawful reception of devotional Communion, with the exception of the law of the Eucharistic fast, are also required for the lawful reception of Holy Viaticum. Hence

[104] Decr., 12 dec. 1821, ad 23—*Fontes*, n. 864; *Collect.*, n. 879.

[105] 11 dec. 1838 (C. G.), n. 23: "... quoad vero communicantes in azymo, concedantur facultates prout in decreto S. O. 12 dec. 1821."—*Fontes*, n. 4778.

[106] Litt. ap., *Orientalium*, 30 nov. 1894, II—*Fontes*, n. 627.

[107] 14 sept. 1912, n. V—*Fontes*, n. 698.

[108] S. C. de Prop. Fide pro negotiis ritus orientalis, decr. *Cum Episcopo*, 17 aug. 1914, art. 25—*AAS*, VI (1914), 462.

[109] Cf. can. 866.

one must have some intention of receiving the sacrament and at the same time be free from sin. In addition to these two, there is required a third condition for the reception of Holy Viaticum, namely that the recipient be in at least a probable danger of death, which danger may arise either from an intrinsic or from an extrinsic cause.

But it may also be stated as a general rule that the conditions required for the fruitful reception of Holy Viaticum are less exacting than those required for the fruitful reception of devotional Communion. The requisite of the state of grace demanded in all communicants alike is of course a point regarding which no difference obtains under any given circumstances. The Eucharist may never be fruitfully received by anyone who is in a state of mortal sin. Such a person can indeed receive It sacramentally, but he cannot do so fruitfully.[110]

Further general conditions demanded of the recipient of Holy Viaticum concern the actual recognition of and belief in the real presence of Christ in the Blessed Sacrament, and insurance against the danger of irreverence. With regard to the former, a reply of the Holy Office given in 1861 ruled that Holy Viaticum was not to be administered to dying adult neophytes unless they were able to distinguish the spiritual from the material food, and actually believed in the real presence of Christ in the Sacred Host.[111]

One may also be incapable of belief in the presence of Christ under the sacramental species in consequence of his never having possessed the use of reason. It was generally agreed that such persons should not be allowed to receive Holy Viaticum. Thus Suarez taught that these, since they

[110] Conc. Trident., sess. XIII, *Decretum de Sanctissimo Eucharistiae Sacramento*, c. 8—Schroeder, *Canons and Decrees of the Council of Trent*, p. 354.

[111] S. C. C. Off. (Tchely Meridio-Oriental.), 10 apr. 1861, ad 1: "Praeterea hisce neophytis moribundis non esse administrandum Viaticum nisi saltem discernant cibum spiritualem a corporali, cognoscendo et credendo in Sacra Hostia praesentiam Christi Domini."—*Fontes*, n. 965; *Collect.*, n. 1213.

were incapable of the devotion with which the sacrament should be received, should be denied It.[112]

Opinion was divided on the point whether one who had not always been insane could receive Holy Communion in danger of death, when at the time of death he had not enjoyed the use of reason for some time past. Suarez taught that such persons could be allowed to receive,[113] while De Lugo contended that, if the dying insane person had manifested his intention and desire to receive prior to his becoming insane, there was no reason why Viaticum should not be administered.[114]

Further support of the affirmative opinion was given by Barbosa (1589-1649). He maintained that Viaticum was not to be denied to such a person as long as it was not certain that he had lost the use of reason while complacently in a state of mortal sin, inasmuch as he was to be regarded as having interpretatively requested the Eucharist in the danger of death.[115] Later the Council of Alba (1850) decreed that Holy Viaticum was not to be denied them as long as it could be prudently judged that while they were sane they had expressed the desire to fulfill the precept, and as long as Holy Communion could be administered without danger of irreverence.[116]

The negative opinion, however, seemed to find favor with Gasparri (1852-1934). While not condemning the contrary opinion, he advised a denial of Holy Viaticum to such insane persons despite a previously expressed intention or desire to receive it.[117]

[112] *De Sacramento Eucharistiae,* q. 80, art. 9, disp. 68, sect. 6—*Opera Omnia,* XXI, 520.

[113] *Loc. cit.*

[114] *De Eucharistia,* disp. 13, sect. 3, n. 4—*Disputationes Scholasticae et Morales,* IV, 59. Cf. *The Catechism of the Council of Trent, supra,* p. 38.

[115] *De Officio et Potestate Parochi Descriptio,* pars II, cap. XX, n. 43.

[116] Tit. IV, decr. VII—*Coll. Lac.,* IV, 434.

[117] *De Eucharistia,* II, n. 1124.

Those who had the use of reason, but only in a feeble and vapid manner (*semifatui*), were allowed to receive Holy Viaticum if they were able to distinguish between the sacrament and common bread and were capable of some measure of devotion towards the Eucharist.[118]

With regard to the other general condition, namely that the danger of irreverence be obviated, the Roman Ritual warned that Holy Viaticum was not to be given to those from whom on account of their frenzy, or in consequence of their persistent cough, or because of some similar malady, irreverence was to be feared.[119]

Barbosa asserted that the delirious patient could be admitted to Holy Viaticum if he was capable of receiving It without any danger of irreverence. The giving of an unconsecrated particle in order to explore the possible presence of such a danger was recommended.[120] Noldin (1838-1922) also recommended the experiment with an unconsecrated particle, and stated that only during the enjoyment of a lucid interval could Holy Viaticum be administered.[121]

With regard to the other potential sources of irreverence, St. Alphonsus (1696-1787) remarked that if coughing was so severe as to render the swallowing of the Host impossible, the administration of Holy Viaticum should not be attempted. If the danger of vomiting was feared, an unconsecrated particle was to be given by way of experiment. If the patient was unable to retain it, then on no account was Viaticum to be administered, and in the case of one who was subject to vomiting apart from the taking of food he required that a period of six hours should elapse between the last attack and the administration of the sacrament.[122]

118 Suarez, *loc. cit.;* St. Alphonsus Liguori, *Theologia Moralis,* Lib. VI, n. 303; Gasparri, *De Eucharistia,* II, n. 1123.

119 *Rituale Romanum, Pauli V iussu editum et a Benedicto XIV auctum et castigatum,* Baltimore: John Murphy, 1873), tit. IV, cap. IV, n. 5.

120 *Loc. cit.*

121 *Summa Theologiae Moralis* (5. ed., 3 vols., Oeniponte: F. Rauch, 1904), III, n. 139.

122 *Theologia Moralis,* Lib. VI, n. 292.

The opinion of St. Alphonsus seems to lean to the side of severity. A six-hour delay would in many cases be impossible, and in many cases hardly necessary. Noldin, on the other hand, stated that one hour would be sufficient, but that the Eucharist was not to be administered if there remained any danger that vomiting might occur.[123]

Relative legislation on the matter of the dispositions required for the fruitful reception of Holy Viaticum are to be found in the Synod of the Vicariate of Suchow (1803). Here it was decreed that Viaticum was not to tbe administered if there was any evident danger of irreverence to the sacrament. It was not to be administered to the unworthy to the scandal of others. According to the fathers of the synod, the unworthy were those who were given to the practice of usury, those who lived in concubinage, and notorious criminals. To such persons Holy Viaticum was not to be administered until they had confessed their sins and as far as possible had repaired the scandal.[124]

With regard to those who were notoriously excommunicated, they were not to be denied Viaticum as long as they had given some sign of repentance and had been absolved from the censure.[125]

B. Children as the recipients

It has already been seen that the Council of Trent defined that the reception of Holy Viaticum was not necessary for children who had not reached the use of reason.[126] From that statement of the Council it may be inferred that It is necessary for those children who have already acquired the use of reason; It is necessary in the sense that such children are bound by precept to receive It. Since the time of the Council it had been the common doctrine that such children of tender age be admitted to Holy Viaticum, even

[123] *Loc. cit.*

[124] Cap. IV, n. 10—*Coll. Lac.*, VI, 602.

[125] Barbosa, *De Officio et Potestate Parochi Descriptio*, pars II, cap. XX, n. 43.

[126] Cf. *supra*, p. 36.

though in the ordinary course of events they would not have been admitted to first Holy Communion for some time.

De Lugo, following the teaching of Suarez, professed the opinion that dying children who had reached the use of reason should not be denied the Eucharist.[127]

During the post-Tridentine period, the theologians disputed the age at which a child attained the use of reason. Many were of the opinion that the age of discretion for the reception of Holy Communion was attained only between the tenth and twelfth year, while others asserted that children began to enjoy the use of reason at about the seventh year.[128]

Pope Benedict XIV, after a close examination of the various current opinions, concluded that a less advanced age was required for the reception of the Eucharist as Viaticum. Pastors were to be admonished not to let all young children alike die without the sacrament. It was the duty of the latter to diligently examine the dying child with a view to ascertaining its capability to discern the Eucharist from common food and to recognize the presence of Christ in the Sacred Host. Ultimately it was to be left to the judgment of the pastor to decide whether the child was a fit subject for the reception of Holy Viaticum.[129]

A less perfect disposition was required of children who received the Eucharist in danger of death. St. Alphonsus pointed out that the acquired use of reason not only sufficed but also called for the reception of Holy Viaticum on the

[127] *De Sacramento Eucharistiae*, disp. 13, sect. 4, n. 37—*Disputationes Scholasticae et Morales*, IV, 63.

[128] De Lugo taught that they reached the requisite age of reason when they were capable of distinguishing the Eucharist from common food, and hence in the danger of death were from that point onward bound to receive It—*De Sacramento Eucharistiae*, disp. 13, sect. 4, n. 39—*op. cit.*, IV, 63; St. Alphonsus Liguori, *Theologia Moralis*, Lib. VI, n. 301. Cf. Crotty, *The Recipient of First Holy Communion*, The Catholic University of America Canon Law Studies, n. 247 (Washington, D. C.: The Catholic University of America Press, 1947), pp. 14-20.

[129] *De Synodo Dioecesana*, Lib. VII, cap. 12, n. 3.

part of dying children in view of the divine precept which bound them, and in view also of the fact that the immense utility of the Holy Eucharist in such a circumstance does not postulate any larger measure of disposition for It.[130]

The substance of the legislation enacted by the various local councils of the post-Tridentine period followed that of the authors. In general, in the ordinary course of events, some children who were not allowed to receive Holy Communion by reason of the lack of required knowledge or by reason of their tender age were nevertheless allowed to receive Holy Viaticum. Provided that they had some knowledge of the mysteries of faith, and especially of the real presence of Christ in the Eucharist, they were not to be denied Holy Viaticum at death.[131]

The II Plenary Council of Baltimore (1866) reminded priests that in danger of death a less mature age was required of children for the reception of Holy Communion. Priests who allowed such children of conspicuous intelligence to die without Holy Viaticum for no other reason than that they had not been admitted to first Holy Communion were guilty of grave sin. Children who became seriously ill were to be imbued with the knowledge of the Eucharist, and unhesitatingly given the divine food, provided they were capable of discerning It from common food, and capable also of a due measure of devotion according to their limited power of appreciation.[132]

On August 8, 1910, the Sacred Congregation of the Sacraments issued the celebrated decree *Quam singulari,* the most important piece of legislation relative to the present mat-

[130] *Theologia Moralis,* Lib. VI, n. 301.

[131] Cf. Provincial Council of Bordeaux (1850), tit. III, cap. IV, n. 3 —*Coll. Lac.,* IV, 570; Provincial Council of Albi (1850), tit. V, decr. VII—*Coll. Lac.,* IV, 434; Provincial Council of Auch (1851), tit. III, cap. I, sect. 3—*Coll. Lac.,* IV, 1186; II Provincial Council of Quebec (1854), decr. X, sect. 7—*Coll. Lac.,* III, 643; Provincial Council of Urbino (1859), pars I, tit. VI, n. 27—*Coll. Lac.,* VI, 14; Provincial Synod of Utrecht (1865), tit. IV, cap. VIII—*Coll. Lac.,* V. 825.

[132] *Acta et Decreta,* n. 261.

ter that had been issued since the Council of Trent. The decree, issued with the specific approval of Pope Pius X, regarded the practice which allowed children who had reached the use of reason to die without Viaticum as an utterly detestable abuse, and decreed that the ordinary was to proceed severely against those who did not abandon that practice.[133]

The decree did not, however, distinguish between the knowledge required for the reception of simple Holy Communion and that required for the reception of Holy Viaticum. It merely directed that the prospective child-recipient was required to have a knowledge of the truths necessary as an essential means for salvation and an ability to distinguish the Eucharist from ordinary food.[134]

C. Persons under capital punishment

It seems that up to the time of the Council of Trent there was no uniform practice which regulated the administration of Holy Viaticum to persons under capital punishment. In Italy and in Germany such persons were allowed to receive It on the day of execution or on the day preceding, while in France and Spain Viaticum was always denied them.[135]

De Azpilcueta stated that, in accordance with the com-

[133] N. VIII: Detestabilis omnino est abusus non ministrandi Viaticum et Extremam Unctionem pueris post usum rationis eosque sepeliendi ritu parvulorum. In eos, qui huiusmodi more non recedant, Ordinarii locorum severe animadvertant."—*AAS*, II (1910), 583.

[134] N. III: "Cognitio religionis quae in puero requiritur, ut ipse ad primam Communionem convenienter se praeparet, ea est, qua ipse fidei mysteria necessaria necessitate medii pro suo captu percipiat, atque eucharisticum panem a communi et corporali distinguat ut ea devotione quam ipsius fert aetas ad SS. Eucharistiam accedat."—*AAS*, II (1910), 582; *Fontes*, n. 2103.

[135] Cf. G. Juenin (†1713), *Commentarius Historicus et Dogmaticus de Sacramentis in Genere et in Specie* (Lugduni, 1696), *De Eucharistia*, cap. IV; L. Pilati (1705-1755), *Origenes Iuris Pontificii ad Carolum sextum* (Tridenti, 1739), Lib. II, tit. IV, *de Eucharistiae Sacramento*, p. 186; Martinus de Azpilcueta (Navarrus) (1493-1586) *Consilia et Resonsa iuxta Ordinem Decretalium* (Lugduni, 1594), Tom. II, lib. V, *de poenitentiis et remissionibus*, consilium XL, n. 1.

mon law, persons about to be executed for a capital crime were not to be denied the Eucharist. In France and Spain, however, it was customary not to make the sentence of death known to the criminal until the actual moment of execution. Under such circumstances the administration of Holy Viaticum was denied out of reverence for the Eucharist. Moreover, it was not certain whether the criminal was really in danger of death as long as his fate was unknown. If, however, there were positive indications that the penalty of death would be inflicted, then Holy Viaticum was to be administered.[136]

It appears that the practice of denying Holy Viaticum to persons who awaited execution still prevailed in many places long after the Council of Trent. In 1821 the Sacred Congregation of the Holy Office decreed that in danger of death any member of the faithful who gave signs of repentance was not to be refused the last sacraments. Relative to persons under capital punishment, Viaticum was not to be denied them unless there was a custom to the contrary. The Sacred Congregation reserved its opinion concerning the lawfulness of such a custom.[137]

In 1841 the Sacred Congregation for the Propagation of the Faith ruled that Holy Viaticum could be administered to the faithful and to priests who had been condemned to death because of the faith, and It was to be administered on the day preceding their execution.[138]

A second question, which was submitted at the same time, asked if Holy Communion could be brought to those who had been justly or unjustly condemned to death, if they had received absolution, and especially if they had asked for Holy Communion. The reply was: "In the affirmative, and *ad mentem,* namely, that the Vicar Apostolic

[136] *Loc. cit.*

[137] 9 maii 1821—*Collect.,* n. 757.

[138] (C. P. pro Sin.—Tunkin. Occident.), 21 iul. 1841—*Fontes,* n. 4789; *Collect.,* n. 928.

should take care that those who had been condemned to death would be nourished with this heavenly food.[139]

Many local councils found occasion to legislate against the practice of refusing Viaticum to anyone merely on the grounds that he had committed a crime worthy of death. From the location of these various councils it appears that the abuse had spread outside of France and Spain to Italy and to Canada. The substance of the various conciliar decrees was that persons who had been condemned to death were not to be denied Viaticum, provided that they had repented and that in the act of Its administration there was no danger of irreverence.[140]

In the light of these enactments it can readily be seen that the practice was entirely foreign to the mind of the Church. There was no reason why such persons, if they were truly repentant of their crimes, should be denied the strength and comfort that a death-cell reception of the Eucharist would provide. The authors, however, were careful to note that all danger of irreverence was to be precluded, and that a sufficient length of time to allow for the dissolving of the Sacred Species was to elapse before the infliction of the death penalty. St. Alphonsus stated that the authorities responsible for the infliction and execution of the death-sentence were bound to make allowance for the proper reception of Holy Viaticum.[141]

[139] *Loc. cit.*

[140] Cf. Provincial Council of Lyons (1850), sect. XXI, n. 10—*Coll. Lac.*, IV, 480; II Provincial Council of Quebec (1854), decr. X, n. 3—*Coll. Lac.*, III, 642; Provincial Council of Ravenna (1855), pars II, cap IV, n. 6—*Coll. Lac.*, VI, 156; Provincial Council of Auch (1851), tit. III, cap. 1, 3—*Coll. Lac.* IV, 1186.

[141] *Theologia Moralis*, Lib. VI, n. 293; Cf. Laymann, *Theologia Moralis*, Lib. VI, tract. IV, cap. 6, n. 13; Pirhing, *Jus Canonicum*, Lib. V, tit. 18, *de furtis*, n. 30—V, 249.

PART TWO

CANONICAL COMMENTARY

In the foregoing portion of this work the writer discussed the historical development of the ecclesiastical legislation surrounding the institute of Holy Viaticum. In the remaining portion the institute will be further examined in the light of the current legislation as outlined in the Code of Canon Law. Within the framework of the Code legislation it is possible to distinguish three types of Communion of the sick: 1) Communion of the sick when administered in a public manner; 2) Communion of the sick when administered in a private manner; 3) Communion when received by the sick who are in danger of death (Holy Viaticum). Only the latter type shall be dealt with in this dissertation.

Again, according to the mind of the Church as evidenced by the Code of Canon Law, it is possible to consider Holy Viaticum in a twofold sense. Taken in its strictest sense this term simply denotes that Communion which is prescribed by divine and ecclesiastical precept for a person who is in danger of death.[1] Taken in a broader sense it denotes the repeated reception of Holy Communion by one who is in danger of death and who accordingly is not obliged by the law of the Eucharistic fast.[2]

It shall be within the scope of this dissertation to discuss Holy Viaticum from both of these view-points.

[1] Can. 864, § 1.

[2] Can. 864, § 3. Cf. T. Bouscaren-A Ellis, *Canon Law, A Text and Commentary* (Milwaukee: The Bruce Publishing Co., 1946), p. 204.

CHAPTER IV.

THE CANONICAL PRECEPT TO RECEIVE HOLY VIATICUM

ARTICLE 1. THE NATURE OF THE PRECEPT

It has already been seen that among the pre-Code authors there prevailed a difference of opinion regarding the precise nature of the precept that binds one to receive Holy Communion when one is in danger of death.[1] While there were some few who denied the existence of any such special precept, the authors quite generally acknowledged the existence of some kind of precept, but sought in addition to determine the nature of the existing precept. The vast majority inclined towards the opinion that the precept was one of divine origin.

Whatever may be the relative merits of the opinions of the pre-Code authors and commentators regarding the nature of this precept, the positive enactment of the Code of Canon Law leaves no room for further doubt or discussion concerning the actual existence of a precept.

> In danger of death, from whatever cause it may proceed, the faithful are bound by precept to receive Holy Communion.[2]

But while the Code does decide the issue precisely on this point, it does not state whether that precept is by nature divine or ecclesiastical. While modern authors continue to hold varying opinions, it immediately becomes evident that the vast majority, upholding the majority opinion of the pre-Code authors, regard this precept as one that derives its binding force from the divine law. In fact, the writer has found only one modern author, Augustine (1872-1943), who departed from the common view by holding that the

[1] Cf. *supra*, pp. 40-45.

[2] Can. 864, § 1.

obligation derives from a purely ecclesiastical precept.[3] This isolated opinion of Augustine can hardly be considered as of much consequence in opposition to an otherwise unanimous consensus of the authors.

In general, an obligation may arise either from a necessity that is inherent in the very nature of man, or from a precept that is imposed by lawful authority, whether human or divine. Man of his very nature is obliged to take food in order to conserve the life of the body. That exists as an essential means. On the other hand, man is obliged by divine precept to adore God in order to attain to eternal life. That necessity exists in consequence of a divine precept. The two obligations reflect in common a quality of indispensability in the work of achieving a given end. They differ, however, in the source from which they immediately emanate.

Theologians have long disputed the point regarding the exact nature of man's obligation to receive the Holy Eucharist. Merkelbach (1871-1942), representing the common teaching of the theologians, stated it as a principle that the sacrament of the Eucharist in itself is not absolutely necessary as an essential means for salvation.[4] With regard to little children who have not attained the use of reason, that doctrine stands confirmed by the Council of Trent, which declared that infants, regenerated by the waters of baptism and incorporated with Christ, cannot at that age(that is before attaining the use of reason) lose the grace of the sons of God already acquired,[5] and anathemetized anyone who insisted that communion of the Eucharist was necessary for little children before they have attained the years

[3] Charles Augustine, *A Commentary on the New Code of Canon Law* (8 vols., Vol. IV, 2. ed., St. Louis: Herder Book Co., 1921), IV, 242 (hereafter cited *A Commentary on Canon Law*).

[4] *Summa Theologiae Moralis* (3 vols., 3. ed., Romae: Desclée, 1939), III, n. 291.

[5] Sess. XXI, *de communione sub utraque specie et parvulorum*, c. 4—Schroeder, *Canons and Decrees of the Council of Trent*, p. 134.

of discretion.[6] With regard to adults, it is a *certain* proposition that the sacrament of the Eucharist is not absolutely necessary as an essential means for salvation, for the Eucharist is one of the sacraments of the living and as such can be fruitfully received only by those who are already in a state of grace.[7]

On the other hand, in the light of the words of Christ: "Unless you eat the flesh of the Son of Man and drink His blood, you shall not have life in you,"[8] it is also to be regarded as a certain proposition that the Eucharist is necessary in consequence of a divine precept.[9]

Precisely when and how often during life that precept was binding, Christ did not say. The Church, whose right it is to determine more accurately a general divine command, has by its positive legislation decreed that the faithful are bound to receive Holy Communion several times (*semel in anno*) during life and when they are in danger of death.[10]

It is to be noted, however, that the wording of canon 864, § 1, still leaves some room for doubt. It does not state that in danger of death one is bound by divine precept to receive Holy Communion; it merely states, without more clearly determining the nature of the matter, that one is bound by precept. In the absence of any authentic interpretation regarding the nature of the precept spoken of in canon 864, one must have recourse to a doctrinal interpretation, as arising from the common and constant opinion of the authors.[11]

Cappello[12] and Coronata,[13] representing the common opinion, declare that the precept to receive the Holy Eucha-

[6] Sess. XXI, can. 4: "Si quis dixerit, parvulis, antequam ad annos discretionis pervenerunt, necessarium esse Eucharistiae communionem: anathema sit."—Schroeder, *op. cit.*, p. 135.

[7] Merkelbach, *loc. cit.*

[8] John, VI: 54.

[9] Merkelbach, *op. cit.*, III, n. 293.

[10] Can. 859, § 1; can. 864, § 1.

[11] Cf. cans. 6, 18 and 20.

[12] *De Sacramentis*, I. n. 421.

[13] *Tractatus Canonicus de Sacramentis* (3 vols., Romae: Marietti, 1943-1945), I, n. 330 (hereafter cited *De Sacramentis*).

rist when one is in danger of death is an obligation arising from the command of Christ. Their method of argumentation proceeds along the line of the pre-Code authors to the effect that, if Christ did at any time give a divine command that was to bind the faithful to a reception of the Eucharist at some time during life, it is beyond all doubt that that command surely becomes operative when one is in danger of death, a time in which one feels most keenly the need for such special help as a means for resisting the onslaughts of Satan.

In line with this opinion of Cappello and Coronata are a host of modern theologians and canonists who are emphatic in their assertions that the precept spoken of in canon 864, § 1, is one which derives its binding force from the command of Christ Himself.[14] In view of this teaching of so many modern leading theologians and canonists one must perforce accept the interpretation which regards canon 864, § 1, as reflecting a divine precept written into the positive law of the Church.

[14] A. Van Hove, *Tractatus de Sanctissima Eucharistia* (ed. altera, Mechliniae: H. Dessain, 1941), capt. VI, art. 3, p. 208 (hereafter cited *De Eucharistia*); A. Blat, *Commentarium Textus Codicis Iuris Canonici* (5 vols. in 6, Vol. III, pars I (*De Sacramentis*), 2 ed., Romae: Ex Typographia Pontificia, 1924), Lib. III, pars I, n. 183 (hereafter cited *Commentarium*); L. Fanfani, *De Iure Parochorum* (Romae: Marietti, 1924),n. 287; E. Regatillo, *Ius Sacramentarium* (2 vols., Santander: Sal Terrae, 1945-1946), I, n. 342; H. Noldin-A. Schmitt, *Summa Theologiae Moralis* (3 vols., Vol. III, 26. ed., Ratisbonae, Romae et Neo Eboraci: Pustet, 1940), III, n. 137 (hereafter cited *Theologia Moralis*), Dom. M. Prümmer, *Manuale Theologiae Moralis* (7. ed., 3 vols., Friburgi-Brisgoviae: Herder and Co., 1931-1933), III, n. 208; Merkelbach, *Summa Theologiae Moralis*, III, n. 294; H. Davis, *Moral and Pastoral Theology* (4. ed., 4 vols., London: Sheed and Ward, 1943), III, 218 and 227; J. Aertnys-C. Damen, *Theologia Moralis* (13. ed., 2 vols., Taurini-Romae: Marietti, 1939), II, n. 139; T. Iorio, *Theologia Moralis* (3 vols., Vol. III, 3. ed., Neapoli: D'Auria, 1947), III, n. 147; A. Tanquerey, *Synopsis Theologiae Dogmaticae* (3 vols., Vol. III, 21. ed., Parisiis: Desclée et Socii, 1929), III, n. 918; F. Wernz-P. Vital, *Ius Canonicum ad Codicis Normam Exactum* (7 vols. in 8, Vol. IV, Pars I, Romae: Apud Aedes Universitatis Gregorianae, 1934), IV, n. 109.

Vermeersch (1858-1936), indicating a preference for the theory of St. Thomas concerning the necessity of the Eucharist, followed a somewhat different opinion. St. Thomas in discussing the question distinguished between the necessity of actually receiving the sacrament and the desire to receive it. Man, he asserted, was bound to the reception of the Eucharist as an essential means at least in his desire; but this in turn would lose all its meaning and import if it were left unfulfilled when opportunity was offered for its fulfillment.[15] This same doctrine was later expounded in the Catechism of the Council of Trent.[16]

Adopting this theory and applying it to the present question, Vermeersch argued that one in danger of death is bound to receive the Eucharist if an opportunity to do so presents itself, lest his desire be frustrated. In that case the reception of the Eucharist becomes a matter of inherent necessity regardless of any precept. While admitting that the opinion of modern authors overwhelmingly regarded the reception of Holy Viaticum as necessitated simply by divine precept, he charged that these authors did not offer any cogent reason for their stand, and stated that they drew their strongest argument from the keen spiritual need felt by a man in danger of death, which need he cannot neglect with impunity.[17]

This theory of Vermeersch, however, is of little more than academic importance, for it matters little whether a person fails to attain to eternal life consequent upon his lack of desire to receive the Eucharist or as a result of his failure to

[15] *Summa,* Pars III, q. 73, art. 3, and q. 80, art. 11.

[16] Nn. 51-52: "We say that this sacrament (of the Eucharist) imparts grace, because even the first grace which all should have before they presume to approach this sacrament, lest they 'eat and drink judgment to themselves,' is given to none unless they desire to receive the Holy Eucharist, which is the end of all the sacraments, the symbol of ecclesiastical unity and brotherhood, to which anyone must belong if he is to attain to divine grace." Callan and McHugh, p. 243.

[17] *Theologiae Moralis, Principia, Responsa, Concilia* (4 vols., Vol. III, 3. ed., Romae: Università Gregoriana, 1933), III, n. 369 (hereafter cited *Theologia Moralis*).

obey a divine precept. In either case the result is the same.[18]

It is to be noted, moreover, that Vermeersch himself, while propounding the thory, seemed to be content to vindicate the note of necessity that arises from the precept alone. In the *Epitome* both he and Creusen defined Holy Viaticum in the strict sense to mean that Communion which one who is in serious danger of death must receive in fulfillment of the divine and ecclesiastical precept.[19] This does not involve a self-contradiction on the part of the author, Vermeersch, for if a thing is necessary as an essential means, is it not also necessary in consequence of a divine precept? In either case the conclusion is the same.

The New Roman Ritual quotes verbatim the prescriptions of the Code, without, however, adding any further explanation.[20] O'Kane-Fallon, in their interpretation of the rubric, stated that all are bound by divine precept to receive Holy Communion when in danger of death from any cause whatsoever.[21]

A further argument for the divine origin of this precept may be deduced from the common and constant practice of the Church from the very earliest times. Whenever there exists such a long-standing and universal custom from which the Church is not wont to dispense and with reference to which the Church disclaims the power to do so, that in itself appears to be a positive indication that the precept is not merely of ecclesiastical origin.[22]

In the *Ecclesiastical Review* for 1941 there was reported an article written by the Reverend B. van Achen in the

[18] Cf. J. Stadler, *Frequent Holy Communion*, The Catholic University of America Canon Law Studies n. 263 (Washington, D. C.: The Catholic University of America Press, 1947), p. 44.

[19] *Epitome Iuris Canonici* ,3 vols., Vol. II, 6. ed., Mechliniae-Romae: H. Dessain, 1940), II, n. 114, 4 (hereafter cited *Epitome*).

[20] Tit. IV, cap. 4, *de communione infirmorum*, n. 1.

[21] *Notes on the Rubrics of the Roman Ritual* (Revised ed., Dublin: James Duffy and Co., 1943), n. 738 (hereafter cited *Notes on the Ritual*).

[22] Cf. Van Hove, *De Eucharistia*, cap. VI, art. 3. p. 208. Noldin-Schmitt, *Theologia Moralis*, III, n. 137.

Theologisch-praktische Quartalschrift for the year 1940, treating of this particular question. In support of the now common opinion, the author drew his arguments from the conciliar decrees, from the consistent ecclesiastical practice, and from the teaching of the theologians. In his concluding remarks he stated:

> If the Church is convinced that there is a divine command prescribing the reception of Holy Viaticum, why is nothing said about it in the Catechism? The answer is, that from her experience of two thousand years the Church knows full well that the reception of the sacraments is a matter of intelligent and zealous priestly activity; hence the Church is constantly reminding her priests, the dispensers of the Holy Mysteries, that they have the grave duty to give Holy Viaticum to the faithful in danger of death.... One might say: 'Very probably there is a *divine* command to receive Holy Viaticum in danger of death.' Certainly there is an *ecclesiastical* precept to this effect; and it would be desirable to have this law of the Church mentioned in the Catechism. For if the faithful were more thoroughly instructed in this matter, the number of those who would die without the viaticum would not be so great.[23]

What seems to be an argument in favor of the view that the precept to receive Holy Viaticum is one of ecclesiastical law may be drawn from the apparent conflict between this prescription of canon 864, § 1, and various other laws of the Church which forbid the reception of the Eucharist to

[23] *The American Ecclesiastical Review* (Vols. I-XXXII, Philadelphia, 1895-1905 (*AER*); *The Ecclesiastical Review*, Vols. XXXIII-CIX, Philadelphia, 1905-1943 (*ER*); *The American Ecclesiastical Review*, Vols. CX-, Washington, D. C., 1944-), CV (1941), 229. The translation is that of Francis J. Connell. In the recent revised edition of the Baltimore Catechism, question 376 reads: "When are we obliged to receive Holy Communion?" Answer: "We are obliged to receive Holy Communion during Easter time each year and when in danger of death." It is to be regretted that the Catechism does not better emphasize and more fully explain the nature of the latter obligation.

certain classes of persons.[24] If it be assumed that canon 864, § 1, is a prescription of the divine law, is it then logical to condition its observance on the prior fulfillment of what appear to be merely ecclesiastical prohibitions?

In actu primo, the divine precept to receive Holy Viaticum binds all men—those who have been baptized, in a direct manner; and those who have not been baptized, in an indirect manner by first binding them to a reception of the sacrament of baptism. *In actu secundo,* however, it binds only those who are fit subjects of the sacrament of the Eucharist.[25] The prohibitions which touch either non-Catholics who are baptised or also unworthy Catholics do not in any way remove the obligation to receive Holy Viaticum, but simply show their unworthiness and indicate that they should remove that unworthiness so that they too may be able to receive the sacrament rightfully and legitimately.[26]

In the light of the foregoing considerations, the following conclusion seems justifiable. The prescription of canon 864, § 1, is but a restatement of the divine law in this regard. Moreover, the obligation of receiving Holy Viaticum derives from the divine law in a fully determined manner, while the obligation of receiving the Eucharist once a year is not ultimately determined by the divine law, and it receives this determination only through the intervention of ecclesiastical authority. This common explanation is clearly stated by Jorio, now Cardinal Prefect of the Sacred Congregation of the Sacraments:

> Precisely how many times one must receive Holy Communion in order to satisfy the divine precept, Jesus did not say. But it is beyond discussion that the moment in which the divine precept urges in all its force is precisely when man girds himself for that

[24] Can. 731, § 2; can. 855.

[25] S. Romani, *Institutiones Iuris Canonici* (2 vols. in 3., Vol. II, Sectio prior, Romae: Editrice "Iustitia," 1944), II, n. 262.

[26] G. Michiels, *Normae Generales Iuris Canonici* (2 vols., Lublin: Universitas Catholica, 1929), I, n. 288.

great journey to eternity, that is, in danger of death; for then is his eternal destiny at stake in the final war waged by the spirit of evil, who is determined in this last assault to make him his victim.[27]

It follows that the obligation to receive Holy Viaticum is indeed a grave one. Consequently, only a correspondingly grave cause will excuse from its observance. The reception of Holy Communion when one is in danger of death is certainly the minimum requirement that arises from the words of Christ Himself. His command urges at least once in the lifetime of every Catholic who has attained the use of reason, and perhaps several times in the lives of many.

Article 2. The Manner of its Fulfillment

Section 1. The Danger of Death

From the wording of canon 864, § 1, it becomes unmistakably clear that the precept which binds the faithful to the reception of Holy Viaticum becomes operative only when one is in at least a probable danger of death. Consequent upon this prescription of law there arises the need of some norm whereby it can be determined when one is to be regarded as being in danger of death.

In their efforts to supply this norm, authors are wont to make a distinction between the danger of death (*periculum mortis*) and the point of death (*articulus mortis*). The former admits of a wide application, while the latter is much more restricted in its meaning and implication. In 1859 the Holy Office was asked when persons could be said to be in danger of death or at the point of death. In its reply the questioner was referred to the approved authors.[28] The indiscriminate use of both phrases even by authors of the present day presents no particular difficulty, inasmuch as the Code itself uses the wider terminology (*in periculo mortis*) and thus precludes, at least with reference to the

[27] *La Comunione agl' Infermi* (Romae: Pustet, 1931), n. 2. Translation by Joseph N. Stadler).

[28] S. C. S. Off. (Cincinnati), 13 sept. 1859—*Fontes*, n. 955.

administration of Holy Viaticum, any value which the distinction may have. For if one is bound in danger of death, as the Code states, then surely one is also bound at the point of death to receive Holy Viaticum.[29]

Modern commentators, almost unanimously, define the phrase *periculum mortis* in the words of D'Annibale's comprehensive definition.[30] The Code does not, indeed could not, define the emergency in more specific terms. In relation to the administration of Holy Viaticum it means that whenever the state of a person's health or the particular condition in which a person may find himself inspires serious uneasiness concerning his life, and gives reason to fear that the issue will prove fatal, then such a person can rightly be regarded as being in a danger of death. The actual judgment whether the emergency be of this character in a particular case is the responsibility of the individual priest who is the subject of the right to administer Holy Viaticum according to the canons of the Code.[31]

The use of the phrase *periculum mortis* rather than *articulus mortis* by the Code further indicates that the danger need neither be imminent nor as yet morally certain. Consequently a probable danger of death is all that is required in order that one may be regardad as a fit subject for the reception of Holy Viaticum.[32] A reasonably prudent judgment that the danger of death is present satisfies the requirements of the law on this point. Speaking of the danger of death in relation to extreme unction, Genicot-Salsmans declared that a man can be in a probable danger of death even though the likelihood of recovery is even more probable.[33] In a similar pattern Vermeersch-Creusen observed that the common opinion demands nothing more than a

[29] Cf. Jorio, *La Comunione agl' Infermi*, n. 4.

[30] Cf. *supra*, p. 45.

[31] Cappello, *De Sacramentis*, I, n. 432; Durieux, *The Eucharist, Law and Practice* (translated from the French by O. Dolphin, Chicago: The Lakeside Press, 1926), p. 174 (hereafter cited *The Eucharist*).

[32] Noldin-Schmitt, *Theologia Moralis*, III, n. 138; Cappello, *De Sacramentis*, I, n. 432; Coronata, *De Sacraemntis*, I, n. 330.

[33] *Institutiones Theologiae Moralis* (2 vols., Bruxellis: Dewit, 1927), II, n. 422.

probable judgment or a positive doubt that death will or may follow in this emergency.[34] According to Coronata, the degree of probability that death will follow is to be measured according to the frequency with which death has in the past followed under similar circumstances.[35]

The concept involved in the phrase *periculum mortis* is not indeed something that can be determined with mathematical accuracy. It seems more in accord with the mind of the Church to reckon the danger of death morally. According to Joseph F. Connolly,[36] the formula whereby the danger of death may be so determined involves two elements. The first element is an absolute and physical one, that is, there must be verified in fact a cause that is prudently judged to involve a probable danger of death. The second element is a relative and moral one, that is, the danger of death must be considered in relation to the present need of the prospective recipient.

Relative to the first element, authors prior to the promulgation of the Code of Canon Law, in their consideration of the causes productive of a danger of death, inclined to the opinion that a cause that was extrinsic to the recipient did not create the same amount of urgency as one that was intrinsic. The majority, however, held that the danger of death that arose from any cause was sufficient to demand the administration of Holy Viaticum.[37]

Subsequent to the positive enactment of canon 864, § 1, it is now certain that any cause, whether it be intrinsic or extrinsic to the recipient, is sufficient to produce a danger of death warranting the administration of Holy Viaticum.[38]

[34] *Epitome*, II, n. 225.

[35] *De Sacramentis*, I, n. 330.

[36] "The Emergency Powers of Canons 1043, 1044, and 1045 and Some War-time Considerations," *The Jurist*, V (1945), 26.

[37] Cf. *supra*, pp. 45-46.

[38] Canon 864, § 1: In periculo mortis, *quavis ex causa procedat*, fideles sacrae communionis recipiendae praecepto tenentur. (The italics are the writer's own).

It follows that the field of causes is so wide as to defy any exhaustive enumeration. The textbooks commonly list the following more by way of example than by way of attempt at an all-inclusive listing: serious sickness, imminent battle, childbirth (at least when it is the mother's first parturition or any parturition under difficult conditions), serious surgical operation, the iminence of a death sentence, extreme old age, serious bodily injury, dangerous fires or floods, serious epidemics, hostile invasions, dangerous journeys, etc.[39]

Older theologians were wont to list the undertaking of a long journey as a cause productive of a danger of death. But in view of the modern means of transportation, this cannot any longer be admitted, so that the average modern voyage by ship or airplane does not give rise to a danger of death than can be regarded as even probable.[40] Merkelbach, however, considers in danger of death any aviator or navigator making a new journey or exploring new lands.[41]

With regard to imminent battle, the Sacred Penitentiary, on May 29, 1915, issued a response to the effect that every soldier who is in a state of warlike assembly (mobilization) can *ipso facto* be considered to be in danger of death, so that he can be absolved by any priest.[42] Although the response of the Sacred Congregation was given in connection with a matter other than that which is here under discussion, its fundamental object is one with the fundamental object of this discussion, namely, the danger of death in relation to the administration of a sacrament. A general decree of the Sacred Congregation of the Sacraments given

[39] Cf. Cappello, *De Sacramentis*, I, n. 421; Coronata, *De Sacramentis*, I, n. 330; Aertnys-Damen, *Theologia Moralis*, II, n. 139; Durieux, *The Eucharist*, p. 174; O'Kane-Fallon, *Notes on the Ritual*, n. 740; Noldin-Schmitt, *Theologia Moralis*, III, n. 138; Merkelbach, *Summa Theologiae Moralis*, III, n. 294.

[40] Cappello, *De Sacramentis*, I, n. 421; Durieux, *The Eucharist*, p. 174; Merkelbach, *Summa Theologiae Moralis*, III, n. 585.

[41] *Loc. cit.*

[42] *AAS*, VII (1915), 282.

on February 11, 1915, did directly touch upon the matter of administering Holy Viaticum in circumstances of war, and declared that soldiers *ad proelium vocati* could receive Holy Communion after the manner of Holy Viaticum.[43] Some doubt as to the precise import of the phrase *ad proelium vocatos* prevailed among contemporary writers. One writer interpreted the concession as applying only to those soldiers who were mobilized and already under orders to proceed to some unknown front. Obviously it had no import for those who were already at the battle-front, since for them there patently exists a very probable danger of death, which would automatically cause them to fall under the general provisions of law. Rather the response of the Holy See seemed to concern itself with those soldiers who as yet were not in actual danger, will not be for some considerable time, in fact may conceivably never be in danger at all. But they were liable to proceed to the front any moment and for those men the last chance to receive Holy Viaticum would be before their departure for their respective stations. It is prudently admitted that the danger of death is physically present once a soldier gets aboard the transport.[44]

A more recent reply of the Sacred Penitentiary seems to bear out this conclusion. Notwithstanding the provisions of the war-time faculties that permitted the granting of a general absolution when fighting is imminent, the question was asked: what is to be done if sometimes the circumstances are such that it is foreseen that it will be morally impossible or very difficult to absolve the soldiers in a body? The Sacred Penitentiary replied that in such circumstances it is allowed to absolve the soldiers in a body as soon as it is judged necessary to do so.[45]

[43] *AAS*, VII (1915), 97.

[44] O'Donnell, "Administration of the Viaticum to Soldiers Ordered to the Front," *The Irish Ecclesiastical Record* (Dublin, 1864-), 5. series, VI (1915), 626 (hereafter cited *IER*).

[45] 10 December, 1940—*AAS*, XXXII (1940), 571; Bouscaren, *The Canon Law Digest* (2 vols. and Supplement, Milwaukee: Bruce, Vol. I, 1934, Vol. II, 1943, Suppl., 1949), II, 146.

A writer in the *Ecclesiastical Review* applied the concession to crews of submarines and of other warships when on active duty and to the crews of merchantmen whose courses were charted through submarine- or mine-infested waters.[46] On the same principle, it must be made applicable to the crews of bomber- and fighter-planes going into active combat.

Theologians and canonists generally consider a person who is about to undergo a serious surgical operation as being in danger of death. It is to be noted, however, that due to the advance of medical science many operations which were formerly considered as serious may now be classed as minor ones. An operation can be regarded as serious if the patient will probably die in the event that the operation proves unsuccessful. Such a patient can rightly be regarded as being in a danger of death sufficient to warrant the administration of Holy Viaticum. With regard to the time at which the sacrament should be administered, there is no ruling that prevents its administration on the morning of the operation. In that case, however, it should be administered at least one hour prior to the operation. But very often doctors are opposed to any interference with the patient on that morning and consequently, unless it be an emergency case, there is no reason to delay the administration until that morning.[47]

There are still many deaths whose causes remain unaccounted for in the textbook listings of causes. Death very frequently results from the circumstances of one's occupation, from occupational hazards. That many occupational hazards involve a danger of death will be readily admitted.[48]

[46] Twomey, "The Eucharistic Fast," *ER*, CII (1940), 416.

[47] Woywod, "Answers to Questions," *Homiletic and Pastoral Review*, (New York, 1900-), XXXIII (1932-1933), 637 (hereafter cited *HPR*); Twomey, "The Eucharistic Fast," *ER* (CII (1940), 416; and the article—"Last Sacraments before Surgical Operation," *ER*, LXXXIV (1931), 633-634.

[48] Cf. Connolly, "The Emergency Powers of Canons 1043, 1044, and 1045 and Some War-Time Considerations," *The Jurist*, V (1945), 27-

But to maintain that whole classes of people habitually engaged in occupations that are fraught with mortal danger are so habitually bound by the divine precept to receive Holy Viaticum could lead only to conclusions bordering on the absurd. And while the law itself and its interpreters allow a wide latitude in the causes and circumstances productive of a danger of death that induces a divine precept to avail oneself of the spiritual aid at one's disposal, there are obviously certain limits beyond which one must not go. Thus, for example, a mere possible danger of death in which a person may habitually find himself would hardly warrant the administration of Holy Viaticum. Similarly all warrant seems wanting when a danger of death is only remotely probable. There is postulated rather a danger that is both probable and, to a certain extent, proximate.[49]

The second element in the formula is the relative and moral element, that is, even though the danger is physically absent as yet, it is morally present if there is the likelihood of objective circumstances which will prevent the availability of the accustomed spiritual aid if it be not availed of here and now. The authors envision precisely such a case and state that the victim of such circumstances may here and now be regarded as being in a danger of death sufficient to warrant the administration of Holy Viaticum. Given a chance to serve his spiritual needs now, the chance must be grasped at without scruple and without hesitation.[50]

In the experience of every pastor of souls, cases which are wrapt in the mists of doubt will certainly arise. It will be his responsibility to solve that doubt by relying either upon

---

32, who draws freely on the ratings of insurance companies, and lists among others the following examples: test pilots, automobile drivers—racing and speed testing, submarine workers, certain classes of workers in steel plants, shot-firers in the mining industry, steeplejacks, electrical workers, etc.

[49] J. Ferreres, *Compendium Theologiae Moralis* (2 vols., 14. ed., Barcinone: Ex Typis Eugenii Subirana, 1928), II, n. 420.

[50] Blat, *Commentarium*, Lib. III, pars I, n. 138; Fanfani, *De Iure Parochorum*, n. 287; Cappello, *De Sacramentis*, I, n. 421.

the aid of professional counsel, or upon the advice of those present, or upon his own reasonable judgment. Should the doubt remain, it may always be resolved in favor of the recipient even though he be not fasting.[51]

As a result of the foregoing study one must take cognizance of the very notable difference between the circumstances that justify the administration of Holy Viaticum and those that justify the administration of extreme unction. In the latter case only two justifying causes are admitted, namely sickness and old age.[52] The reason for this may be found in the high value set upon the reception of Holy Viaticum as a preparation for the journey to eternity and in the effects proper to each of these sacraments. Moreover, a difference obtains in favor of the administration of Holy Viaticum in the light of a comparison between the obligations that enjoin the reception of each. But while the law admits of a very liberal interpretation in the matter of administering Holy Viaticum, one must not go so far as to err on the side of laxity by overlooking the necessary factor of probability that must be present in each case.

Section 2. The Element of Time

The temporal element in the fulfillment of the precept to receive Holy Viaticum is a factor that has been much discussed by both old and modern authors alike.[53] In the light of modern commentary, however, it is certain that the obligation can be fulfilled at any point of time during which the danger of death lasts. In other words, the obligation begins with the beginning of the danger of death and lapses upon

[51] Benedictus XV, Litt. ap. *Sodalitatem*, 31 maii, 1921: "... ut qui in discrimine ultimo versantur, sacri Viatici et extremae Unctionis susceptionem ne eo usque remorentur cum sensum amissuri iam sunt, sed, contra, quemadmodum Ecclesia docet ac praecipit, iis roberentur Sacramentis vixdum, ingravascente morbo, prudens fiat de periculo mortis iudicium."—*AAS*, XIII (1921), 345; Cappello, *De Sacramentis*, I, n. 485; Vermeersch, *Theologia Moralis*, III, n. 262; Vermeersch-Cruesen, *Epitome*, II, n. 122.

[52] Can. 940, § 1.

[53] Cf. *supra*, pp. 45-50.

the cessation of the danger. One who fails to satisfy the demands of the divine law within that time is indeed guilty of sin, but one is not bound to supply the deficiency by a later reception of the Eucharist.[54]

The obligation, moreover, is satisfied through a single reception of Holy Communion, so that the subsequent acts of reception the while the danger of death lasts are only in a loose sense to be regarded as acts of the reception of Holy Viaticum. Authors are agreed that the reception of Holy Communion in the nature of Viaticum in no way depends upon a consciously manifested will or intention of the recipient, so that the precept can be fulfilled apart from any formally invoked actual intention. So too they regard it as a matter of indifference whether the recipient is aware of his present danger, whether he wishes to fulfill the precept by this particular reception of the sacrament, whether Holy Communion was indeed administered as Viaticum but received as simple Holy Communion of devotion, or whether the formula proper to the administration of Holy Viaticum was employed.[55] In the light of that teaching, one is led to the conclusion that the obligation is satisfied by the first reception of the Eucharist subsequent to the emerging of the danger of death. Vermeersch, however, seemed to indicate a preference for the contrary opinion, for he stated that during the danger of death one could receive Viaticum of devotion both *before* and after one's reception of the Viaticum of precept.[56] In the light of the foregoing, this opinion of Vermeersch seems hardly admissible.

It is still problematic whether a person who has received Holy Communion a few days previously with the object of satisfying his devotion is bound to receive again by way of Viaticum when he has fallen into a danger of death. Noldin-Schmitt assert that the question finds its solution in the

[54] Regatillo, *Ius Sacramentarium,* I, n. 354; Coronata, *De Sacramentis,* I, n. 330; Cappello, *De Sacramentis,* I, n. 421.

[55] Cappello, *De Sacramentis,* I, n. 481; Regatillo, *Ius Sacramentarium,* I, n. 342.

[56] *Theologia Moralis,* III, n. 362.

current positive legislation,[57] which enacts that the precept urges only in danger of death, and not also a short time before.[58] Furthermore, it is the mind of the Church that this precept urge only in an actual danger of death, so that the faithful would be fortified against spiritual enemies by this divine safeguard. Hence the fulfillment of the prescribed work at a time when the obligation did not yet exist falls short of a fulfilling of the obligation when it has become binding. This doctrine receives a resonable support from various authors and thus has at least the value of a probable opinion.[59]

On the other hand, there are authors who with an even greater degree of probability for the correctness of their doctrine hold that one who a short time previous (six or eight days) to the emerging danger of death received Holy Communion of devotion or of precept (Paschal precept) would not be bound to repeat his reception upon falling into a danger of death. They argue that the divine precept is already substantially fulfilled through the prior reception of the Eucharist, and at the same time the purpose for which the near-death reception was intended has been achieved. From a morally acceptable viewpoint such a person could be regarded as already in the danger of death even though he himself was ignorant of it.[60]

In the mind of the writer this latter opinion has much to recommend it. It seems possible, at least by analogy, to apply the prescription of canon 864, § 2, and to arrive at the conclusion that, while there is no strict obligation to receive again in danger of death, it is certainly the mind of the Church that one should do so. Moreover, this opinion is more in consonance with the fact that, if Holy Viaticum

[57] Cf. can. 864, §§ 1 and 2.

[58] *Theologia Moralis*, III, n. 138, 2.

[59] Fererres, *Compendium Theologiae Moralis*, II, n. 421; Iorio,*Theologia Moralis*, III, n. 147; Aertnys-Damen, *Theologia Moralis*, II, n. 140, I; O'Kane-Fallon, *Notes on the Ritual*, n. 738.

[60] Cappello, *De Sacramentis*, I, n. 433; Coronata, *De Sacramentis*, I, n. 330; Regatillo, *Ius Sacramentarium*, I, n. 354.

cannot be received when the danger of death has already commenced, as in childbirth or in a battle, it is possible and obligatory to receive It sometime beforehand.

The positive enactment to the effect that, even though one may have received Holy Communion on the same day, one is strongly advised to receive again if in the course of that day one is beset with a danger of death,[61] precludes any ground for further doubt in the heretofore much disputed question whether one who received Holy Communion in the morning could or should receive again at a later hour on the same day in order to fulfill the precept of Holy Viaticum. In the light of this directive norm it is evident that the Church does not wish to impose a strict obligation for a repeated reception of the Eucharist within the course of the same day, but at the same time strongly recommends that the faithful avail themselves of the concession which the law allows in favor of those who have become aware of the seriousness of their physical state. Coronata contends that the disposition of the Code seems applicable to those who received while already in ill health but later became ill to the extent that the danger of death intervened, and to those who suddenly become dangerously ill after a morning reception of the Eucharist when they were in a state of perfect health. Holy Viaticum can be given to them not only in the course of the same day but even in the course of the same morning, for the Code does not make any distinction that would bar such a double reception.[62]

Van Hove in commenting upon this canon stated that one can now forget the former controversy that centered around this point and rather keep in mind the term *suadendum* of the Code. Thus there rests upon the priest an obligation to exhort the sick person to again receive the Eucharist in the course of the same day if the state of his health or the condition in which he finds himself is productive of a probable danger of death. Furthermore, he states that canon

[61] Can. 864, § 2. [62] *De Sacramentis*, I, n. 330.

857 and canon 858, § 1, are to be interpreted in the light of this present prescription as contained in canon 864, § 2.[63]

The pre-Code authors were generally agreed that Holy Viaticum could be repeated during the same danger of death. They differed, however, as to the amount of time that should elapse between each reception. While some were of the opinion that a period of eight days should intervene between one reception and the next, the more common opinion allowed a daily reception.[64] Relative to the repeated reception of Holy Viaticum during the same danger of death, the Code of Canon Law states that the faithful may, on the prudent advice of the confessor, receive Holy Viaticum repeatedly on different days.[65]

It is proper to note here the precise wording of the canon. With the use of the term *licet* the canon definitely precludes anyone's future denial of an admissible repeated reception of Holy Viaticum during the same danger of death. It is now certain that with the use of the term *decet* the canon points to the becomingness of such a practice and to its evident utility. While a repeated reception of Holy Viaticum apart from unusual circumstances which give rise to new and distinct dangers of death within the course of the same day is not permissible, the canon by its use of the phrase *distinctis diebus* sets no limit as to the number of times that one may receive It on successive days; on the contrary, it points to a daily reception as very desirable.[66] In these repeated acts of reception Holy Communion is ad-

[63] *De Eucharistia*, p. 208; Cf. Blat, *Commentarium*, Lib. III, pars I, n. 183; Cappello, *De Sacramentis*, I, n. 433.

[64] Cf. *supra*, pp. 66-67.

[65] Can. 864, § 3: Perdurante mortis periculo, sanctum Vaiticum, secundum prudens confessarii concilium, pluries, distinctis diebus, administrari et licet et decet.

[66] Blat, *Commentarium*, Lib. III, pars I, n. 183; Cappello, *De Sacramentis*, I, n. 434; Coronata, *De Sacramentis*, I, n. 331; Vermeersch-Cruesen, *Epitome*, II, n. 133; Noldin-Schmitt, *Theologia Moralis*, III, n. 137.

ministered after the manner of Holy Viaticum, and hence the recipient is not obliged to observe the Eucharistic fast.[67]

Section 3. Relaxation from the Law of the Eucharistic Fast

The Church, ever mindful of the grave obligation that binds all of the faithful to partake of the Eucharist when they are in danger of death, and ever conscious of the extreme importance that attaches to such a deathbed reception, has allowed various relaxations of its laws in order to expedite such receptions. Not the least of these concessions has been the relaxation of the law of the Eucharistic fast. From the very earliest times the Church has allowed this relaxation in favor of those who were in danger of death.[68]

Current legislation in keeping with the older practice of the Church decrees that those who are in danger of death are allowed to receive Holy Viaticum even though they have not observed the natural fast from midnight.[69] It has already been seen that the danger of death which warrants the reception of Holy Viaticum may arise either from an intrinsic or from an extrinsic cause.[70] Relative to the observance of the Eucharistic fast, Augustine was of the opinion that only those who are in danger of death from an intrinsic cause come under the provisions of canon 858, § 1. He accordingly regarded these provisions as not applicable to soldiers going into battle or to persons about to suffer capital punishment.[71]

Even a strict interpretation of the law hardly warrants the making of such a distinction. Canon 858 makes no mention of the fact that the contemplated danger of death must

[67] Can. 858, § 1; Cf. Woywod, *A Practical Commentary on the Code of Canon Law* (2 vols., 10. printing, New York: Joseph F. Wagner, 1946), I, n. 764 (hereafter cited *A Commentary*).

[68] Cf. *supra*, pp. 32-34.

[69] Can. 858, § 1.

[70] Cf. *supra*, p. 86.

[71] *A Commentary on Canon Law*, IV, 234.

have arisen from an intrinsic cause. If the law makes no distinction, no distinction should be drawn.[72]

But while there is certainly no justification for such a distinction in the law, there may be some justification for it in fact. Thus authors readily agree that, if a person who is in danger of death from an extrinsic cause can easily observe the law which requires fasting from midnight, then he should do so.[73] Prümmer felt that Holy Viaticum should not be administered apart from the observance of the Eucharistic fast even to those who are in danger of death from an intrinsic cause, as long as the administration of It could be postponed with reasonable ease to a time when they would be able to receive while observing the law of the fast.[74]

A negative response given by the Sacred Congregation of the Sacraments in 1915 to a question proposed by the Cardinal Archbishop of Lyons in the following terms: "Whether soldiers *in procinctu,* or, as they say, mobilized for war, ought to be considered as constituted in the near danger of death, so that Holy Communion may be administered to them while not fasting," denies the lawfulness of a general custom of administering Holy Communion to such men while they are not fasting.[75]

The reason for the indicated distinction is to be found in the fact that those who are in danger of death by reason of some intrinsic cause (sickness) will usually be in a condition that renders the observance of the law of fast very difficult if not impossible. On the other hand, persons who are in danger of death by reason of some extrinsic cause will in most cases experience no difficulty in the observance of the law. For them, prior to all unqualified exemption from

[72] Woywod, *A Commentary,* I, n. 764.

[73] Vermeersch, *Theologia Moralis,* III, n. 362; Vermeersch-Cruesen, *Epitome,* II, n. 123; Cappello, *De Sacramentis,* I, n. 485; Noldin-Schmitt, *Theologia Moralis,* III, n. 153.

[74] *Manuale Theologiae Moralis,* III, n. 152.

[75] Cf. *Le Canoniste Contemporain* (Paris, 1878-1922; *Le Canoniste* 1924-1926), XXXVIII (1915), 455.

fasting for Holy Communion when they are in danger of death, as the exemption is stated in canon 858, it is more strongly desired that fasting for the reception of Holy Viaticum be observed if indeed they can do so without grave inconvenience.[76]

In the last analysis it is to be left to the prudent judgment of the minister to determine when Viaticum can be given apart from an observance of the law of the fast, to determine whether there is any likelihood for the emergence of an abuse, and to take steps to prevent it. In a particular case he would be justified in refusing the sacrament to a prospective recipient if there existed a well-grounded fear of the emergence of irreverence or of scandal from the non-observance of the law.[77]

Whatever be the relative merits of the foregoing opinions, the fact remains that the Code of Canon Law demands for the reception of Holy Viaticum simply the presence of a danger of death. The words of canon 858, § 1, as well as those of canon 864, § 1, are to be understood as referring to a probable as well as to a certified danger of death. Furthermore, if one consider canon 858 in relation to canon 864, § 3, one sees no reason why Holy Viaticum cannot be administered even daily to one who is not fasting. And this seems certainly applicable in all cases in which it would be inconvenient to postpone the administration of the sacrament to a time when the recipient can be fasting for its reception. It seems immaterial whether the inconvenience arise on the part either of the minister or of the recipient. In a case of doubt relative to the existence of a danger of death, Viaticum may and should be administered to those who are not fasting, for the priest need not hesitate to act on a concession granted by both the Code of Canon Law and the Roman Ritual.[78]

[76] Genicot-Salsmans, *Institutiones Theologiae Moralis*, II, n. 202.

[77] Cf. V. J. Coucke, "De Ieiunio Eucharistico," *Collationes Brugenses* (Brugis Flandorum, 1896-), XXXIV (1934), 380-386; Anglin, *The Eucharistic Fast*, p. 100.

[78] Tit. IV, cap. 4, *de communione infirmorum*, n. 4; Vermeersch,

The consideration given to a few practical questions may help to further clarify the extent of the relaxation of the law of the Eucharistic fast. Moralists and canonists alike teach that a person who is about to undergo a serious surgical operation is certainly in danger of death. Consequently such a person may receive Holy Communion after the manner of Viaticum, which in turn means that he may receive Holy Communion even though he be not fasting. It is not demanded that one inquire into the physical condition of the patient for the purpose of assuring oneself of the actual presence of a danger of death, for all that the law demands is that there be at least a probable danger. Yet the mere possability that death may ensue is a factor that is vastly divergent from the extant probability that death will ensue. It is the latter of these that suffices as a requisite for the reception of Holy Viaticum apart from the observance of the law of the Eucharistic fast.[79]

With reference to soldiers going into battle, Augustine held that they were not automatically exempt from the law of the Eucharistic fast unless they were already seriously wounded.[80] This rule of Augustine hardly lends itself to a universal application. It has already been seen that soldiers who are now at the battle-front or those who are under orders to proceed to some unknown front are rightly regarded as being in danger of death. For that reason they too would be the beneficiaries of the concession allowed by the law, and could therefore receive Holy Communion even though they were not fasting, provided it was reasonably probable that this was the last opportunity that would pre-

---

"Administratio Viatici Infirmo non Ieiuno," *Periodica de Re Canonica et Morali utili praesertim Religiosis et Missionariis* (Brugis, 1905-; ab anno 1927: *Periodica de Re Morali, Canonica, Liturgica*), XIV (1925), 102-112 (hereafter cited *Periodica*); Coucke, "Casus de Viatico Suscipiendo," *Collationes Brugenses*, XXVI (1926), 457-461.

[79] Noldin-Schmitt, *Theologia Moralis*, III, n. 153; Woywod, "Answers to Questions," *Homiletic and Pastoral Review*, XXXIII (1932-1933), 638; "Last Sacraments before Surgical Operation," *ER*, LXXXIV (1931), 633-634; Anglin, *The Eucharistic Fast*, p. 100.

[80] *A Commentary on Canon Law*, IV, 236.

sent itself. The next day they could again receive Holy Viaticum while not fasting, and daily thereafter could do so as long as the threat of combat lasted.[81]

A final question may be raised regarding the admissibility of a priest's saying Mass while not fasting when his reason for doing so is to provide Holy Viaticum for a dying person who would otherwise be deprived of the sacrament. Among the pre-Code theologians there were many who indicated a preference for the negative opinion. Their supporting arguments were for the most part based upon the extreme importance which the Church attaches to the law of the Eucharist fast. Even though the precept which required the reception of Holy Viaticum was regarded as being of divine origin, and the prescription which required fasting as a condition for its reception as a purely ecclesiastical law, yet this prescription was deemed most important for its safeguarding of the reverence due to the Blessed Sacrament, a reverence which was not to be sacrificed for the sake of the sick, since this sacrament is not indispensable to salvation. Moreover, the sick in such circumstances were thought not to be obliged to receive Holy Viaticum when they could do so only at the expense of a departure from a strict ecclesiastical law.[82]

Among modern authors, however, the affirmative opinion seems to be the more acceptable one. Its defenders base their arguments on the fact that a divine precept does take precedence over a purely ecclesiastical one, that is to say, the precept to receive Holy Viaticum, being divine in its nature, outweighs any consideration of the merely ecclesiastical one requiring the observance of a natural fast as a preparation for Holy Communion. Moreover, if ecclesiastical law allows one who is in danger of death to receive the Holy Eucharist

[81] O'Donnell, "Administration of the Viaticum to Soldiers Ordered to the Front," *IER*, 5. series, VI (1915), 626.

[82] Cf. St. Alphonsus, *Theologia Moralis*, Lib. VI, n. 286; Laymann, *Theologia Moralis*, Lib. V, tract. IV, cap. VI, n. 21; Gasparri, *De Eucharistia*, I, n. 309.

while not fasting, it is but reasonable to expect that the Church would also allow a priest to celebrate Mass while not fasting if such a celebration is the only means whereby the Church's solicitude for the dying can continue to operate effectively.[83]

[83] Cappello, *De Sacramentis*, I, n. 486; Iorio, *Theologio Moralis*, III, n. 171; C. Marc-F. Gestermann-J. B. Raus, *Institutiones Morales Alphonsianae*) 18. ed., 2 vols., Lugduni: Typis Emmanuelis Vitte, 1927-1928), II, n. 1560, II.

CHAPTER V.

THE MINISTER OF HOLY VIATICUM

ARTICLE 1. HOLY VIATICUM IN ITS ADMINISTRATION A RESERVED PAROCHIAL FUNCTION

By virtue of his power of orders and in the light of positive ecclesiastical legislation, it is certain that the valid administration of the sacrament of the Eucharist lies within the ordinary competence of any priest.[1] But the trend of the post-Tridentine legislation was definitely in favor of reserving to the pastor certain rights in the matter of the administration of the sacraments in general and in the administration of Holy Viaticum in particular.[2] The law of the Code, in keeping with the pre-Code trend, prescribes that the administration of Holy Viaticum, whether It be brought in a public or in a private manner, pertains to the pastor, though allowance is to be made for certain exceptions.[3] These exceptions will form the subject matter of the following article. The law as it touches upon the strict right of the pastor will be dealt with in the present article.

It may be stated as a general rule that it is the right and duty of the pastor to administer Holy Viaticum to any member of the faithful who is actually residing within the limits of his parish. Thus his right extends not only over his own parishioners but also over non-subjects who are found to be in danger of death while residing in or passing through his parish.[4]

The administration of the last sacraments is a function which postulates in the minister both the power of orders and the power of jurisdiction. Inasmuch as the pastor pos-

[1] Can. 845, § 1.

[2] Cf. *supra*. pp. 52-54..

[3] Can. 850; can. 462, n. 3.

[4] Can. 848, § 1: Ius et officium sacram communionem publice ad infirmos etiam non paroecianos extra ecclesiam deferendi, pertinet ad parochum intra suum territorium.

sesses both of these powers the right to administer Holy Viaticum naturally belongs to him. A priest other than the pastor or the local ordinary, lacking as he does the power of jurisdiction relative to the recipient, can lawfully exercise this pastoral function only with the permission, at least presumed, of the local pastor or the local ordinary. In a case of necessity the universal law of the Church automatically grants him this permission, so that it becomes not only allowable but to a certain extent also obligatory for him to perform this priestly ministration.[5]

It is proper to note that the administration of Holy Viaticum calls for the local rather than the proper pastor. This conclusion is to be gathered from the phrase *intra suum territorium* as contained in canon 848, § 1, which is constituted the norm of interpretation for canon 850. The use of the phrase *in propria paroecia* as contained in canon 462, n. 2, gives added strength to the right of the local pastor. The Roman Ritual is even more explicit in upholding the right of the pastor of the place as against that of the proper pastor, inasmuch as it mentions only the former as being the subject of the right to administer Holy Viaticum.[6]

Concerning the right of the proper pastor the law is silent. Coronata expresses the opinion that his right cannot be interpreted in a manner that would restore to him any rights relative to the administration of Holy Viaticum over those members of his flock who actually reside outside the limits of the parish. And such would be the case even if the sick person were nearer his own parish church than that of the parish in which he happens to be, a condition

[5] Can. 848, § 2. Cf. Van Hove, *De Eucharistia,* Cap. V, art. 2, p. 153; Coronata, *De Sacramentis,* I, n. 297; Cappello, *De Sacramentis,* I, n. 300. C. Augustine, *The Pastor according to the New Code of Canon Law* (2. ed., St. Louis: Herder, 1924), p. 93; C. Koudelka, *Pastors, Their Rights and Duties,* The Catholic University of America Canon Law Studies, n. 11 (Washington, D.C.: The Catholic University of America, 1921), pp. 98-99; Jorio, *La Comunione agl' Infermi,* n. 94.

[6] Tit. IV, cap. 4, *de communione infirmorum,* n. 9: Sacram Communionem per modum Viatici sive publice sive privatim ad infirmos deferre, pertinet ad parochum loci, in quo degunt infirmi.

which may easily arise in cities where there are a number of parishes.[7]

By reason of canon 451, § 2, the following are to be regarded as equivalent to pastors in the possession of all their rights and duties, and hence as beneficiaries of the right to administer Holy Viaticum:

(a) Quasi-pastors (can. 216, § 3);
(b) The acting vicar constituted in charge of a parish whose title has become vested in a moral person such as a religious community or a chapter (can. 471);
(c) The priest appointed as administrator of a vacant parish (can. 472, n. 1);
(d) The curate lawfully constituted to act as pastor when the parochial office has fallen vacant (can. 472, n. 2);
(e) The vicar-substitute, who is appointed to govern the parish in the absence of the pastor, provided that the local ordinary or the pastor has not set a limitation upon this right (can. 474, can. 465, §§ 4 and 5);
(f) The adjutant vicar who is deputed with full powers (can. 475).[8]

With regard to the assistant pastor (*vicarius cooperator*), his powers derive, as a general rule, from the diocesan statutes, from the letter of his appointment, or from the commission given to him by the pastor. The better interpretation of canon 476, § 6, favors the opinion that the office of the assistant pastor is not an ecclesiastical office in the strict sense, so that all of his powers are simply of a delegated character.[9]

But in cases where any express stipulation as to his rights and duties is lacking the law gives him the right to supply for the pastor in all things pertaining to the spiritual minis-

[7] *De Sacramentis*, I, n. 297.

[8] Cf. M. Ramstein, *A Manual of Canon Law* (Hoboken, N. J.: Terminal Printing Co., 1947), pp. 277-280.

[9] Cf. C. V. Bastnagel, *The Appointment of Parochial Adjutants and Assistants*, The Catholic University of America Canon Law Studies, n. 58 (Washington, D.C.: The Catholic University of America, 1930), pp. 143-144.

tration of the parish with the exception of the *Missa pro populo.*[10] Consequently, he would share with the pastor the right to administer Holy Viaticum. Moreover, if one is to follow the opinion of Kelly in his interpretation of the phrase *"nisi aliud iure caveatur"* of canon 462, it seems wholly within the power of the bishop through the medium of a diocesan statute to grant to the assistant pastor a right equal to that of the pastor in the matter of administering Holy Viaticum.[11]

Relative to the gravity of a violation of the pastoral rights in the administration of Holy Viaticum, a difference of opinion prevails among the authors. In the eyes of many a deliberate infringement upon this domain of pastoral rights constitutes a grave sin.[12] Cappello, however, regards this opinion as leaning to the side of severity, and asserts that rarely will a mortal sin be involved unless an express prohibition of the pastor is violated simply out of contempt.[13]

The tenor of modern ecclesiastical discipline favors a milder attitude towards religious who as priests presume to administer Holy Viaticum without the requisite permission of the pastor. Under the pre-Code law the religious who did so incurred the penalty of excommunication reserved to the Holy See.[14] Since this penalty is not re-enacted in the

[10] Can. 476, § 6.

[11] *The Functions Reserved to Pastors,* The Catholic University of America Canon Law Studies, n. 250 (Washington, D.C.: The Catholic University of America Press, 1947), pp. 56-60. According to the author a broad interpretation of the term *ius*" is the more acceptable one, with the consequent result that intermediate legislators may enact legislation governing parochial functions, either by way of derogation or amplification, provided that the particular statute does not conflict with extant universal law. There would hardly be any such conflict in the present matter.

[12] Van Hove, *De Eucharistia,* Cap. V, art. 2, p. 153; Marc-Gestermann-Raus, *Institutiones Morales,* II. n. 1537; Iorio, *Theologia Moralis,* III, n. 132; O'Kane-Fallon, *Notes on the Ritual,* n. 762.

[13] *De Sacramentis,* I, n. 301.

[14] Pius IX, const. *Apostolicae Sedis,* 12 oct. 1869, II, 14—*AAS,* V (1869), 297.

Code, one must conclude that in virtue of canon 6, n. 5, it is no longer of application.

The distinction referred to earlier in this work[15] between Viaticum in the strict sense and Viaticum in a broader connotation has a practical value in the consideration of the right of the pastor with respect to Its administration. The former is that Communion which is prescribed by divine and ecclesiastical law when one falls into the danger of death; the latter is that Communion which one receives out of devotion while still seriously ill. The precise point at issue here is the question whether the administration of the Viaticum of devotion is also reserved to the pastor.

The authors who try to provide the answer are divided in their opinions. Some maintain that the administration is reserved to the pastor, others, however, deny it. Writing in the *Irish Ecclesiastical Record* of 1931, Father O'Neill reached the following conclusions: (1) The administration of Holy Viaticum both of devotion and of precept is a function that is reserved to the pastor; (2) in a case of necessity the law becomes divested of its normal binding force, so that any priest could and should administer It; (3) in a case of evident utility, when an express permission of the pastor cannot be had, one may lawfully presume such a permission. Thus the right of the pastor and the spiritual good of the parishioner can be amply safeguarded.[16]

O'Neill is stoutly supported in his view by Fallon. The latter censures the indicated distinction as "strange and arbitrary," and one which is not warranted by a proper interpretation of the relative canons of the Code. To allow such a distinction would only facilitate the depriving of the pastor of his legal right, for the *Viaticum latius acceptum* may frequently be also the *ultimum sacramentum*.[17]

Vermeersch, on the other hand, is among the most ardent supporters of the view that Viaticum of devotion is in Its

[15] Cf. *supra*, p. 106.

[16] "The Administration of Holy Viaticum, A Function Reserved to the Pastor," *IER*, 5. series, XXXVII (1931), 515-517.

[17] O'Kane-Fallon, *Notes on the Ritual*, n. 762.

administration not reserved to the pastor, and the support which he receives from such recognized authors as Aertnys-Damen,[18] Cappello[19] and Coronata[20] lends added weight to his opinion. Drawing his arguments from a strict interpretation of canon 850, from the use of the term *confessor* rather than the term *pastor* in canon 864, § 3, and from the common practice of the Church, Vermeersch concludes that it would be contrary to the mind of the legislator to render more difficult the procuring of the sacramental nourishment by those who have the greatest need of it by reserving to the pastor the administration of Holy Viaticum in all cases. Consequently it would be lawful for another priest to administer Viaticum of devotion subsequent to the pastor's administration of Viaticum of precept. Unless this be allowed it could frequentlyhappen, as a consequence of prejudice or timidity, that the faithful would be deprived of the daily help of this heavenly food.[21]

Some few authors were content to regard the opinion of Vermeersch as a merely probable one, or, at any rate, as one which could be safely followed in practice.[22]

Article 2. Exceptions to the Right of the Pastor

Section 1. The Minister of Holy Viaticum in a Case of Necessity

Under the universal law of the Church, pastors are accorded the right to administer Holy Viaticum to all those living within the confines of the parish. But at the same time one must note that it was not the intention of the legis-

[18] *Theologia Moralis*, II, n. 255.

[19] *De Sacramentis*, I, n. 300.

[20] *De Sacramentis*, I, n. 297.

[21] *Theologia Moralis*, III, n. 355; "De Iure Parochi et Iterata Viatici Ministratione," *Periodica*, XXII (1933), 213-215.

[22] Fanfani, *De Iure Parochorum*, n. 289; P. Raus, *Institutiones Canonicae* (2. ed., Lugduni: Vitte, 1931), n. 158.

lator to so inflexibly determine that right as to preclude any sharing of it with others. The law does make allowance for several exceptions.[23]

The first of these exceptions becomes operative in what the legislator terms *a case of necessity.* Then the right of the pastor lapses and the right of any priest to perform the function arises. Since the first exception is couched in rather general terms through the use of the cited phrase, a more exact determination of its implications at once becomes imperative. It is sufficiently clear that the legislator in drafting this canon envisioned a case of necessity that is most apt to arise due to the illness or absence of the pastor. But a similar need may arise apart from the intervention of either of those factors. Thus it may happen that the pastor justly or unjustly refuses to exercise his right and to perform his duty, or the sick person perhaps declines the proffered ministrations of the pastor in preference for another priest. There too there is a case of necessity productive of the same urgency as that contemplated by the canon, and one may reasonably expect that the right of the pastor would yield to an even greater right on the part of the sick person. In general, a case of necessity can be said to be operative when, if one were to depend entirely on the pastor, one would probably be deprived of the saving help of Holy Viaticum.

Relative to the minister who may act when such a case of necessity arises, the common law grants to all priests the authority to do so.[24] Thus it would be permissible for the faithful to request the services of a priest who is an *excommunicatus vitandus*, or a *toleratus* whose excommunication is accompanied with a condemnatory or a declaratory sentence, if there is no other priest available.[25] Such a priest,

[23] Cf. can. 848, § 2, and can. 850.

[24] Can. 848, § 2.

[25] Can. 2261. Cf. H. A. Ayrinhac-P. J. Lydon, *Penal Legislation in the New Code of Canon Law* (New York: Benziger Brothers, 1936), p. 91; Coronata, *Institutiones Iuris Canonici* (5 vols., Vols. I-II, 2. ed., 1939; Vol. III, 2. ed., 1941; Vol. IV, 2. ed., 1945; Vol. V, 1936, Taurini: Marietti), IV, n. 1780.

however, could not take the initiative, but he may accede to any request without having to enquire into the motives which prompted it. It is allowed him to inform the faithful of the permission which the law grants him under such circumstances.[26]

With reference to the deacon as the minister of Holy Communion, the law designates him as the extraordinary minister. He may act in that capacity only on the fulfillment of a double condition, namely in the presence of a grave cause in consideration of which the permission of the local ordinary or of the pastor has been obtained.[27] The authors determine only by means of examples what constitutes a grave cause. They point out that the urgency of administering Holy Viaticum to a dying person is certainly a cause grave enough to warrant the granting of the requisite permission.[28]

The Code itself further prescribes that in a case of necessity the deacon need not seek the required permission, and in turn allows him to act on a presumption of law that the permission has been granted. In the case of necessity as contemplated in canon 845, § 2, there is undoubtedly included the necessity of administering Holy Viaticum to a dying person who would otherwise be deprived of the sacrament.[29]

The Roman Ritual directs the deacon who acts as the extraordinary minister of Holy Viaticum to follow the rite which is prescribed for the ordinary minister.[30] This includes the Eucharistic benediction both at the house of the recipient and afterwards in the church, for the Code clearly states that the deacon can impart this blessing when acting

[26] Jorio, *La Communione agl' Infermi,* n. 100.

[27] Can. 845, § 2. Pre-Code authors allowed the deacon to act only in a case of necessity and with the permission of the local ordinary or of the pastor; cf. Gasparri, *De Eucharistia,* II, n. 1079.

[28] Coronata, *De Sacramentis,* I, n. 291; Noldin-Schmitt, *Theologia Moralis,* III, n. 125; Cappello, *De Sacramentis,* I, n. 303; Vermeersch, *Theologia Moralis,* III, n. 354.

[29] Coronata, *loc. cit.;* Noldin-Schmitt, *loc. cit.;* Augustine, *A Commentary on Canon Law,* IV, 214.

[30] Tit. IV, cap. 4, *de communione infirmorum,* n. 28.

as the minister of Holy Viaticum.[31] When no consecrated particle remains in the pyx after Holy Viaticum has been administered, he imparts the blessing with his hand, using the formula prescribed by the Ritual.[32]

While it is perfectly in accordance with the prescriptions of law for a deacon to act as the extraordinary minister of Holy Viaticum, it is here necessary to explore the further possibility of allowing the subdeacon, inferior clerics and members of the laity to act in the same capacity. The law does not explicitly grant to them the right to do so even in a case of necessity. At the same time the law does not explicitly forbid them to so act. It is certain that clerics inferior to the deacon do not derive any power to administer the Eucharist in virtue of their ordination, a fact which is evident from tradition and which is implicitly confirmed by the Code.[33] The question can only be discussed in the light of opinions of the approved authors.

Among the older authors there were many who denied that the lower clerics or lay people could allowably act in the absence of a priest or of a deacon. It was contended that such an action would be contrary to the universal practice of the Church, and also unwarranted inasmuch as the reception of Holy Viaticum was not essential for salvation.[34]

Among modern authors, however, the affirmative opinion prevails. In justification of the position taken by them these authors assert that the divine law which in the case obliges the person in danger of death to receive Holy Viaticum prevails over the ecclesiastical law which under the circumstances calls for the reception of the Eucharist from the hands of a priest or of a deacon. Reception from the

[31] Can. 1274, § 2: Minister vero benedictionis Eucharisticae est solus sacerdos, nec eam impertire diaconus potest, nisi in casu quo, ad normam ca. 845, § 2, Viaticum ad infirmum detulerit.

[32] The Commission for Interpretation, July 13, 1930—*AAS*, XXII (1930), 365; Bouscaren, *The Canon Law Digest*, I, 404.

[33] Can. 345, § 2.

[34] De Lugo, *De Sacramento Eucharistiae*, disp. XVIII, sect. I, n. 22, IV, 172; Laymann, *Theologia Moralis*, Lib. V, tract. IV, cap. VII, n. 2.

hands of a lower cleric or of a lay person is not something that is evil in itself, nor is it forbidden by either the divine law or the ecclesiastical law. It is not contrary to the universal practice of the Church, for the reception of Holy Viaticum from lay hands was a practice which continued until the tenth century.[35]

The practice of the Church in modern times is certainly indicative of a milder attitude in the matter of allowing the lower clerics and the pious members of the faithful to administer Holy Viaticum in the absence of a priest or of a deacon. In 1927 the Sacred Congregation of the Sacraments granted to Mexican ordinaries the faculty to make use of a pious layman who had a common good reputation for moral character to carry the Blessed Sacrament to the sick and to the dying whenever a suitable priest, deacon or subdeacon could not be had. The sick person could receive the Sacred Species with his own hands, but if he was unwilling or unable to do so, the ministering of Holy Viaticum was to be undertaken by the visiting lay person who thereupon was to wash or purify his hands.[36]

In cases wherein the administration of Holy Viaticum calls for a special dexterity (administering It to patients who are affected with a cancerous condition of the mouth or of the throat), a priest could commit Its administration to a hospital sister, who would deposit the Sacred Species in the mouth of the recipient by means of a spoon.[37]

Though one admit that the lower clerics or even lay persons can administer Holy Viaticum in cases of extreme necessity when a priest or a deacon cannot be had, one may further ask whether they require a special mandate from the bishop in order to do so, or whether the presumed permission of the bishop or of the pastor is sufficient. Cappello

[35] Cappello, *De Sacramentis,* I, n. 305; Coronata, *De Sacramentis,* I, n. 291; Noldin-Schmitt, *Theologia Moralis,* III, n. 125.

[36] Bouscaren, *The Canon Law Digest,* II, 28; Coronata, *Interpretatio Authentica Codicis Iuris Canonici ab anno 1916 usque ad annum 1940* (Romae: Marietti, 1940), p. 193 (hereafter cited *Interpretatio*).

[37] Noldin-Schmitt, *Theologia Moralis,* III, n. 125.

answers that such an explicit mandate would not be required, except perhaps in time of pestilence, so that the bishop might verify the existence of a true necessity. If recourse cannot be had, one may rightly act on a simply presumed permission.[38]

Likewise authors are agreed that priests, deacons, the lower clerics and even the laity can administer the Holy Eucharist to themselves in order to satisfy the divine precept to receive Holy Viaticum in circumstances where the proper minister could not be had and provided that the factors of scandal and irreverence did not intervene.[39] Their reasons for this stand were drawn from the practice of the early Church and from the authority of the Sacred Congregation of the Propagation of the Faith, which expressly declared such action to be lawful for persons who had been imprisoned because of their profession of the true faith.[40]

Section 2. *The Minister of Holy Viaticum in Religious Houses*

The second exception to the right of the pastor relative to the administration of Holy Viaticum obtains in favor of the superior, the chaplain or the ordinary confessor of religious communities. In all clerical religious communities

[38] *De Sacramentis,* I, n. 305.

[39] Cappello, *De Sacramentis,* I, n. 308; Coronata, *De Sacramentis,* I, n. 295; Noldin-Schmitt, *Theologia Moralis,* III, n. 125; Van Hove, *De Eucharistia,* cap. V, art. 2, pp. 154-155.

[40] The following doubt was proposed to the Sacred Congregation: "3. An permitti potest in hoc persecutionis tempore ut fidei confessores ad mortem propter fidem damnati, et quibus in carceres defertur Sanctissimae Eucharistiae sacramentum occulte, possint illud suis manibus accipere et sese occulte communicare, ne sacerdos illos more ordinario communicans a persecutoribus agnoscatur et prehendatur; vel satiusne est in illo casu ab illis confessoribus communicandis abstinere, maximo cum illorum animae detrimento?"

On July 21, 1841, the Sacred Congregation replied: "Ad 3. Affirmative quoad primam partem, dummodo nullo irreverentiae aut conculcationis periculo tantum Sacramentum exponitur."—*Fontes,* n. 4789. A similar faculty was granted by the Sacred Congregation of the Sacraments to the Mexican ordinaries in 1927. Cf. *supra,* p. 153.

the superior has the right and the duty to administer, either in person or through another priest, Holy Viaticum and extreme unction to the professed members of the community as well as to others who live day and night in the religious house, either as servants, or for the purpose of education, or as guests, or on account of ill health.[41] To determine more precisely this right of the religious superior it is necessary to subject the general provisions of canon 514, § 1, to closer scrutiny.

The term *religious house* is to be interpreted in the sense of canon 488, n. 5, as meaning any house in which a religious community habitually dwells and discharges its proper duties under the guidance of a religious superior. But it must be noted that the various classes of persons mentioned in canon 514, § 1, fall under the jurisdiction of the superior even though they do not occupy the same building with him. It is sufficient that they dwell within the property confines of the religious house. Thus the canon would not apply to schools and summer residences situated elsewhere than on the premises of the religious house, and the religious superior could not in this matter vindicate his rights with regard to persons living in those buildings.[42] On the contrary, the residents of a filial house lacking moral personality remain under the jurisdiction of the religious superior and receive the last sacraments from his hands[43]

The subjects of the religious superior relative to his right to administer Holy Viaticum fall into two general classes. To the first class belong the professed religious and the novices. To the second class belong: (1) Servants who are actually in service and are residing fixedly on the premises, to the exclusion of workmen who live off the premises at

[41] Can. 514, § 1.

[42] U. Beste, *Introductio in Codicem* (3. ed., Collegeville: St. John's Abbey Press, 1946), p. 341; Fanfani, *De Iure Religiosorum ad normam Codicis Iuris Canonici* (2. ed., Romae: Marietti, 1925), n. 415.

[43] T. Schaefer, *De Religiosis ad normam Codicis Iuris Canonici* (4. ed., Romae: Typis Polyglottis Vaticanis, 1947), n. 567 (hereafter cited *De Religiosis*).

night; (2) persons who for reasons of study and education are living on the premises in an abiding fashion, such as the students, associates, oblates, and members of the apostolic school; (3) those who are staying in the convent or the monastery by reason of the latter's hospitality, such as the guests, the parents who come to visit their children, or the persons who board in the religious house while attending the religious exercises;[44] (4) those who are staying in the religious house in view of their infirmity—the sick in the infirmary.[45]

Authors are of the opinion that the length of time during which persons have to stay in the religious house in order to come under the jurisdiction of the superior does not exceed one full day, or that one needs to have at least the intention of remaining for that length of time. Thus, if one who had the intention of remaining for a shorter period falls into the danger of death, the right of the pastor of the place to administer Holy Viaticum to him would remain intact.[46]

Within the limits of the foregoing interpretation of canon 514, § 1, the religious superior —he who in his own name or in the name of another exercises a dominative power or the power of jurisdiction in the religious house—has the right to administer Holy Viaticum. The law constitutes him as pastor in this regard, and no further intervention, concession or communication either from the local pastor or from the local ordinary is necessary for the exercise of this right. Its loss on the part of the local pastor entails

[44] It is the practice of certain religious houses to give shelter to refugees. If these live in places that are independent of the house they are not members of the household nor are they guests; if they have been received into the religious house itself, they belong to the category of members of the household and come under the provisions of canon 514.—Cf. J. Creusen, *Religious Men and Women in the Code* (3. English ed. by A. Ellis, Milwaukee: The Bruce Publishing Co., 1940), n. 60.

[45] Cf. Schaefer, *loc. cit.;* J. Creusen, *Religious Men and Women in the Code,* n. 60.

[46] Schaefer, *op. cit.*, n. 566; Woywod, *A Commentary,* I, n. 391.

a corresponding relief from the duty of responding to the spiritual needs of the religious subjects.

In 1931 the Pontifical Commission for the Authentic Interpretation of the Code was asked whether canon 514, § 1, was to be understood in the sense that, in a clerical religious institute, superiors had the right and duty of administering Holy Viaticum and extreme unction to all persons mentioned in that canon when they were ill outside of the religious house. The Commission replied in the affirmative as regards professed religious and novices, but without prejudice to canon 848; otherwise in the negative.[47]

This response further determines the ambit of pastoral power enjoyed by the religious superior in virtue of canon 514, § 1. The question was prompted by the difference of opinion that hitherto prevailed among the authors. The distinction as made in the reply has its basis in the fact that professed religious and novices are the personal subjects of the religious superior, so that such a relationship is entirely independant of the circumstances of place. On the other hand, the second class of persons mentioned in the canon are not religious subjects, and the right of the superior to administer Holy Viaticum to them while living in the religious house does not flow from any personal power but rather from a local circumstance. When that local circumstance no longer intervenes, the power of the religious superior lapses. And even with regard to the professed members of the community and the novices who are living outside the property confines of the religious house, the right of the superior is restricted to the extent that he requires the permission, at least presumed, of the pastor or of the local ordinary to carry the Blessed Sacrament in a public manner.[48]

[47] 16 iun. 1931—*AAS*, XXIII (1931), 353; Bouscaren, *The Canon Law Digest*, I, 204; *Commentarium pro Religiosis* (Romae, 1920-; ab anno 1935: *Commentarium pro Religiosis et Missionariis*), XII (1931), 335.

[48] Cf. P. Maroto, "Animadversiones de Ultimis Sacramentis Ministrandis," Commentarium pro Religiosis, XII (1931), 335-346.

In the house of nuns (women religious with solemn vows), the ordinary confessor or the priest who takes his place has the same right and duty as the religious superior in the clerical religious house.[49] From the wording of the canon it would appear that the ordinary confessor enjoys this right only in houses of nuns which according to law are to be regarded as women religious professed with solemn vows.[50] But the Code also takes into consideration women religious who according to their institute are ordered to make solemn profession but who in some places must by order of the Apostolic See take simple vows.[51] These latter, while they may be subject to the local ordinary, fall under the provision of canon 514, § 2, so that it is the right of their ordinary confessor to administer Holy Viaticum to them.[52]

Unlike the legislative prescriptions governing the minister of Holy Viaticum in the clerical religious community, the Code here makes provision for the contingency in which the ordinary confessor, in consequence of illness or absence, will be prevented from exercising his right, stating that the right will then be vested in the priest who habitually or provisionally replaces him in the interim. It need not necessarily be the chaplain or the extraordinary confessor, for the ordinary confessor, in virtue of the power accredited to him is free to depute for this purpose any priest of his choice.[53]

In lay institutes the right and duty to administer Holy Viaticum belongs to the pastor of the place unless, through the intervention of the ordinary, the community has been withdrawn from parochial jurisdiction. In such a case the right belongs to the chaplain.[54] Privileges of exemption from parochial jurisdiction enjoyed by religious communi-

[49] Can. 514, § 2. [50] Can. 488, n. 7. [51] Can. 488, n. 7.

[52] Cf. Coronata, *Institutiones Iuris Canonici*, I, n. 540.

[53] Cf. Creusen, *Religious Men and Women in the Code*, n. 150: A. Larraona, "Commentarium Codicis," *Commentarium pro Religiosis*, IX (1928), 108.

[54] Can. 514, § 3, and can. 464, § 2.

ties prior to the promulgation of the Code retain their force, unless they were explicitly revoked in the canons of the Code.[55]

Although not explicitly excepted in canon 850, all persons residing in the seminary must also be regarded as exempt from parochial jurisdiction in the matter of administering the last sacraments, and so there is conferred upon the rector of the seminary a right similar to that enjoyed by the religious superior.[56] The seminary enjoys this local exemption from the moment of its canonical erection, and this favor applies to both the major and the minor seminary. Furthermore, the text of the law as contained in canon 1368 indicates a personal exemption which is enjoyed by all who are attached to the seminary, and live there day and night. Thus, in addition to the seminarians, the teachers, the officials, the domestic servants, and also the sisters employed in culinary or medical duties become the subjects of the rector in this regard. But unlike the religious house, a summer villa serving the needs of the seminary would partake of the exemption accorded to the seminary itself.[57]

Section 3. The Minister of Holy Viaticum in Hospitals

In order to take care of the spiritual needs of large Catholic hospitals, the local ordinary usually resorts to the expediency of appointing a hospital chaplain. This he does along the line indicated in canon 464, § 2, which entitles him to withdraw certain institutions from parochial jurisdiction. In the simple appointment of hospital chaplains, however, there is seldom any express reference to any such exemp-

[55] Can. 4. In Belgian dioceses the chaplain of all lay religious administers the last sacraments to the professed, the novices, the postulants, and to all other persons who habitually live in the convent. Sometimes the ordinary, in the document which contains the appointment of the ordinary confessor of men reliigous, includes the power of administering the last sacraments,—Creusen, *op. cit.*, n. 150.

[56] Can. 1368.

[57] Cf. Beste, *Introductio in Codicem*, pp. 684-685.

tion either in the letter of appointment or in the diocesan statutes. The exemption may best be described as an interpretative or tacit one, and it results in the withdrawal of the pastor's rights in those matters which made the appointment of the chaplain necessary.[58]

The designation of a hospital chaplain through the simple mode of appointment evidently carries with it the right to administer Holy Viaticum. The law allows that any priest may administer Holy Viaticum in a case of necessity or with the reasonably presumed permission of the local pastor or the local ordinary.[59] What the bishop can grant by individual permission, it seems he can also grant by general delegation. Such general delegation is normally implied in the appointment of the hospital chaplain.

Fundamentally the right of the local pastor to administer Holy Viaticum to the patients remains intact. Customary usage or the traditional procedure as well as the consideration of courtesy may impose a moral obligation on the pastor to refrain from any intervention. In the last analysis, the right of the chaplain would obtain in virtue of a mutual agreement. Furthermore, the local pastor retains the right to bring the Blessed Sacrament from the hospital chapel.[60] The convenience and propriety of bringing the Blessed Sacrament from the nearest place of reservation form the basis for this latter right of the pastor. A similar right would belong to the religious superior who would administer Holy Viaticum to his religious subjects who are patients in the hospital.

It is not evident from the wording of canon 1368 whether the rector of the seminary has the right to administer Holy Viaticum to the seminarians who are patients in the hospital. Such a right does indeed belong to the religious superior with regard to the professed religious and novices,[61]

[58] Cf. Drumm, *Hospital Chaplains*, pp. 88-89.
[59] Can. 850 and can. 848, § 2.
[60] Can. 483, n. 2.
[61] Cf. *supra*, pp. 158-159.

But a similar claim can hardly be made by the rector of the seminary inasmuch as the seminarians cannot be regarded as his personal subjects both on and off the seminary campus.

Hospitals may enjoy further exemption from parochial jurisdiction through some application of the common law or in consequence of an Apostolic indult. In virtue of the common law, hospitals maintained and used exclusively for clerics regular enjoy the same exemption as the community itself, whether they constitute part of the religious house or form a religious house in themselves.[62] Similarly hospitals or infirmaries, when established for the exclusive use of clerical religious who are not exempt and when constituting part of the religious house, enjoy the same exemption from parochial jurisdiction in the matter of the administering of the last sacraments.[63]

While the foregoing exemptions are clearly indicated in the law, the status of hospitals of clerical communities which are maintained for the use of externs is not so clear. If, however, such a hospital constitutes part of the religious house through its erection on the same premises, it too would evidently enjoy the exemption outlined in canon 514, § 1.[64]

Since such a hospital obtains its exemption from the local pastor's care only by reason of its forming part of the religious house, it is important to determine when this condition is fulfilled. Woywod stated that it need not be the same house in the physical sense, and that it is sufficient that if it is erected on the grounds of the religious house.[65] Drumm is of the opinion that an interpretative norm may be drawn from canon 497, § 3, which requires an additional permission of the local ordinary over and above that required for the erection of a religious house for the erection

[62] Can. 615.

[63] Can. 514, § 1.

[64] Cf. Augustine, "Hospitals—Their Chaplains, Confessors, Pastors," *ER*, LXVI (1922), 185-192.

[65] *A Commentary*, I, n. 391.

of a school, hospice, etc., if it be separate from the religious house. A separation which makes such an additional permission necessary precludes the enjoyment of the rights mentioned in canon 514, § 1,[66] The exemption, if any, would then obtain in virtue of canon 464, § 2, rather than in virtue of canon 514, § 1.

An exemption may furthermore derive from a privilege either Apostolic or episcopal in its origin. Apostolic privileges oblige not only the local pastor but also the local ordinary to respect the exemption thus conferred. Prior to the Code the Apostolic privilege was an important source of exemption.[67] Now, however the common law plainly authorizes the bishop to exempt a hospital or a similar institution from parochial jurisdiction.[68] Consequently the practical need for a direct intervention on the part of the Holy See has been considerably diminished. Where such a privilege has been granted, either by Apostolic or episcopal authority, the rights of the respective institution and the rights of the chaplain who may be appointed to take care of its spiritual needs can be determined only through a careful perusal of the respective indult.

Section 4. The Minister of Holy Viaticum to the Bishop and to the Pastor

The fourth exception to the right of the pastor relative to the administration of Holy Viaticum obtains in regard to Its administration to the bishop. The law prescribes that this duty be discharged by the ranking dignitary of the cathedral chapter.[69] In places where cathedral chapters do not exist, as is the case in this country, their function, relative to the government of the diocese, is discharged by the body of diocesan consultors.[70] The administration of Holy Viati-

[66] *Hospital Chaplains*, p. 83.
[67] Cf. *supra*, pp. 75-76.
[68] Can. 464, § 2.
[69] Can. 397, n. 3. For the rules of precedence, cf. can. 408.
[70] Can. 427.

cum to the bishop hardly pertains to the government of the diocese, and consequently the law does not transfer to the body of diocesan consultors the right to administer It to the bishop. Accordingly, in this country it appears that the right of the local pastor to administer Holy Viaticum to the bishop remains intact. It is always the latter's right to administer It to titular bishops and to cardinals who are not residential bishops.[71]

Strangely enough the law makes no explicit provision for the administration of Holy Viaticum to the pastor himself. Canon 447, § 3, however, points very definitely to the rural dean as having the duty, as soon as he learns of the serious illness of any pastor in his deanery, to see to it that the latter receives the necessary spiritual care. If it is the duty of the rural dean to provide for the spiritual needs of the sick pastor, as this canon indicates, then it seems that he has the corresponding right to administer the last sacraments, through which in large measure those needs will be supplied. This right and duty he may discharge either personally or through another priest.

Article 3. The Obligation to Administer Holy Viaticum

The foregoing articles were devoted to a consideration of the right that is vested in pastors and certain other priests to administer Holy Viaticum. It now remains to consider the corresponding obligation that flows from that right. As a general rule, pastors and other priests who have the care of souls are bound in justice to administer the sacrament of the Eucharist to their subjects, not only when these subjects are bound by precept to receive the Eucharist, but also when they reasonably petition for a reception of the sacrament in order to satisfy their devotion.[72]

The Code of Canon Law, however, not content with establishing the general obligation that binds the pastor to administer the sacrament of the Eucharist, wishes to par-

[71] Fanfani, *De Iure Parochorum,* n. 289.

[72] Can. 467, § 1.

ticularize with reference to the administration of Holy Viaticum, thereby reflecting the solicitude of the Church for the sick and the dying. Thus the Code prescribes that the pastor shall take special care of the sick members of his flock, above all when they are near death, give them the last sacraments, and commend their souls to God.[73] Furthermore, pastors are warned that the administration of Holy Viaticum is not to be unduly deferred. Rather they must seek out the sick in order that their spiritual needs may be supplied while they are still in possession of their senses, so that they may ensure for themselves a more fruitful reception of the last sacraments.[74]

The Roman Ritual, in keeping with the spirit of the law, reminds the pastor that not the least of his duties is to care for the sick. Upon learning of the illness of any of his parishioners he should not wait to be called, but he should go at once to the sick person's home. Neither should he be satisfied with one visit, but he should repeat his visits as often as there is need for them. If the danger of death is evident, the pastor is to warn the sick person not to allow himself to be deceived through the astuteness of the devil or the idle flattery of his relatives or of the doctor, but rather to prepare himself for the due reception of the sacraments while he is still in full possession of his senses.[75]

The authors are agreed that a pastor is bound to administer the sacraments of baptism and penance to those who are in grave spiritual necessity, even if the fulfillment of such a duty were to entail a danger to his own life, as long as the spiritual need of the recipient is certain and there is every reason to hope that the reception of these sacraments will carry with them their proper effects. The evident gravity of this obligation arises from the fact that the reception of the one or the other of these sacraments may be necessary for salvation. Relative to the administration of Holy Viaticum under the same circumstances, the

[73] Can. 468, § 1.

[74] Can. 865.

[75] Tit. V, cap. 4, *de visitatione et cura infirmorum*, nn. 1 and 10.

authors are not agreed as to the existence of a similar obligation. If one bear in mind that the reception of Holy Viaticum is not an essential means of salvation, it seems that the negative opinion may be sustained, at least in theory. In practice, however, the refusal to administer Holy Viaticum on the part of the pastor on the grounds of the prospective recipient's being afflicted with a contagious disease can scarcely be regarded as constituting less than a grave sin. The advance of modern medical science considerably minimizes the inherent risk to the pastor's own life, so that the latter's obligation is proportionately increased. On the other hand, the concomitant risk of scandal arising from such a refusal would be sufficient to outweigh the danger to life.[76]

The weight of authority that supports the negative opinion, however, precludes a definitely certified obligation on the part of the pastor to administer Holy Viaticum when to do so involves a danger to his own life. The authors who support the negative opinion propose as a basis for their argument a decree of the Sacred Congregation of the Council, which was issued in the year 1576. According to its provisions, a pastor was bound to administer only the sacraments of baptism and penance to persons who were afflicted with a contagious disease. Inasmuch as the decree carried with it the approval of the reigning pope, Pope Gregory XIII (1572-1585), it is certainly indicative of the mind of the Church on the matter.[77]

Priests who do not have the care of souls are bound in charity to administer Holy Viaticum whenever there is a necessity for their so doing. Although the sacrament is not essential for salvation, yet in the light of the fact of its being commanded by a precept of the divine law, the obligation in charity may likewise be a grave one. It differs, however, from the obligation arising from the virtue of justice

[76] Coronata, *De Sacramentis*, I, n. 294.

[77] Cappello, *De Sacramentis*, n. 54; Noldin-Schmitt, *Theologia Moralis*, III, n. 34; A. Sabetti-T. Barrett, *Compendium Theologia Moralis* (27. ed., New York: Pustet, 1919), n. 688.

inasmuch as one is much more easily excused from its fulfillment.

The Code enacts severe penalties against pastors who are found to be negligent in their duties regarding the administration of the last sacraments and their assistance at the bedside of the dying. First they are to be reminded by the ordinary of the gravity of their obligation and the punishments to which their neglect exposes them. If such an admonition fails to produce the desired effect, the bishop should issue a reprimand and impose some penalty proportionate to the gravity of the fault. Should this also prove ineffective, a pastor who is not irremovable should be deprived of the fruits of his parish either in whole or in part, and as a last resort the bishop may invoke the expediency of effecting his removal from the parish.[78]

Impressed with the importance of the sacraments of penance and extreme unction for those who are in danger of death, priests are apt to lose sight of the gravity of the obligation that also binds one to receive Holy Viaticum, and of their own responsibility in ensuring that one is given the opportunity to receive It. While not denying the greater dignity of Holy Viaticum, they show a tendency to subordinate Its administration to that of the sacraments of baptism and penance. It must ever be borne in mind that, if the faithful are bound by a divine precept to receive Holy Viaticum, the corresponding obligation of the pastor must indeed be a grave one.

While the obligation of ensuring that those who are in danger of death are afforded an opportunity of receiving Holy Viaticum rests directly upon those who are charged with the care of souls, Catholic doctors and nurses, by reason of their close association with the sick, share in this responsibility. The obligation to notify the priest of the patient's illness will often fall upon them. For this reason they must bear in mind the importance of the last sacraments and the divine precept that binds one to a reception

[78] Can. 2382 and cans. 2182-2185.

of Holy Viaticum. They must bear in mind too the connotation of the phrase "danger of death" as employed in the law of the Church in contrast to its implications in medical and nursing terminology. In the latter it indicates that death is imminent, in the former it indicates that there is a resonable anticipation that death may ensue from the patient's condition, even though it is not expected to occur within a few hours. A proper knowledge and appreciation of the priceless spiritual aids which the Church brings to its sick and dying children should certainly be possessed by every Catholic doctor and nurse.[79]

[79] Cf. C. J. McFadden, *Medical Ethics* (2. ed., Philadelphia: F. A. Davis Company, 1949), p. 386.

CHAPTER VI.

THE RECIPIENT OF HOLY VIATICUM

Article 1. Adults as the Recipients

Section 1. General Legislation

The term "adult," if it be considered in the light of the meaning that attaches to it when the Code employs this term with reference to baptism,[1] points simply to those persons who enjoy the use of reason. But in order that one may be presumed to be in possession of the faculty of reason one must have completed his seventh year of age.[2] The writer has found it convenient, however, to treat in this aritcle of only those persons who have completed their seventh year and in addition possess the use of reason. He leaves to a later article the consideration of those persons who, although not yet seven years of age, nevertheless have gained possession of the faculty of reason.[3]

Relative to the recipient of the Eucharist in general, the Code lays down the rule that all those who have been validly baptised and who are not otherwise debarred by law may and must be admitted to the reception of Holy Communion.[4] The limitation referred to in canon 853 may arise either from the divine or from the ecclesiastical law. The fundamental requirement of a valid baptism is a condition set by the divine law for the valid reception of any of the other sacraments. Baptism is the door through which the faithful are admitted to a participation in the benefits shared by the members of Christ's Mystical Body, the Church.

But the precept to receive Holy Viaticum, being a precept of the divine law, binds all men, in a direct manner, those

[1] Can. 745, § 2, n. 2: Adulti autem censentur, qui rationis usu fruuntur....

[2] Can. 88, § 3.

[3] Cf. *infra*, pp. 146-149.

[4] Can. 853.

who have been validly baptised, and in an indirect manner, those who have not yet received that sacrament, in that it obliges them to a reception of the sacrament of baptism itself.[5]

Thus, in so far as the divine law is concerned, it seems that nothing further is required for the valid reception of the sacrament of the Eucharist than a prior reception of the sacrament of baptism. But in cases of doubtful baptism, when the doubt cannot be resolved, the subject is not to be deprived of his right to receive the Eucharist. When there is question of the privation of a certain right which one who is certainly baptised possesses, there must be certainty as to the existence of the cause which warrants the privation. In the case of the doubtfully baptised that certainty is lacking.[6] In practice, however, such a one is to be baptised conditionally.

The ecclesiastical law has added limitations not contained in the divine law. The Church has the obligation of ensuring that due reverence is paid to Christ in the Eucharist, and may therefore in its judgment introduce regulations which are conducive to that end. With the exceptions of the law of the Eucharistic fast and the law forbidding a second reception of the sacrament within the day, all the regulations which the Church lays down for the valid and lawful reception of the Eucharist in general find a similar application with regard to the valid and lawful reception of Holy Viaticum. It is to be expected, however, that these regulations will be less exacting when there is question of fulfilling the divine precept which calls for the reception of Holy Viaticum, than they would be when there is question of a mere devotional reception of the Eucharist. These mitigating modifications will be considered in a later section.[7]

[5] S. Romani, *Institutiones Juris Canonici*, Vol. II, Sectio Prior, n. 262.

[6] Cappello, *De Sacramentis*, I, 399; Coronata, *De Sacramentis*, I, n. 302.

[7] Cf. *infra*, pp. 136-146.

One of the conditions which the Church establishes for the lawful reception of Holy Communion is that a person be free from mortal sin.[8] This is obviously a condition which admits of no exceptions under any circumstances; freedom from mortal sin is as necessary a prerequisite for the fruitful reception of Holy Viaticum as it is a necessary prerequisite for the fruitful reception of simple Holy Communion.

Canon 856 further prescribes that ordinarily a sacramental absolution is required before one approaches the Holy Eucharist, even though one might be convinced that his act of contrition had restored the state of grace to his soul. The canon, however, does not call for an iron-clad enforcement of the latter rule, so that when there exists a real necessity for the receiving of Holy Communion, and when at the same time no suitable confessor is available, a person may without sin receive Holy Communion after having elicited an act of perfect contrition. Cappello mentions that the danger of death along with the impossibility of confessing or of receiving absolution would constitute an urgent necessity.[9]

For the valid reception of the sacraments, with the exception of the sacrament of the Eucharist, there is required in adults a true intention of receiving them. The Eucharist, however, can be truly received independently of any inten-

[8] Can. 856. This law was taken from the Council of Trent, sess. XIII, *de Eucharistia*, c. 7: "Si non decet ad sacras ullas functiones quempiam accedere nisi sancte, certe quo magis sanctitas et divinitas coelestis huius sacramenti viro christiano comperta est, eo diligentius cavere ille debet, ne absque magna reverentia et sanctitate ad id percipiendum accedat, praesertim cum illa plena formidinis verba apud Apostolum legimus: *'Qui manducat et bibit indigne, iudicium sibi manducat et bibit, non diiudicans corpus Domini.'*"—Schroeder, *Canons and Decrees of the Council of Trent*, p. 354. Fundamentally this law is of divine origin.

[9] *De Sacramentis*, I, n. 441. The exemption arising from the lack of a suitable confessor certainly excludes the obligation of confessing to: (1) A priest ignorant of the only language of the penitent; (2) A priest who is under excommunication as a *vitandus;* (3) an accomplice *in peccato turpi;* Cf. Vermeersch, *Theologia Moralis*, III, n. 290.

tion on the part of either the recipient or the minister. The Eucharist, unlike the other sacraments, possesses an element of relative permanency. But for the fruitful reception of the Eucharist some intention is required on the part of the recipient.[10] Theologians and canonists agree that an implicit habitual intention is required and suffices for the fruitful reception of Holy Viaticum.[11] Such an intention is found in the act of the will that is directed towards a conduct of life in accordance with the teachings of Christ and His Church.

But such an intention postulates the further need of a certain amount of knowledge of what the Eucharist is in order that one's reception be fruitful. What amount of knowledge is necessary the Code does not state. By analogy, from the requirements demanded of children,[12] one may conclude that the ability to distinguish the Eucharist from common bread and to understand the essential notion of the real presence of Christ in the Blessed Sacrament would be demanded as an absolute minimum. That in turn would entail some degree of knowledge regarding the mystery of the Incarnation, for some degree of knowledge of that mystery is a necessary preamble to any possession of knowledge regarding the mystery of the Blessed Eucharist.

Theologians are not in agreement as to whether an explicit faith in the doctrines of the Redemption and of the Blessed Trinity is absolutely necessary for salvation. The question is a theological rather than a canonical one. A reply of the Holy Office given on January 25, 1703, stated that missionaries were bound to explain the mysteries which are necessary as an essential means for salvation, such as the mysteries of the Trinity and the Incarnation, to dying

[10] Tanquerey, *Synopsis Theologiae Dogmaticae,* III, nn. 307-308.

[11] Cappello, *De Sacramentis,* I, n. 74; Noldin-Schmitt, *Theologia Moralis,* III, n. 135; Durieux, *The Eucharist,* p. 176; A. De Smet, *Tractatus Dogmatico-Moralis de Sacramentis in Genere, De Baptismo et Confirmatione* (ed. altera, Brugis: Beyaert, 1924), pp. 134-135; Regatillo, *Ius Sacramentarium,* I, 23.

[12] Can. 854, § 2.

persons who are not incapable of receiving such instruction.[13] In practice, an explicit faith in these doctrines should be demanded of adults.

The question of administering Holy Viaticum to dying non-Catholics may now be discussed. In the very first canon dealing with the sacraments, the Code forbids their administration to heretics and schismatics, even though they are in good faith and request the sacraments, unless they first renounce their errors and are reconciled with the Church.[14] The prohibition of this canon is general; it admits of no exceptions when there is question of heretics or schismatics who are not in danger of death.[15] Thus it points to the fact that, under normal circumstances at least, the sacrament of the Eucharist cannot be administered to such persons prior to their formal conversion. Here, however, there is question of an administration of the Eucharist, not under normal conditions but in danger of death.

The case wherein a formal conversion has taken place presents little difficulty. As a first requisite, the minimum of knowledge and belief referred to in the foregoing paragraphs must be demanded of non-Catholics, and cannot be postulated except perhaps in the case of schismatics and some High Church Anglicans. Apart from these two exceptions, not notwithstanding an otherwise devout life, some instruction is called for. But in the case wherein a formal conversion is lacking does indeed present a difficulty. As a general rule, a formal heretic or schismatic who is in possession of his senses, even though he be in danger of death, cannot be given absolution unless he retracts his errors and submits to the Church, and consequently he cannot receive any of the other sacraments. But if the question turns about a purely material heretic or schismatic (one who is

[13] Ad 2: "Non sufficere promissionem, sed missionarium teneri adulto etiam moribundo, qui incapax omnino non sit, explicare mysteria fidei quae sunt necessaria necessitate medii, ut sunt praecipue mysteria Trinitatis et Incarnationis."—*Fontes*, n. 764.

[14] Can. 731, § 2.

[15] Vermeersch-Creusen, *Epitome*, II, n. 16.

in good faith), it sems that the prescription of canon 731, § 2, more easily admits of an exception when the danger of death is present and when the risk of scandal does not intervene. Given such a case, there are authors who hold that the sacrament of penance can be administered conditionally, so that thus the door may be opened to the reception of any other sacrament warranted by the need and disposition of the recipient.[16] The administration of the other sacraments including Holy Viaticum should not be undertaken apart from a formal abjuration of error. In most cases a warning to the effect that such an abjuration should be made will be readily complied with. If it be prudently feared that the warning will go unheeded and would serve only to disturb the good faith of the dying person, it may be altogether omitted.[17] But such an omission of the request for a formal abjuration and reconciliation does not in addition mean that the sacraments may then be administered. Rather it should be the endeavor of the minister to so dispose the recipient for the proper reception of the other sacraments.

There are several responses of the Holy Office touching upon this matter. The first of these, given on January 13, 1864, stressed the need of some token that could serve to establish at least a reasonable doubt in favor of the heretic's or schismatic's desire for reconciliation.[18] The second response, given on July 20, 1898, allowed the administration of the sacrament of penance to schismatics who were in good faith and in danger of death, but solely on the condition that all scandal was efficaciously removed.[19] The third response was a private reply to the Bishop of Linz, given on May 27, 1916. It stated that material heretics and schismatics, even though they were in danger of death and asked

[16] Coronata, *De Sacramentis*, I, n. 72; Cappello, *De Sacramentis*, I, n. 62; Vermeersch, *Theologia Moralis*, III, n. 180; Genicot-Salsmans *Institutiones Theologiae Moralis*, II, n. 298.

[17] Regatillo, *Ius Sacramentarium*, I, n. 23.

[18] *Fontes*, n. 975.

[19] *Fontes*, n. 1203.

for the sacraments, could not be allowed to receive them until they had in some way rejected their errors and had made a profession of faith. If destitute of their senses, the sacraments of penance and extreme unction could be administered conditionally, provided that there was some basis for the conjecture that they had, implicitly at least, rejected their errors and provided also that scandal was removed through the fact that it was made known to the bystanders that the Church supposes such to have returned to the unity of the Church in their last moments.[20]

What was stated in this response was later confirmed by the response of the Holy Office of November 15, 1941. It too stressed the need of an abduration of error and a profession of faith. It is sufficient that these acts be implicit and as such may be contained in acts of the penitent by which he manifests his sorrow for sin and shows himself ready to do all things necessary for salvation.[21]

Whenever an implicit abjuration of error takes place, at least a conditional absolution may be given. If a devout schismatic ardently desires to receive Holy Viaticum from a Catholic priest who alone is present, Vermeersch-Creusen think that ordinarily It is to be denied him.[22] However, there can arise circumstances in which from the very denial there will be danger that his good faith will be disturbed. In this case some are of the opinion that there is room for *epikeia*, if scandal is removed.[23]

Some authors consider the question particularly in relation to Protestants, and are inclined to be a little more strict in their opinions.[24] While the reverence due to the sacraments of penance and extreme unction can be protected by means of a conditional administration, such a procedure is not possible in the case of the sacrament of the

[20] Cf. *Theologisch-praktische Quartalschrift*, LXIX (1916), 693.

[21] Bouscaren, *The Canon Law Digest*, Supplement through 1948, pp. 102-104.

[22] *Epitome*, II, n. 16.

[23] Vermeersch-Creusen, *loc. cit.;* Regatillo, *Ius Sacramentarium*, I, n. 20.

[24] Cf. Woywod, *A Commentary*, I, nn. 625-626.

Eucharist. Consequently one must satisfy himself that a prospective recipient possesses the necessary dispositions before one undertakes to administer Holy Viaticum to him. In the present matter it is difficult to establish hard and fast rules. Each individual case will have to be examined on its own merits, but it is to be borne in mind that the canons of the Church are to be interpreted, not only with a scholastic wisdom but also with an understanding heart.[25]

Another general limitation imposed upon the recipient of Holy Communion is to be found in canon 855, § 1. There the Code prescribes that all those who are publicly known to be unworthy, such as have been excommunicated, interdicted, or those who are manifestly of ill fame, must be refused Holy Communion until they have repented and formed the purpose of amendment, and until satisfaction has been made for the public scandal that has been given. The Code lists as being publicly unworthy the persons who are excommunicated, the interdicted, and also the manifestly infamous. Now, it is only external offences that are punishable under the penal law of the Code.[26] Excommunication and interdict carry with them the effect of unworthiness only after a condemnatory or a declaratory sentence of the court, or after a general disclosure of the fact in question.[27] The infamy may be notorious either in law or in fact.[28]

[25] Cf. Umberg, "De Haereticis et Schismaticis in Mortis Periculo Constitutis," *Periodica,* XVIII (1928), 108-122; I. Szal, *The Communication of Catholics with Schismatics,* The Catholic University of America Canon Law Studies, n. 264 (Washington, D.C.: The Catholic University of America Press, 1948), pp. 152-163; King, *The Administration of the Sacraments to Dying Non-Catholics,* pp. 112-113.

[26] Can. 2195, § 1: Nomine delicti, iure ecclesiastico, intelligitur externa et moraliter imputabilis legis violatio cui addita sit sanctio canonica saltem indeterminata.

[27] Can. 2232. Cf. Ayrinhac, *Penal Legislation,* n. 57.

[28] Delicts are legally notorious after a judicial sentence of the competent judge or as a result of a judicial confession of guilt. Notoriety of fact exists when the crime is publicly known or was committed in such circumstances of time and place that it cannot be concealed through the use of any subterfuge or excused by means of any legal principle.

But the mandate of canon 855 cannot, it seems, be limited by the definitions of the penal law of the Code. The Roman Ritual, containing an analogous prohibition,[29] now omits the list contained in the pre-Code edition which enumerated among the manifestly infamous such persons who were prostitutes, usurers, sorcers, blasphemers, or who lived in concubinage. Coronata explains the omission in the present edition of the Ritual by pointing out that the repentance of such sinners is to be presumed upon their request for the sacraments.[30] Persons who are known to be living in concubinage or in an invalid marital union, those who belong to forbidden societies, and those who are engaged in works that are gravely sinful are to be regarded as being publicly unworthy of the sacrament of the Eucharist.[31] Before such a sinner can be admitted to Holy Communion the law demands that he give proof of a sincere conversion and purpose of amendment and that he promise to repair the scandal.[32] Even in danger of death Holy Viaticum cannot be administered to a dying person unless his repentance is attended with some effort to repair the scandal or to remove the voluntary occasion of sin.[33] It is for the prudent judgment of the confessor to decide the extent of that obligation in each individual case, taking into consideration the condition of the penitent and the extent of the scandal occasioned by his sinful conduct. Whenever reparation is possible the penitent ought not to be allowed to receive the Eucharist until he has satisfied the obligation. When such reparation is not possible here and now, the dying person must reject his sinful way of life in the presence of witnesses or at least,

[29] Tit. IV, cap. ., *de sanctissimo Eucharistiae Sacramento*, n. 8.

[30] *De Sacramentis*, I, n. 313.

[31] Ayrinhac, *Legislation on the Sacraments in the New Code of Canon Law* (New York: Longmans, Green and Co., 1928), n. 145 (hereafter cited *Legislation on the Sacraments*).

[32] Can. 855, § 1.

[33] *Rituale Romanum*, Tit. IV, cap. 4, *de Communione infirmorum*, n. 2: "Cavendum autem in primis est, ne ad indignos cum aliorum scandalo [Sanctum Viaticum] deferatur, nisi sese prius sacra confessione purgaverint, et publicae offensioni, prout de iure, satisfecerint."

he should authorize the confessor to make known the fact of his conversion and repentance.[34] In addition, he must seriously promise to repair any scandal that may have been occasioned by his past sinful way of life. For the administration of Holy Viaticum such a promise will suffice but the confessor must satisfy himself as to its sincerity.

Should doubt prevail concerning the note of sincerity the confessor will usually be able to resolve it in favor of the penitent, and the spirit of the Code legislation is not averse to such a procedure. Vermeersch-Creusen recommend that recourse to the ordinary should be made if circumstances allow, and they point to the necessity of exercising the greatest caution in this matter.[35] A similar doubt concerning the necessity of making due reparation of scandal may also be referred to the ordinary.[37]

Relative to the administration of Holy Viaticum to occult sinners, the Code directs that priests refuse to administer the Eucharist to such sinners whenever they privately petition Its reception. If, however, they publicly request the sacrament, Its administration cannot be refused, for under such circumstances it is likely that a refusal would lead to the scandal of the faithful and to the loss of the recipient's reputation.[38] Before one bring these rules to bear upon the administration of Holy Viaticum, one must first determine whether the petition for Viaticum in a given case is to be regarded as a public or as a private petition. Ordinarily the request for the sacrament will be known only to the immediate members of the sick persons's family and on that account would hardly take on the characteristics of a public request. Consequently the factors of scandal or of the loss of reputation would not intervene so as to compel the priest to accede to the request. In practice, a petition for the last

[34] Vermeersch-Creusen, *Epitome*, II, n. 117; Coronata, *De Sacramentis*, I, n. 313.

[35] *Loc. cit.*

[37] Cf. reply of the Sacred Congregation of the Council, 18 November, 1922—Bouscaren, *The Canon Law Digest*, I, 408-409.

[38] Can. 855, § 2.

sacraments on the part of an occult sinner can generally be taken as an indication that the sinner is now repentant and has therefore removed the only obstacle that stands in the way of his receiving these sacraments.

All too frequently it happens that habitual sinners, when beset with a danger of death, will not hesitate to call the priest and indicate their desire to be reconciled with the Church, though past experience has clearly shown that a recovery is likely to entail a falling back into their former way of life. But even though such past experience gives reason to fear a lack of proper dispositions, it will seldom constitute a ground for refusal of the last sacraments. Following the pattern of the ruling of the Sacred Congregation of the Council,[39] the priest may refer the matter to the ordinary if circumstances allow a sufficient time for recourse to be made. Should the condition of the patient be such as to demand an immediate decision, the minister of the last sacraments could safely resolve the doubt in favor of the recipient and accede to his request.[40]

No reason however grave will justify the administration of the sacraments to one who is certainly unworthy and whose petition for them was prompted simply by a contempt of religion. In the absence of any such contempt on the part of the recipient, the theologians allow the administration of Holy Viaticum if a denial of It is fraught with fatal consequences for the priest.[41]

Section 2. Abnormal Cases

A. Abnormal cases arising from mental disorders

While the general law of the Church regulating the reception of Holy Viaticum may be clearly understood, one is apt to encounter some difficulty in the handling of cases

[39] Cf. *supra*, p. 135.

[40] Cf. Coronata, *De Sacramentis*, I, n. 314; Vermeersch, *Theologia Moralis*, III, n. 178; Ayrinhac, *Legislation on the Sacraments*, n. 146.

[41] Vermeersch, *op. cit.*, III, n. 179; Cappello, *De Sacramentis*, I, n. 60; Coronata, *loc. cit.*

which have not been so clearly envisioned by the legislator. In general, such abnormal cases may likewise find their solution in an application of the general principles of the law and in the light of the teaching of the theologians and canonists. Moreover, these cases are so many and varied that the most that can be hoped for is a treatment of the ones that are of most common occurrence.

The study of the general law of the Church revealed the necessity not only of the use of reason in the recipient of Holy Viaticum, but also of the presence of certain spiritual and intellectual dispositions. The absence of the former qualification, however, may not at all times warrant the refusal of Holy Viaticum, provided that there is no danger of irreverence to the Sacred Species. The latter condition is one which plays an important part in the matter of determining whether one, when laboring under abnormal mental or physical conditions, is capable of receiving Holy Viaticum. In order to avoid needless repetition, the writer wishes to be understood that, when in this section he states that a certain type of abnormal person may be admitted to Holy Viaticum, he means that such persons may receive It provided that they possess the necessary dispositions and provided that there is no danger of irreverence.

There can never be any question of administering Holy Viaticum to persons who have been totally insane from birth. In law such persons enjoy the standing of children who have not yet reached the age of discretion.[42] It may happen, however, that a person insane from birth is not totally but only partially so. A person's insanity may be limited to one particular sphere while in all other spheres he may enjoy the outlook of a normal person. Provided that the special object of his insanity is not the Eucharist, such an abnormal person may possess all of the necessary dispositions, and consequently would certainly be entitled to receive the Eucharist in danger of death.[43]

[42] Can. 88, § 3.

[43] Cappello, *De Sacramentis,* I, n. 402; Coronata, *De Sacramentis,* I, n. 304; Regatillo, *Ius Sacramentarium,* I, n. 178.

Little difficulty will be encountered in the case of the insane who enjoy lucid intervals. The Roman Ritual explicitly states that such persons may be allowed to receive Holy Communion during the intervals in which their mental disorders have abated.[44] The dispositions demanded of children of tender age who are in danger of death would also constitute a sufficient preparation for the reception of Holy Viaticum on the part of the insane who enjoy such intermittent periods of sanity.[45]

But should such a person be beset with the danger of death while not actually enjoying a period of sanity, could Holy Viaticum still be administered to him? As O'Kane-Fallon pointed out, the words of the rubric of the Ritual leave its meaning somewhat ambiguous, but all doubt as to what can be done in practice is removed by the common teaching of the theologians to the effect that Holy Viaticum can be administered to such persons even while they are actually insane.[46] What is allowable for the recipient becomes mandatory for the minister, but the latter must bear in mind that he can take action only on the supposition that the recipient, prior to his lapsing into insanity, expressed the desire to receive the sacrament and has not revoked it.

The same principle finds a similar application in the case of those who have lost the faculty of reason and who have never, even to the slightest degree, recovered it. They too can be admitted to Holy Viaticum provided that, prior to their becoming insane, they had evidenced pious and religious sentiments which afford a solid basis for the presumption that they have the requisite intention of receiving

[44] Tit. IV, cap. 1, *de sanctissima Eucharistiae sacramento,* n. 10: "Amentibus praeterea, seu phreneticis communicare non licet; licebit tamen, si quando habeant lucida intervalla, et devotionem ostendant, dum in eo statu manent, si nullum indignitatis periculum adsit."

[45] Can. 854, § 2.

[46] Coronata, *De Sacramentis,* I, n. 304; Cappello, *De Sacramentis,* I, n. 402; Noldin-Schmitt, *Theologia Moralis,* III, n. 135.

the Eucharist in danger of death, the duration of the insanity being of no import.[47]

The possibility of administering Holy Viaticum to delirious patients may now be considered. If circumstances allow, then the priest should await the return of sanity, and be prepared to avail himself of the first opportunity that presents itself for the due administration of the sacrament. But should it be apprehended that death may overtake the sick person prior to his recovering his senses, the minister may proceed to administer Holy Viaticum, since there are sufficient grounds for believing that the reception will be reverent, especially in the case of those who have led a good religious life. Given the necessary dispositions, such a reception may be beneficial to the recipient even though he be unconscious of what is taking place.[48]

Cappello recommends the practice of exploring the danger of irreverence through the administration of an unconsecrated particle. It seems to the writer that this procedure, while it may be eminently suited for exploring the danger of irreverence as arising from some physical disorder, cannot be adopted in the present case without running the risk of material idolatry, inasmuch as the patient may still retain some powers of reason. Should a doubt concerning the danger of irreverence remain, the priest should abstain from administering the sacrament.

Akin to the mental condition just discussed is the condition which arises from a loss of consciousness due to the near approach of death. Is it lawful, and if so, is it obligatory for the priest to administer Holy Viaticum to one who is already unconscious? From the point of view of lawfulness, the law does not decide the issue. The authors try to solve the question on the basis of analogous prescriptions of the Code.[49]

[47] Cf. O'Kane-Fallon, *Notes on the Ritual*, n. 750.

[48] Cf. Connell, "The Hospital Chaplain and the Administration of the Eucharist," *AER*, CXIX (1948), 24; Cappello, *De Sacramentis*, I, nn. 405-406; Noldin-Schmitt, *Theologia Moralis*, III, n. 136.

[49] Can. 854, § 2.

A strict interpretation of both of these prescriptions seems to render unlawful a reception of Holy Viaticum by one who is unconscious, since there is not present the ability to distinguish between the sacramental and material food as well as the potential use of the faculty of reason. On the other hand, there are some authors who hold that the prescription of the Ritual in forbidding the administration of Holy Communion to persons who are actually insane does not contain an absolute prohibition which forbids also the administration of Holy Viaticum.[51] If it may be assumed that the person could lawfully have received Holy Communion prior to his becoming unconscious, and that even now he can do so without irreverence, then there is no obstacle to a lawful reception of Holy Viaticum despite his present state of unconsciousness. Granted the lawfulness of such a reception, it follows that it would be obligatory on the part of the priest to administer It.[52]

To the final class of mentally deficient persons belong those who, though not really insane, approach a condition of insanity, so that they enjoy the use of reason only in a vapid manner (*semifatui*). The decision to grant or to refuse such a person permission to receive Holy Viaticum will hinge upon the presence or absence of the dispositions enumerated in canon 854, § 2. Usually such a person will have the requisite minimum of dispositions, and may, according to the common opinion of the authors, receive Holy Communion when in danger of death. Any doubt relative to the presence of these required dispositions may be resolved in favor of the recipient, so that the priest need not scruple about administering Holy Viaticum to him.[53]

[50] Tit. IV, cap. 1, *de sanctissima Eucharistiae sacramento*, n. 10.

[51] Cf. *supra*, p. 138, footnote n. 46.

[52] Cf. E. J. Mahoney, "Viaticum to the Unconscious," *The Clergy Review* (London, 1931-), XXXII (1949), 267-269 (hereafter cited *CR*); Sabetti-Barrett, *Compedium Theologiae Moralis*, n. 695.

[53] Coronata, *De Sacramentis*, I, n. 305; Van Hove, *De Eucharistia*, cap. VI, art. 1, p. 174; Noldin-Schmitt, *Theologia Moralis*, III, n. 135.

B. Abnormal cases arising from physical disorders

Similar problems relative to the administration of Holy Viaticum may arise from disorders that are of a purely physical nature. The presence of a persistent cough, a tendency to vomit, or a cancerous condition of the mouth or of the esophagus may all be potential sources of irreverence. It is precisely this danger of irreverence that the Ritual has in mind when it warns against the administration of Holy Viaticum to persons who are so afflicted.[54]

When coughing is so persistent as to render the patient incapable of swallowing, then the administering of Holy Viaticum is completely out of the question. But apart from such an aggravated condition it will seldom constitute an obstacle to the valid and lawful reception of the Eucharist. The physical make-up of man is such that the phlegm ejected as a result of coughing comes not from the esophagus or passage to the stomach, but from the trachea or passage to the lungs. Consequently, even should a fit of coughing follow closely on the reception of the Sacred Species, there is little danger that They will be ejected.[55]

Perhaps the danger of irreverence most to be feared in communicating the sick is that which arises from vomiting. In this case the resultant irreverence is of such a nature that the presence of any reasonable doubt must deter the priest from administering Holy Viaticum. In order to explore the possible danger, the authors recommend the giving of an unconsecrated particle after first making sure that the patient is aware of the experimental quality of such a reception. If after the unconsecrated particle has been swallowed no vomiting has taken place for at least half an hour, the minister of Holy Viaticum may reasonably assure himself that there is no danger of irreverence, and then proceed

[54] Tit. IV, cap. 4, *de Communione infirmorum,* n. 4: "... id tamen, diligenter curandum est, ne [Viaticum] iis tribuatur, a quibus ob phrenesim, sive ob assiduam tussim, aliumve similem morbum, aliqua indecentia cum iniuria tanti Sacramenti timeri potest."

[55] O'Kane-Fallon, *Notes on the Ritual,* n. 751; Regatillo, *Ius Sacramentarium,* I, n. 179; Cappello, *De Sacramentis,* I, n. 407.

to administer the sacrament. Even a certain amount of risk is justified if otherwise it is to be feared that the patient will die without Viaticum.[56]

Vomiting may occur as the result of the taking of food or drink, or it may occur independently of either of these actions. The required period of freedom from vomiting will differ in each case. In the former case a period of a half-hour would be sufficient, and the opinion of older theologians who required a longer period cannot any longer be sustained.[57] In the latter case, when vomiting occurs at irregular intervals, there is required a much longer period of at least six hours.[58] In practice, the advice of the attending physician may be sought with evident utility. He, knowing the cause of the malady, will best be able to judge the length of time that must have elapsed if one is to conclude that all serious danger of irreverence to the Blessed Sacrament has been obviated.

It may happen, despite all precautionary measures, that the Sacred Species will be ejected. If the Host still appears entire or is easily decernible, It should be reverently taken up and carried to the church where It is allowed to corrupt. If It cannot be distinguished, all the matter that is ejected should be taken up and burned and the ashes disposed of in the sacrarium.[59]

A further problem, relative to the admissibility of a reception of Holy Viaticum that can be effected only in an artificial manner, namely through the use of a tube inserted into the esophagus or directly into the stomach, may logically be discussed here. The crux of the problem centers on the question whether such an artificial reception is sufficient to include the notion of the *manducatio* that is essential to the valid reception of the sacrament of the

[56] Cf. Connell, "The Hospital Chaplain and the Administration of the Eucharist," *AER*, CXIX (1948), 23; O'Kane-Fallon, *loc. cit.*

[57] Cf. *supra*, p. 68.

[58] Regatillo, *Ius Sacramentarium*, I, n. 179; O'Kane-Fallon, *Notes on the Ritual*, *loc. cit.*

[59] O'Kane-Fallon, *op. cit.*, n. 752.

Eucharist. According to the opinion of most of the authors, it is essential to the notion of *manducatio* that the Sacred Species be taken into the stomach, and that the taking of the Sacred Species into the mouth is merely an integral part of the action of eating.[60] Cappello, however, expresses the opinion that if one takes the Host into the mouth with the intention of swallowing It, one receives the grace of the sacrament by that very action and prior to the action of swallowing the Sacred Species.[61]

Consequently, a reception of the Eucharist in an artificial manner does not seem to destroy the essential notion of eating. If the esophagus itself is artificial, Holy Communion can and should be administered, for there is then preserved the complete action of eating and there is precluded any irreverence to the sacrament. The same conclusion is possible when there is question of administering the Eucharist by means of a tube inserted into the esophagus.

A number of responses of the Holy Office seem to rule out the possibility of administering Holy Viaticum by means of a tube that is inserted directly into the stomach. The first response, given on January 27, 1886, stated that the administration of Holy Viaticum through the use of such artificial means was not expedient. A second response, given on November 27, 1919, again denied the permission to receive in this manner. These responses of the Sacred Congregation, given in particular cases and in a private manner, are not sufficient to constitute a definite ruling on the matter, and many authors continue to hold that it is still possible to make use of this artificial means, at least when there is question of administering Holy Viaticum.[62]

When the use of such artificial means of administration

[60] Cf. Cappello, *De Sacramentis*, I, n. 359.

[61] *Op. cit.*, I, n. 358.

[62] Cappello, *op. cit.*, I, n. 359; Prümmer, *Manuale Theologiae Moralis*, III, n. 185; Sabetti-Barrett, *Compendium Theologiae Moralis*, n. 691; Davis, *Moral and Pastoral Theology*, III, 233; Connell, "The Hospital Chaplain and the Administration of the Eucharist," *AER*, CXIX (1948), 24.

is excluded, would it still be possible for a patient who is suffering from a malignant or cancerous growth in the esophagus to validly and lawfully receive the Eucharist? The condition of the recipient may be considered under a twofold aspect: (1) when the esophagus is completely closed; (2) when the esophagus is only partially closed. With regard to the former case, if one is to follow the opinion of Cappello concerning the notion of *manducatio,*[63] then the reception of the Host into the oral cavity and the change that It there undergoes will satisfy that notion . One cannot, however, too readily accept this opinion of Cappello, inasmuch as he stands alone in his view. Nor does the present writer in any way subscribe to it for it seems altogether pragmatic whether such an opinion can be sustained. With regard to the latter case, namely when the esophagus is only partially closed, the swallowing of a very minute quantity of food, such as a little water with a particle of a host, will not be impossible. It seems indicated to make an experiment with an unconsecrated particle and a little water. If vomiting does not follow, the food may have come in contact with parts of the esophagus that are already dead, so that it decomposes without supplying any nourishment to the organism. But it is more probable that it comes in contact with parts of the esophagus that are still active, and then undergoes a kind of assimilation which can be regarded, to some extent at least, as equivalent to digestion and nutrition. Thus the patient is able to receive Holy Communion in a way that very probably fulfills the conditions essential to Its sacramental effects.[64]

In cases similar to those discussed in the foregoing paragraphs, a reception of Holy Viaticum under the species of wine would certainly facilitate matters. But in view of the prescription of canon 852, which rules that the Holy Eucharist is to be administered to the faithful under the species

[63] Cf. *supra*, p. 143.

[64] Cf. J. Schwienbacher, "The Administration of Viaticum in Cases of Cancer of the Esophagus," *The Casuist* (A Collection of Cases in 5 vols., Vol. IV, revised ed., New York, Wagner, 1925), IV, 128-134.

of bread alone, there seems to be excluded any such procedure. Yet an examination of this law of the Church, in the light of tradition and in the teaching of the authors, reveals that the prohibition is not so absolute as to exclude any and all exceptions.

The practice of administering Holy Communion under both species, for a long time common to both the Eastern and the Western Church, fell into desuetude in the Western Church during the eleventh and twelveth centuries. The Council of Constance 1414-1418) and of Trent (1545-1563) approved the contrary custom and formed the basis for the present law of the Latin Church. For grave but not dogmatic reasons the Latin Church introduced and maintained this discipline. None of these reasons, however, would form a motive for the refusal to administer Holy Viaticum under the species of wine alone if that were the only means of communicating a person who is in danger of death.

The authors who discuss the question are divided in their opinions, some maintaining that Viaticum can be administered in this manner,[65] others denying any such concession.[66] The precept to receive Holy Viaticum, inasmuch as it is divine in its nature, should not be conditioned on the prior observance of a precept that is merely ecclesiastical.

The last type of abnormality arising from a physical cause is present in those persons who lack one or more of the faculties of sight, speech, and hearing. Gasparri taught that persons who lacked all three faculties from birth were not fit subjects of the sacrament of the Eucharist.[67] Whatever may have been the value of Gasparri's opinion in the age in which it was formulated by him, it is certain that, in the light of modern methods of imparting knowledge to persons who are so physically handicapped, which methods

[65] Cappello, *De Sacramentis*, I, n. 385; Coronata, *De Sacramentis*, I, n. 301; Ayrinhac, *Legislation on the Sacraments*, n. 138.

[66] Vermeersch, *Theologia Moralis*, III, n. 388; Vermeersch-Cruesen, *Epitome*, II, n. 115.

[67] *De Eucharistia*, II, n. 1123.

demonstrate the fact that these persons are capable of acquiring a certain amount of knowledge, it cannot be sustained today. Again, the criterion regulating the lawfulness of communicating such persons is simply the presence or the absence of the minimum of disposition as it is stated in canon 854, § 2. That minimum of knowledge and of devotion would seldom be wanting in such defectives.

Article 2. Children as the Recipients

As a result of well-defined legal principles, a child which has completed its seventh year of age is presumed to be in possession of the faculty of reason; prior to that age the presumption points to the contrary.[68] In either case the presumption of the law will yield to the actuality of fact established to the contrary. Now, the age of discretion with respect to the reception of Holy Communion is determined by the law as the age when a child can distinguish between the Eucharist and common food. At that age the child has a right to receive Holy Viaticum regardless of its completion of the seventh year of age.[69]

The decree *Quam singulari*, issued by the Sacred Congregation of the Sacraments in 1910, condemned as an utterly detestable abuse the practice of allowing children who had reached the use of reason prior to their completion of the seventh year to die without Holy Viaticum, and instructed local ordinaries to proceed severely against all those who failed to abandon the practice.[70]

The decree, however, did not set any explicit demand regarding the dispositions required of a child which is to be admitted to Holy Viaticum. In this regard the Code is more explicit in demanding as the only requirements that the child be able to distinguish between the sacrament of the Eucharist and common food, and to adore It with such de-

[68] Can. 88, § 3.
[69] Can. 854, § 2.
[70] Cf. *supra*, pp. 71-72.

votion as can be expected of children of such tender age.[71] It is to be noted that the conditions laid down for the fruitful reception of Holy Viaticum are less exacting than those required for the fruitful reception of first Holy Communion. In the latter case the Code demands a more careful preparation, which evinces some knowledge of the mysteries of faith that are essential to salvation, over and above the requirements already noted for the reception of Holy Viaticum.[72]

If it be assumed that the child which is in danger of death possesses the requisite dispositions, the Code not only allows Holy Viaticum to be administered, but also enjoins upon the minister a strict obligation to administer It. The use of the terms *possit* and *debeat* leave no room for doubt in this regard. This in turn presupposes that the child not only has the right to receive Holy Viaticum but also is obliged to do so, which obligation arises from the divine law in a determinate manner, while the obligation to receive first Holy Communion becomes determinate only through the intervention of ecclesiastical authority.[73]

While the law itself is clear, a difficulty may arise in its application to individual cases. In the case of children who are near the completion of their seventh year and who have had a good Catholic upbringing, the difficulty will be slight, for invariably such children will be prepared for the fruitful reception of Holy Viaticum. But when the child is no more than five or six years of age, and has had no training in the Catholic religion, then indeed there is room for grave doubt. Before Holy Viaticum can be administered in such

[71] Can. 854, § 2: In periculo mortis, ut sanctissima Eucharistia pueris ministrari possit ac debeat, satis est ut sciant Corpus Christi a communi cibo discernere illudque reverenter adorare.

[72] Can. 854, § 3: Extra mortis periculum plenior cognitio doctrinae christianae et accuratior praeparatio merito exigitur, ea scilicet, qua ipsi fidei saltem mysteria necessaria necessitate medii ad salutem pro suo captu percipiant, et devote pro suae aetatis modulo ad sanctissimam Eucharistiam accedant.

[73] Cf. Coronata, *De Sacramentis*, I, n. 310.

a case, the priest must endeavor to impart the necessary knowledge and foster the requisite devotion. A child of five with average intelligence will be capable of gaining that requisite knowledge and devotion, but the possible preparation of a child of lesser age would on the part of the latter postulate an intelligence above the average.[74] Since the law enjoins upon the pastor the strict obligation of preparing children for the reception of first Holy Communion, it follows that this obligation must bind with equal force when first Holy Communion is received after the manner of Viaticum.[75]

Occasionally, despite the efforts of the pastor to prepare the child for the proper reception of Holy Viaticum, it may remain uncertain whether the prospective recipient has acquired a sufficient use of reason or possesses the disposition required by law. What are the obligations of the ministers when such a doubt arises?

As a solution to the problem, canonists teach that there is no strict obligation to administer Holy Viaticum and no strict obligation on the part of the recipient to receive It when it is not certain that the latter has reached the years of discretion, though the minister is free to do so.[76] But apart from any strict obligation in the matter the authors recommend, as the more laudable practice, that Viaticum be administered in such circumstances.

Since there is question of the child's first reception of the sacrament of the Eucharist, Its reception after the manner of Holy Viaticum notwithstanding, it seems that the prescriptions of canon 854, §§ 4 and 5, will retain their binding force. Consequently the competence to implement the judgment regarding the presence of the needed dispositions would be shared by the parents and the confessor alike.

[74] Cf. Connell, "The Hospital Chaplain and the Administration of the Eucharist," *AER*, CXIX (1948), 25.

[75] Can. 1330, n. 2.

[76] Coronata, *De Sacramentis*, I, n. 330; Cappello, *De Sacramentis*, I, n. 423; O'Kane-Fallon, *Notes on the Ritual*, n. 619; Crotty, *The Recipient of First Holy Communion*, p. 106.

This prerogative, however, is not altogether in their exclusive possession, for the pastor has by law the right to debar from the reception of first Holy Communion the children whom he deems to be insufficiently disposed.

No great degree of devotion and reverence towards the Eucharist can be expected of a child of very tender years. For the reception of first Holy Communion outside the danger of death, the Code demands a display of devotion that is suited to the child's own little way.[77] As a general rule, the amount of devotion will be proportionate to the amount of knowledge possessed by the child.

[77] Can. 854, § 3: ... et devote pro suae aetatis modulo ad sanctissimam Eucharistiam accedant.

CHAPTER VII

THE ADMINISTRATION OF HOLY VIATICUM

ARTICLE 1. THE MANNER OF BRINGING HOLY VIATICUM TO THE SICK

As a general rule, whenever the need of bringing the Blessed Sacrament to the sick arises, It is to be carried in a public and solemn manner. The priest, vested in surplice, stole, cope, and humeral veil, proceeds under a canopy accompanied by clerics or, where clerics are wanting, by a number of the faithful carrying lighted candles. The Blessed Sacrament is carried in a small pyx which is held by both hands before the breast and covered with the extremities of the humeral veil.[1] When performed in this manner, the carrying of the Blessed Sacrament to the sick is a function reserved exclusively to the pastor, and may not be undertaken by any other priest, except in a case of necessity or with the permission, at least presumed, of the pastor or of the local ordinary.[2]

But while the law certainly advocates this public and solemn method, it at the same time leaves room for the use of the private method of taking the Eucharist to the sick whenever the presence of a just and reasonable cause renders such a mode advisable.[3] The Blessed Sacrament is said to be carried privately when the priest who carries It simply wears the stole under his street-dress, bears the pyx on his breast in a secluded manner, and is accompanied by a cleric

[1] Can. 847 gives the law and the exception: Ad infirmos publice sacra communio deferatur, nisi iusta et rationabilis causa aliud suadeat. Cf. *Rituale Romanum*, Tit. IV, cap. 4, *de communione infirmorum*, n. 6, wherein is stated the same law and allowed the same exception, and nn. 10-13, wherein are set down the various requirements when the Holy Eucharist is brought in a public manner.

[2] Cf. cans. 462, n. 2, and 848, § 2.

[3] Can. 847. For the text of this canon, cf. *supra*, footnote 1.

or a member of the faithful.[4] The Code, however, warns that, whenever Holy Communion is administered to the sick privately, due regard must be had for the reverence due to the Sacrament, and directs also that the norms laid down by the Holy See for the safeguarding of that reverence be faithfully observed.[5]

When the Eucharist is carried privately in this manner, the function is not one that is reserved to the pastor, and any priest, with at least the presumed permission of him who has custody of the Blessed Sacrament, may exercise the function.[6] It is to be noted, however, that when there is question of taking the Blessed Sacrament outside of the church in order to administer the Holy Viaticum of precept, the right to do so then belongs to the pastor regardless of whether It is brought in a public or in a private manner.[7]

Cappello is of the opinion that, when the Eucharist is carried with all solemnity in the manner described above but only within the very house where It is reserved, for example in a convent or in a hospital, it is nevertheless to be regarded as a private function.[8] The prescriptions of canon 847, however, would apply in this case.[9] Consequently, the question is asked: Is the priest who administers Holy Communion to the sick in such institutions ever exempted from the obligation of carrying It in a public and solemn manner? Canon 847 requires a sound justifying reason for any departure from the general rule that It be so carried. Moreover, it is hardly conceivable that the reasons which prompted the legal concession in favor of the private mode of bringing the Eucharist to the sick would find any appli-

[4] *Rituale Romanum*, Tit. IV, cap. 4, *de communione infirmorum*, n. 29.

[5] Can. 849, § 2. With regard to the norms prescribed by the Holy See, cf. *supra*, pp. 60-61.

[6] Can. 849, § 1.

[7] Cans. 462, n. 3, and 850.

[8] *Summa Iuris Canonici* (3 vols., Vol. II, 3. ed., Romae: Universitas Gregoriana, 1939), II, n. 509 (hereafter cited *Summa*).

[9] Wernz-Vidal, *Ius Canonicum*, IV, n. 105.

cation under these circumstances, inasmuch as the priest does not leave the precincts of the convent or Catholic hospital.[10]

An adequate concept of the phrase "*iusta et rationabilis causa*" can best be gained in the light of the pre-Code legislation, which allowed a departure from the tradition of carrying the Eucharist to the sick in a public and solemn manner in order to forestall the present danger of contempt on the part of the infidels and of the consequent irreverence to the Sacred Species.[11] It was that same danger that prompted the permission now granted by the universal law of the Church. Other causes listed by the authors as being also just and reasonable are the inconvenience of a too frequent public bringing of the Eucharist to the sick, the opposition that may be offered by the sick person or his family, the desire of the sick person to receive Holy Communion daily when a daily public function is impossible, and the possible danger of a sacrilegious reception that a public administration of the Sacrament might entail.[12]

Because of the varying circumstances of place and person, a uniformity of practice in the matter of carrying the Blessed Sacrament to the sick can hardly be expected. In modern times, however, with the possible exception of Spain, the private mode is employed.[13] In this country the bishops, in the II Plenary Council of Baltimore (1866), regretfully sanctioned the practice of bringing Holy Communion to the sick privately.[14]

In the light of the prescriptions of canon 849, § 1, many theologians and canonists were of the opinion that it was the right of the individual priest who carried the Blessed

[10] Cf. *supra*, p. 87; Coronata, *De Sacramentis*, I, n. 298.

[11] Cf. *supra*, p. 60.

[12] Coronata, *De Sacramentis*, I, n. 298; Augustine, *A Commentary on Canon Law*, IV, 218-219; Vermeersch-Cruesen, *Epitome*, II, n. 114.

[13] Adnotationes Secretarii S. C. de Sacramentis, *Romana et Aliarum*, 5 ian. 1928—*AAS*, XX (1928), 82; Bouscaren, *The Canon Law Digest*, I, 405.

[14] Cf. *supra*, p. 61.

Sacrament to the sick to judge for himself the justness and reasonableness of the cause alleged as warranting a private administration. But many ordinaries, especially in Spain, considering themselves to be thereby deprived of a right that rightfully belonged to them alone, proposed the folowed question to the Sacred Congregation of the Sacraments: "Whether the judge of the just and reasonable cause which, according to canon 847, is required in order that Holy Communion may be brought privately to the sick, is the priest who is administering the sacrament, or only the ordinary of the place?" On December 16, 1927, the Sacred Congregation replied in the negative to the first part, and in the affirmative to the second, but with the added notation of the mind of the Sacred Congregation, namely, if according to common experience and judgment there exists in the diocese, or in any particular place, no objection against the bringing of holy Communion privately to the sick, ordinaries must be on their guard lest by rules that are too rigorous or too universal in requiring that Holy Communion be brought publicly, or by reserving to themselves the faculty of granting permission for the bringing of Holy Communion privately in individual cases, they withhold from the sick the solace of receiving Communion even daily.[15] In virtue of this reply the judgment was left exclusively in the hands of the ordinary.

Yet, notwithstanding, Cappello persists in his opinion that the right to judge the weight and reasonableness of the cause pertains not only to the ordinary but also to the pastor. He states that the Congregation has no power to take from the latter a right which is his by law, and that it has no power ot give an authentic interpretation of the canon in question.[16]

Though the latter assertion is readily vindicated, it is still difficult to uphold Cappello in his view. In the officially

[15] *AAS,* XX (1928), 81; Bouscaren, *The Canon Law Digest,* I, 404-405.

[16] *De Sacramentis,* I, n. 392.

published annotations to the reply, the Secretary of the Sacred Congregation of the Sacraments pointed out that the conformity of the reply with the mind of the legislator was manifestly evident, not only from the many undesirable consequences that would follow if the matter were left to the judgment of individual pastors, but also from the sources themselves of the canon in question. Therefore, he continued, if the ordinaries of places, for just and reasonable causes, either of a general or of a particular nature, judge that in the whole diocese or in some part of it there is room for the exception that is contained under canon 847, the right of the pastor under canon 848, § 1, ceases, and the right of every priest under canon 849, § 1, arises.[17]

In this country, where the practice of taking Holy Communion to the sick in a private manner is universally adopted and at least tacitly approved by the ordinaries of places, the question is of little more than academic importance. Even in those communities which are wholly Catholic, and those are very few, the Eucharist should not be carried publicly because of a present or future danger of irreverence.[18] Any departure from the present prevailing practice would be a matter of no small import, and parishes in which the ordinary might allow the full and public liturgical function are so few as to render its adoption even in those parishes inadvisable.

What has been said, though directly it relates to the taking of Holy Communion to the sick in order that they may satisfy their devotion, is of equal application when there is question of taking Holy Communion to the sick in order that they may fulfill the divine precept to receive Holy Viaticum. And while it would remain the right of the pastor to carry Holy Viaticum whether in a public or in a private manner, it would pertain to the local ordinary to specify the manner in which that is to be done within the limits of his diocese.

[17] *Romana et Aliarum*, 5 ian. 1928—*AAS*, XX (1928), 81; Bouscaren, *The Canon Law Digest*, I, 405-406.

[18] Sabetti-Barrett, *Compendium Theologiae Moralis*, n. 691, ad 3.

What remains to be said concerns only the private mode of conveying the Eucharist to the sick.[19] With regrad to the means of transportation to be employed by the priest, the Ritual is silent. Relative to the public and solemn procedure, however, it is evident that the simple mode of proceeding on foot is contemplated.[20] Obviously such a means is also contemplated when there is question of the private administration. But inasmuch as many American parishes are large in area, the adoption of such a means is in no way feasible. The authors who touch on the question conclude that any means of transportation that is both safe and reverent may be adopted.[21] Undoubtedly the automobile lends itself to such a safe and reverent means of transportation when, in the taking of Holy Viaticum to the sick, a considerable distance has to be traveled.

Among other things, the Ritual observes that the priest is never to go alone on a sick-call, but is always to be accompanied by a cleric or by a layman.[22] In this country it would be frequently inconvenient and often impossible to observe this rule, and custom has now sanctioned the contrary practice. The observance of the rubric requiring the recitation of the psalm *"Miserere,"* and of other psalms and canticles while the priest is on his way to the sick person's house,[23] is of direct application and fulfills a definite need when the Eucharist is brought publicly, but the same observance may fulfill a similar need when the Eucharist is brought in a private manner. O'Kane-Fallon recommend the recitation of the canticles *"Benedictus"* or *Magnificat,"* or of other canticles or psalms which the priest may know by heart.[24]

[19] Cf. *supra*, p. 150, for the rules of the Ritual governing it.

[20] *Rituale Romanum*, Tit. IV, cap. 4, *de communione infirmorum*, nn. 10-13.

[21] Cappello, *De Sacramentis*, I, n. 394; Coronata, *De Sacramentis*, I, n, 299; Vermeersch, *Theologia Moralis*, III, n. 389.

[22] Tit. IV, cap. 4, *de communione infirmorum*, n. 29.

[23] *Rituale Romaunum*, Tit. IV, cap. 4, *de communione infirmorum*, n. 13.

[24] *Notes on the Ritual*, n. 777.

ARTICLE 2. THE PROCESS OF ACTUAL ADMINISTRATION

Section 1. Liturgical Prescriptions

The rubrics of the Roman Ritual relating to the public carrying of the Blessed Sacrament to the sick make provision that the requisites necessary for Its proper administration in the sick room be carried there by the persons who accompany the priest on the sick-call.[25] No such provision, however, is made when Holy Communion is to be taken in a private manner, as is the case in this country. Consequently, it is proper for the pastor to instruct the faithful in the called for preparation of the sick room and to exhort each family to provide itself with the items necessary for the proper discharge of this priestly ministration. But in some cases the priest cannot presume that everything will be in readiness, and on that account he should contrive to take with him or send beforehand these necessary items.

In preparing the pyx (transferring to it a consecrated particle from the large ciborium) it will be necessary for the priest to vest in surplice and stole, as nothing short of a strict necessity will justify him in thus handling the Blessed Sacrament without the use of these prescribed vestments.[26] The mere inconvenience or delay involved in the observance of this rubric will not in itself be a sufficient reason for the nonobservance of the rubrical procedure.[27]

For similar reasons, there must be some justification for any departure from the rule of the Ritual requiring the use of the (cassock) surplice and stole in the sick room.[28] Frequently this rule of the Ritual is overlooked even in circumstances which do not warrant its omission. Little difficulty in complying with the rubric will be experienced, at least

[25] Tit. IV, cap. 4, *de communione infirmorum*, 13.

[26] Cf. II Plenary Council of Baltimore, *Acta et Decreta*, n. 264; O'Kane-Fallon, *Notes on the Ritual*, n. 753; Studies and Conferences, "Bringing Holy Communion to the Sick," *AER*, CIV (1941), 168-169.

[27] Cf. can. 731, § 1: . . . summa in iis [sacramentis] oportune riteque administrandis ac suscipiendis diligentia et reverentia adhibenda est.

[28] *Loc. cit.*

when the patient belongs to a good Catholic family. But when the sacrament has to be administered in the public wards of non-Catholic hospitals, the minister must be on his guard lest by too much ceremonial he excite undue curiosity in the minds of unbelievers and thus expose the sacrament to the danger of ridicule. On the other hand, an over-timid reticence in the matter of Catholic belief and practice must be avoided.

It is difficult to establish hard and fast rules; both methods, the administration of Holy Viaticum by the minister wearing cassock, surplice and stole, and Its administration by him while simply wearing the stole over his street clothes and without the use of lighted candles, may be justified in view of the particular circumstances prevailing in individual places. But it should be borne in mind that the mere desire to make things easier or more expeditious for himself will under no circumstances justify any diminution of the prescribed ceremonies on the part of the minister.[29]

In the apostolic faculties conferred in 1941 by the Sacred Congregation for the Propagation of the Faith, permission was granted to ecclesiastical superiors to allow their priests to administer Holy Viaticum in the homes of the sick without the use of the surplice and stole as long as the use of these vestments would expose either the minister or the recipient to danger.[30] In his commentary on this faculty, Winslow remarks that, "in the assumption that no danger of irreverence to the Blessed Sacrament, or of harm to the person of the priest or his companion, or the sick person, exists or threatens, the rubrics of the Roman Ritual for the

[29] Cf. Connell, "The Hospital Chaplain and the Administration of Baptism and Penance," *AER*, CXVIII (1948), 256.

[30] N. 17: Permittendi suis missionariis ut deferre et administrare valeant christianis aegrotis Ssmam Eucharistiam sine superpelliceo et stola et sine comite, dummodo constet de periculo cui exponerentur si induerent superpelliceum et stolam.—F. J. Winslow, *A Commentary on the Apostolic Faculties* (New York: Field Afar Press, 1946), p. 62.

private administration of Holy Communion should be faithfully observed."[31]

The universality of the prevailing practice in this country of administering Holy Communion to the sick while simply wearing the stole is scarcely justifiable. To say that it can be justified in all cases savors both of irreverence for the sacrament and of disregard for the prescription of the Ritual. At most it may be tolerated in the measure in which it is employed, at least as long as the ordinaries of the various dioceses tacitly approve it inasmuch as it is not forbidden by diocesan statute.[32]

With one notable exception, the prayers and ceremonies prescribed for the administration of simple Holy Communion to the sick are also employed in the administration of Holy Viaticum.[33] The exception obtains in the formula of administration proper to Holy Viaticum, namely, *"Accipe, frater* (VEL *soror*), *Viaticum . . . ." etc.*[34] The use of this formula is determined, not by the fact that the recipient is fasting, but by reason of his being in a probable danger of

[31] *Op. cit.*, p. 64.

[32] Cf. Sabetti-Barrett, *Compendium Theologiae Moralis*, n. 690. An instance of diocesan legislation on the matter is to be found in the first diocesan synod of Toledo, Ohio, decree n. 189, which states that the cassock, surplice and stole are to be worn in the sick room.

[33] In 1929, the Sacred Congregation of Rites issued the following instruction: When Holy Communion is administered to several sick persons who are in the same house or in the same hospital, but in different rooms, the priest who is administering the sacrament shall, only in the first room, recite in the plural number all the prayers that precede the actual administration of the sacrament; in the other rooms he shall say only the prayers, *Misereatur tui . . . ; Indulgentiam . . . ; Ecce Agnus Dei . . . ;* once the *Domine non sum dignus . . . ; Corpus Domini Nostri Jesu Christi. . .* or *Accipe frater* (*soror*) *Viaticum . . . ;* and in the last room he shall add the verse, *Dominus vobiscum,* with its response and the prayer which follows, *Domine Sancte . . .* to be said in the plural number.—*AAS*, XXI (1929), 43; Bouscaren, *The Canon Law Digest*, I, 407-408.

[34] *Rituale Romanum*, Tit. IV, cap. 4, *de communione infirmorum*, n. 19.

death. As long as such a danger lasts, the formula proper to the administration of Holy Viaticum should be used.[35]

Some authors, however, hold that the rubric requiring the use of the proper formula imposes no more than a light obligation, and state that the ordinary formula for the administration of simple Holy Communion may be substituted whenever the condition of the recipient renders its use feasible.[36]

When death is imminent and when there is danger that the patient will be unable to receive Holy Viaticum unless It be administered immediately, the Ritual directs that the preceding prayers, with the exception of the *"Misereatur,"* be omitted in whole or in part, as may be judged necessary, and that the sacrament be administered at once.[37] In practice, if death be so imminent, there will scarcely be any possibility of administering Holy Viaticum. But the apprehension that death may ensue before the Sacred Species are dissolved in the stomach in no way warrants the withholding of the sacrament. If, however, the Host remains in the mouth after death, It is to be removed, carried to the church, allowed to undergo a stage of corruption in a becoming place and then deposited in the sacrarium. But if It be not visible, nothing further need be done.[38]

The authors are agreed that the precept to receive Holy Viaticum, in common with the Paschal precept,[39] is not fulfilled by means of a sacrilegious reception of the Eucharist.[40] Consequently, a person guilty of such a sacrilegious recep-

[35] O'Kane-Fallon, *Notes on the Ritual*, n. 742.

[36] Regatillo, *Ius Sacramentarium*, I, n. 354; Coronata, *De Sacramentis*, I, n. 331; Augustine, *A Commentary on Canon Law*, IV, n. 243; Vermeersch, *Theologia Moralis*, III, n. 362.

[37] Tit. IV, cap. 4, *de communione infirmorum*, n. 21.

[38] O'Kane-Fallon, *Notes on the Ritual*, n. 795.

[39] Can. 861.

[40] Van Hove, *De Eucharistia*, cap. VI, art. 3, p. 208; Noldin-Schmitt, *Theologia Moralis*, III, n. 138; Cappello, *De Sacramentis*, I, n. 421; Coronata, *De Sacramentis*, I, n. 330.

tion would be bound to receive again in the same danger of death.

In this connection some authors speak of a danger of infamy arising from such a repeated reception.[41] According to their statements one who has received Holy Viaticum sacrilegiously can as a result become excused under the danger of infamy from fulfilling the divine precept to receive It worthily. In the light of canon 864, § 3, which allows the repeated administration of Holy Viaticum, it is difficult to see how such a danger of infamy would arise. Moreover, the danger of infamy being self-inflicted, it is hardly reasonable to say that one is now free not to receive Holy Viaticum in order to escape that danger. In practice, any subsequent reception of Holy Communion while the danger of death lasts, provided that the recipient then has the requisite dispositions for a worthy reception, suffices to fulfill the divine precept.

On the other hand, a person who subsequently to the reception of Holy Viaticum falls into serious sin has nevertheless fulfilled his obligation. For altogether incidental reasons (grave temptations) such a person could during the same continued danger of death become subject, not indeed to the obligation of a repeated reception of Holy Viaticum, but to the need of receiving Holy Communion.

It may be asked whether in time of pestilence it would be lawful to administer Holy Viaticum by means of an instrument or by placing It within reach of the sick person so that it becomes possible for him to communicate himself? Among older theologians there were some who allowed such extraordinary methods of administration under the indicated circumstances.[42] In modern times, inasmuch as the danger of infection can be rendered very remote and the contact with the patient is so slight, the use of such extraordinary means would seldom be expedient.

[41] Noldin-Schmitt, *loc. cit.;* Iorio, *Theologia Moralis*, III, n. 148; Durieux, *The Eucharist*, p. 175.

[42] Cf. *supra*, p. 63.

Relative to the relation between the sacraments of Holy Viaticum and extreme unction, it is to be borne in mind that, though both come under the category of the "last sacraments," there easily may arise circumstances in which it will be possible to administer only the one or the other of these sacraments. Thus, one who is about to undergo a sentence of capital punishment may here and now be admitted to a reception of Holy Viaticum, while the administration of the sacrament of extreme unction would have to be deferred until the sentence of death has actually been carried out, if then there is still a period of latent life. On the other hand, circumstances may warrant the administration of the sacrament of extreme unction while a simultaneous administration of Holy Viaticum is precluded by reason of some physical impediment. Conditions of such an usual nature justify a departure from the prescribed order in which the last sacraments are to be administered, namely, the sacrament of penance followed by Holy Viaticum and, lastly, the sacrament of extreme unction.[43] Indeed, inasmuch as the rubric which governs the order that is to be observed in the administration of the last sacraments imposes only a light obligation, any reasonable cause will excuse from its observance.[44]

Section 2. The Factors of Time and Place in the Administration of Holy Viaticum

In the administration of Holy Viaticum, unlike the administration of simple Holy Communion, the factors of time

[43] *Rituale Romanum,* Tit. V, cap. 1, *de sacramento extremae unctionis,* n. 2: "In quo illud in primis ex generali Ecclesiae consuetudine observandum est, ut, si tempus, et infirmi conditio permittat, ante Extremam Unctionem, Poenitentiae et Eucharistiae sacramenta infirmis praebeantur."

[44] Cf. Coronata, *De Sacramentis,* I, n. 566; V. T. Schaaf, "Viaticum without Extreme Unction," *ER,* XCVII (1937), 298; A. Kilker, *Extreme Unction,* The Catholic University of America Canon Law Studies, n. 32 (Washington, D.C.: The Catholic University of America, 1926), pp. 35-38; and *supra,* p. 32.

and place seldom play an important part. In regard to the administration of simple Holy Communion, the law states that It can be administered on any day.[45] But by way of special application the law also states that on Good Friday Holy Communion can be administered only in the form of Holy Viaticum.[46] Consequently, in the light of this general statement of the law and of its special application, it is certain that Holy Viaticum can be administered on any day of the year. It is very probable, however, that the law enunciated in canon 867 is applicable to Holy Viaticum solely as understood in the strict sense.

Theologians and canonists generally agree that it is permissible for a priest to celebrate Mass on Good Friday when his reason for so doing is to provide Holy Viaticum for the dying. The Mass offered should be that of the votive Mass of the Passion.[47] The question, however, will seldom be practical inasmuch as the rubrics found in the Missal for the Mass of Holy Thursday direct that some consecrated particles be reserved for the sick.

For the same reason it would be permissible for the priest to depart from the prescription of canon 821, § 1, which requires that Mass should not be commenced earlier than one hour before dawn or later than one hour after midday, and the prescription of canon 806, § 1, which forbids the celebration of Mass more than once on the same day.[48] Both the Code of Canon Law[49] and the Roman Ritual[50] permit administration of Holy Viaticum at any hour of the day or night. At the same time the Ritual warns that It is not

[45] Can. 867, § 1.

[46] Can. 867, § 2.

[47] Cappello, *De Sacramentis*, I, n. 736; Coronata, *De Sacramentis*, I, n. 231; Prümmer, *Manuale Theologiae Moralis*, III, n. 286; Noldin-Schmitt, *Theologia Moralis*, III, n. 203.

[48] Sabetti-Barrett, *Compendium Theologiae Moralis*, n. 714; Van Hove, *De Eucharistia*, cap. V, art. 3, p. 349.

the Code of Canon Law[49] and the Roman Ritual[50] permit the

[49] Can. 867, § 5: Sacram tamen Viaticum quacumque diei aut noctis hora ministrari potest.

[50] Tit. IV, cap. 1, *de Sanctissimo Eucharistiae Sacramento*, n. 16.

to be carried to the sick by night unless necessity urges.[51] In the latter context, however, there is reference to the public bringing of the Eucharist to the sick. The reason for the admonition becomes apparent from the inherent difficulty of faithfully observing the prescribed external solemnities in the event that a nocturnal administration became necessary. At any rate, in cases wherein necessity urges, Holy Viaticum can be administered in a public manner even at night.

The Code, on the other hand, makes no distinction between the public and the private function and does not demand any special cause in order that Holy Viaticum may be administered at night; the need of the sick person is in itself a sufficient cause, and one may act despite indications that the sacrament may safely be deferred until the following day.[52]

It is probable that the exception which makes allowance for the administration of Holy Viaticum at any hour of the day or night can be invoked only in favor of Viaticum in Its strict sense. Inasmuch as the exception was prompted by a real need of the recipient, it would hardly be in accordance with the mind of the legislator to apply it also when no real need urges. The Code, however, does not place any such restriction, and accordingly there are not wanting some authors who support the contrary opinion.[53]

Relative to the place proper for the administration of the sacrament of the Eucharist in general, the Code states that It may be administered in any place in which Mass may lawfully be celebrated, unless the local ordinary, for just reasons, prohibits Its administration in particular cases.[54]

[51] Tit. IV, cap. 4, *de communione infirmorum*, n. 13: ... noctu autem hoc sacramentum deferri non debet, nisi necessitas urgeat.

[52] Cappello, *De Sacramentis*, I, n. 335; Coronata, *De Sacramentis*, I, n. 373.

[53] Cf. Van Hove, *De Eucharistia*, cap. V, art. 2, p. 162; Coronata, *op. cit.*, I, n. 337, footnote 6.

[54] Can. 869: Sacra communio distribui potest ubicumque Missam celebrare licet, etiam in oratorio privato, nisi loci Ordinarius, iustis de causis, in casibus particularibus id prohibuerit.

Relative to the place proper for the administration of Holy Viaticum in particular, there is scarcely any restriction, provided the place be not repugnant to the holiness of the sacrament. The homes of the sick, no matter how poor they may be, are not in themselves unfit places for the administration of Holy Viaticum.[55]

By virtue of a reply given by the Sacred Congregation of the Sacraments on July 29, 1927, permission was granted to the faithful living in mountain hamlets (or other places not easily accessible) to receive Holy Communion in a sacred place or in any decent or suitable place approved by the ordinary for the celebration of Mass in accordance with the prescriptions of canon 822, § 4, whenever Holy Communion (Viaticum) was brought to the sick in those places. Under similar conditions, Holy Communion could be administered to those who are in the house of the sick person when they are unable to go to a church on that particular day.[56]

Relative to the foregoing reply, Cardinal Jorio, then the Secretary of the Sacred Congregation, added the following annotations: It is beyond doubt that the pious desire of the faithful may be satisfied, if the pastor, as he goes to carry Holy Viaticum to the sick, passes an oratory or other places which can be regarded as suitable for the celebration of Mass and which would certainly be so judged by the ordinary, even though in point of fact Mass is not celebrated there. In the latter contingency it is required that the Blessed Sacrament be legitimately brought there, that is to say, that such places lie along the itinerary of the priest as he goes to administer Holy Viaticum.[57]

Holy Viaticum can seldom be administered during the celebration of Mass, for the law of the Code makes it un-

[55] Cf. *supra*, p. 62.

[56] *AAS*, XX (1928), 79; Bouscaren, *The Canon Law Digest*, I, 391.

[57] Adnotationes Secretarii S. C. de Sacramentis ad *Montis Regalis in Pedemonte*, 5 ian. 1928—*AAS*, XX (1928), 80-81; Bouscaren, *The Canon Law Digest*, I, 391-393. Cf. Beste, *Introductio in Codicem*, p. 502; Jorio, *La Comunione agl' Infermi*, nn. 49-50.

lawful for the celebrant to distribute Holy Communion to those persons who are so far removed from the altar as to entail his losing sight of it.[58] This rule of the Code reiterates an earlier decision given by the Sacred Congregation of Rites on December 19, 1829. In reply to a question regarding the administration of Holy Viaticum during Mass, the Sacred Congregation stated that it would be unlawful to do so under conditions that occasioned the celebrant's losing sight of the altar.[59]

Modern authors generally adopt a mild interpretation of the foregoing legislation. Cappello allows during the celebration of Mass the administration of Holy Viaticum in hospital wards contiguous to the chapel as long as it is possible from the chapel to hear the voice of the celebrant, even though the altar be not visible to the celebrant.[60] Vermeersch, distinguishing between Holy Viaticum of precept and that of devotion, stated that the former could be administered in such places as were sufficiently close to render a removal of the sacred vestments unnecessary. With regard to the latter, he favored the stricter interpretation of the law.[61]

Since there is here a conflict between a divine precept and a merely disciplinary law, it is reasonable to suppose that the latter will give way to the former, so that Holy Viaticum may be administered during the celebration of Mass, canon 868 notwithstanding.

Aside from the foregoing exceptional cases, there may easily arise circumstances in which the prospective recipient of Holy Viaticum may be present in the place where

[58] Can. 868.

[59] *Florentina,* ad I: "... animadvertendum, quod si celebrans pro Viatici administratione intra Missam altare e conspectu suo amittat, hanc administrationem non licere."—*Decreta Authentica Congregationis Sacrorum Rituum ex Actis Eiusdem Collecta Eiusque Auctoritate Promulgata sub Auspiciis SS. Domini Nostri Leonis Papae XIII* (6 vols., Romae: Ex Typographia Polyglotta S. C. de Propaganda Fide, 1898-1927), n. 2672; *Fontes,* n. 5855.

[60] *De Sacramentis,* I, n. 391.

[61] *Theologia Moralis,* III, n. 294.

Mass is being celebrated, for example, in the case of the criminal about to undergo the sentence of death, or where the celebration of Mass is allowed in private homes. Under such circumstances Holy Viaticum may be administered during the celebration of Mass with ceremonies similiar to those employed in the administration of simple Holy Communion, with the exception of the proper formula of administration.[62]

In places affected by a local interdict, whether of a general or of a particular nature, the administration of Holy Viaticum to the dying is permitted. All external pomp and solemnity is to be avoided and the sacrament may be brought only in a private manner.[63] Consequently, in countries where it is customary to take Holy Communion only in such a private manner, the imposition of a general local interdict imposes no restrictions as far as the administration of Holy Viaticum is concerned.

Article 3. The Rite in Which Holy Viaticum is to be Administered

Ecclesiastical law allows the faithful of any rite, even if their act be motivated solely by the consideration of devotion, to receive Holy Communion consecrated in any rite.[64] But when there is question of fulfilling the Paschal precept, the law counsels that that precept be fulfilled by means of a reception in one's own rite.[65] But in what is simply counselled there is not imposed any strict obligation, and even if one should inadvertently or deliberately receive his Easter Communion in a rite other than his own, he nevertheless satisfies the precept and does not incur any guilt of sin.[66]

But when there is question of fulfilling the divine precept

[62] O'Kane-Fallon, *Notes on the Ritual*, n. 816; Cappello, *De Sacramentis*, I, n. 376.

[63] Cans. 2270, § 1, and 2271, n. 2.

[64] Can. 866, § 1.

[65] Can. 866, § 2.

[66] Cf. Cappello, *De Sacramentis*, I, n. 494.

to receive Holy Viaticum, the law does impose a definite obligation on the faithful to receive It in their own rite.[67] According to some authors, the obligation which the law here imposes, when viewed in the light of its purpose and in line with the words which frame the law, is a grave one.[68]

But while canon 866, § 3, states the law on the matter, it at the same time makes allowance for an exception by permitting the reception of Holy Viaticum in any rite whenever necessity urges. The case of necessity here envisaged by the law can and does arise when there is no priest of the prospective recipient's rite present, or, if one is present, there is not available to him any Sacred Host consecrated in his own rite.[69] Coronata was of the opinion that a cause which was sufficient to justify a priest who was not a pastor in administering Holy Viaticum without the pastor's express permission was also sufficient to justify him in the administration of Holy Viaticum to one of a different rite.[70]

In practice, the question will arise only with regard to the faithful of Oriental rites. If an Oriental priest can be procured, this should be done. If not, a Latin priest may then lawfully administer Holy Viaticum to an Oriental subject, and he will do so according to the Latin rite. Once an Oriental Catholic has satisfied the divine precept by his reception of Viaticum in the strict sense, any priest, with at least the presumed permission of him who has custody of the Blessed Sacrament, may then administer to him Holy Viaticum of devotion. Relative to the administration of the last sacraments to Oriental schismatics, a general retractation of error and some acknowledgment of the Catholic Church, at least on the part of those who are in a weakened condition and close to death, will be sufficient to justify the

[67] Can. 866, § 3: Sanctum Viaticum moribundis ritu propria accipiendum est; sed urgente necessitate, fas esto quolibet ritu illud accipere.

[68] Cappello, *loc. cit.;* Coronata, *De Sacramentis,* I, n. 335; Van Hove, *De Eucharistia,* cap. VI, art. 3, p. 209. Regarding the determination of rite, cf. canon 98, § 1.

[69] Cf. can. 851, § 2.

[70] *De Sacramentis,* I, n. 335.

administration of those sacraments which are called for in his present crisis.[71]

Further questions incidental to this present consideration may arise. Can a priest consecrate bread that is proper to another rite in order to administer Holy Viaticum to one who is in danger of death? Among modern theologians the affirmative opinion finds much favor. Their argument is based on the reasonable supposition that an ecclesiastical law such as the one embodied in canon 816 gives way to a divine precept whenever such a precept becomes operative.[72]

Another argument in support of the foregoing opinion is offered by Cappello. He points out that the ruling of canon 851 § 2, which permits a priest in a case of necessity to administer Holy Communion consecrated in another rite, when namely no priest of that rite is present, and that the concession granted in canon 866, which permits the faithful to receive Holy Communion which was consecrated in another rite, even if they do so simply to satisfy their devotion, are indicative of a milder discipline in the Church.[73] In view of canon 816, his attempt to formulate an argument from the silence of the Code seems rather strange. The Code, he states, nowhere contains an explicit or an implicit prohibition concerning the consecration of bread according to the practice of another rite in order to administer Holy Viaticum. Had he desired to set up a prohition, the legislator could easily have given an unmistakable expression of his legislative will.[74] Since the consecration of bread takes place solely at the Mass which the priest celebrates, it is plain that he is to use the kind of bread which his rite calls for.[75] But

[71] Cf. Connell, "The Hospital Chaplain and the Administration of the Eucharist," *AER*, CXIX (1948), 26-27.

[72] Cappello, *op. cit.*, I, n. 261; Davis, *Moral and Pastoral Theology*, III, n. 121; Woywod, *A Commentary*, I, n. 718; Van Hove, *De Eucharistia*, cap. III, art. 1, p. 112; Coronata, *op. cit.*, I, n. 213; Prümmer, *Manuale Theologiae Moralis*, III, n. 171.

[73] *Loc. cit.*

[74] *Loc. cit.*

[75] Cf. can. 816.

even apart from this consideration, it seems that one may safely depart from the ruling of the canon when, in order to administer Holy Viaticum, it becomes necessary to do so.

Is it lawful for a priest to administer Holy Viaticum when the matter of the sacrament and the form of the consecration was proper to a rite other than that of the ministering priest? In the pre-Code law the answer was characterized by a divergence of opinion.[76] The Code of Canon Law[77] has now settled the question by obliging every priest to distribute Holy Communion in the form of bread that is proper to his rite, but leaves room for an exception which becomes operative under the following combined conditions: (1) that there be a case of necessity; (2) that there be no priest of the respective rite present; and (3) that each priest observe the rubrics proper to his own rite. The need of administering Holy Viaticum would certainly constitute a case of necessity which would justify the priest's taking action under the concession allowed by the law. The import of the two remaining conditions is evident; any added explanation would tend to becloud the issue.

[76] Cf. Henry, *The Mass and Holy Communion: Interritual Law*, pp. 78-82.

[77] Can. 851.

CONCLUSIONS

As a result of the foregoing study the following conclusions are offered:

1. It is the first and fundamental conclusion of the writer that the practice of administering Holy Viaticum to the dying is coeval with the Church itself and derives a definite importance in the divine and ecclesiastical order of things; the term, however, possesses a historical and cultural background in the pagan writings of pre-Christian times (pp. 1-13).

2. The promulgation of the Code of Canon Law did not introduce any decisive changes in the legislation governing the canonical institute of Holy Viaticum; consequently pre-Code legislation is still of paramount importance inasmuch as it forms the immediate basis for the canons of the Code which now regulate that same institute (pp. 39-40).

3. Canon 864, § 1, must be regarded as a reflection of a divine command written into the positive law of the Church. Consequently, those of the faithful who are in danger of death are bound to receive Holy Communion by reason of both a divine and an ecclesiastical law (pp. 67-84).

4. The danger of death which warrants the administration of Holy Viaticum need not be a certain one nor need there be indications that death is imminent. It is sufficient that the danger of death be at least probably verified (pp. 84-91).

5. It is certain that the obligation to receive Holy Viaticum can be fulfilled at any point of time while the danger of death lasts, and furthermore this obligation is satisfied through a single reception of Holy Communion, so that subsequent acts of reception while the danger of death lasts are only in a loose sense to be regarded as acts of the reception of Holy Viaticum. Apart from conditions which permit the certain fulfillment of the obligation during the danger of death, it is probable that a reception of the Eucha-

rist which takes place a short time (six or eight days) prior to the emerging danger of death also suffices to fulfill the obligation (pp. 91-96).

6. In order that the relaxation from the law of the Eucharistic fast become operative, the Code of Canon Law simply demands the presence of at least a probable danger of death. As far as the law itself is concerned, it cannot be said that whenever one's physical condition is such that the observance of the fast would not impose any hardship one is bound to observe the law of the Eucharistic fast (pp. 96-101).

7. The dispositions which the fruitful reception of Holy Viaticum demands are generally less exacting than those which the fruitful reception of Holy Communion calls for. With regard to heretics and schismatics, these may not be admitted to Holy Viaticum until they have been first reconciled with the Church and have shown their capacity at least to distinguish the Holy Eucharist from common food. In the case of public sinners, there must be made a reparation for the scandal caused, in so far as that is now possible. Children who are in danger of death can and must be allowed to receive Holy Viaticum even though they have not yet completed their seventh year or been admitted to first Holy Communion, provided that they are able to distinguish the Holy Eucharist from ordinary food and to adore It reverently (pp. 126-149).

8. As a reserved parochial function, the administration of Holy Viaticum is restricted to that Communion which is prescribed by divine and ecclesiastical law when one falls into serious danger of death, and does not extend to other Communions which one may receive out of devotion while one is still seriously ill (pp. 102-106).

9. The judgment as to the sufficiency of a cause warranting the bringing of Holy Viaticum to the sick in a private manner is to be left in the hands of the local ordinary (pp. 152-154).

10. One can receive Holy Viaticum which was consecrated in a form of bread that is proper to another rite only when there is no priest of one's own rite present, or when, though a priest of one's own rite be indeed present, there is available to him only the Holy Eucharist which was consecrated in the form of bread that is proper to another rite (pp. 226-166-169).

11. The marked solicitude of the Church for the sick and the dying is clearly evidenced in its legislation which imposes a grave obligation upon the pastors of souls to attend to their spiritual needs, especially by administering to them the last sacraments (pp. 121-125).

BIBLIOGRAPHY

Sources

Acta Apostolicae Sedis, Commentarium Officiale, Romae, 1909-1929; Civitate Vaticana, 1929-

Acta Sanctae Sedis, 41 vols., Romae, 1865-1908.

Acta et Decreta Conciliorum Recentiorum, Collectio Lacensis, Auctoribus Presbyteris S. J. e domo B. V. M. sine Labe Conceptae ad Lacum, 7 vols., Friburgi-Brisgoviae, 1870-1892.

Bouscaren, T., *The Canon Law Digest,* 2 vols. and Supplement, Milwaukee: Bruce, Vol. I, 1934, Vol. II, 1943, Supplement, 1949.

Bruns, H., *Canones Apostolorum et Conciliorum Saeculorum IV-VII,* 2 vols., Berolini, 1839.

Bullarum Diplomatum et Privilegiorum Sanctorum Pontificum Taurinensis Editio, 24 vols. et Appendix, Augustae Taurinorum, 1857-1872.

Catechism of the Council of Trent for Parish Priests, issued by order of Pope Pius V, English translation by C. J. Callan and J. A. McHugh, tenth printing, New York: Wagner, 1947.

Codex Iuris Canonici Pii X Pontificis Maximi iussu digestus Benedicti Papae XV auctoritate promulgatus, Romae: Typis Polyglottis Vaticanis, 1917.

Codicis Iuris Canonici Fontes, cura Emi Petri Card. Gasparri editi, 9 vols., Romae (Postea Civitate Vaticane): Typis Polyglottis Vaticanis, 1923-1939. (Vols., VII-IX, ed. cura Emi Iustiniani Card. Serédi).

Colectanea S. Congregationis de Propaganda Fide, 2 vols., Romae: Typographia Polyglotta S. C. de Propaganda Fide, 1907.

Collectanea in Usum Secretariae Sacrae Congregationis Episcoporum et Regularium, cura A. Bizzarri, Secretarii, 2. ed., Romae, 1885.

Concilii Plenarii Baltimorensis II, Acta et Decreta, Baltimorae: John Murphy, 1868.

Coronata, Mathaeus Conte a, *Interpretatio Autrentica Codicis Iuris Canonici ab anno 1916 usque ad annum 1940,* Romae: Marietti, 1940.

Corpus Iuris Canonici, Editio Lipsiensis II (Richter-Friedberg), 2 vols., Lipsiae, 1879-1881.

Corpus Scriptorum Ecclesiasticorum Latinorum, 70 vols., Vindobonae: F. Tempsky, 1866-

Decreta Authentica Congregationis Sacrarum Rituum ex Actis eiusdem Collecta eiusque Auctoritate Promulgata sub Auspiciis SS. Domini Nostri Leonis Papae XIII, 6 vols., Romae: Ex Typographia Polyglotta S.C. de Propaganda Fide, 1898-1927.

Decretales D. Gregorii IX, suae Integritati, una cum Glossis Restitutae, Romae, 1582.

Decretum Gratiani emendatum et Notionibus Illustratum, una cum Glossis Gregorii XIII Pontificis Maximi iussu editum, 2 vols., Romae, 1582.

Denzinger, H. Bannwart, C.-Umberg, J., *Enchiridion Symbolorum Definitionum et Declarationum de Rebus Fidei et Morum,* ed. 18-20., Friburgi Brisgoviae; Herder and Co., 1932.

Hardouin, J., *Acta Conciliorum et Epistolae Decretales ac Constitutiones Summorum Pontificum,* 12 vols., Parisiis, 1714-1715.

Hefele, C.-Leclecrq, H., *Histoire des Conciles,* 10 vols. in 19, Paris: Letouzey et Ané, 1907-1938.

Historia Ecclesiastica, Die griechischen christichen Schriftsteller der ersten drei Jahrhunderte, 7 vols. in 10, et. E. Schwartz, Leipzig, 1902-1926, *Eusebius Werke,* Vol. VII, pars 2, 1908.

Jaffé, J., *Regesta Pontificum Romanorum ab condita Ecclesia ad annum post Christum natum MCXCVIII,* 2. ed., cura G. Wattenbach, F. Kaltenbrunner (ad annum 590), P. Ewald (ab anno 590 ad annum 822), S. Löwenfeld (ab anno 822 ad annum 1198), 2 vols., Lipsiae, 1885-1888.

Mansi, J. D., *Sacrorum Conciliorum Nova et Amplissima Collectio,* 53 vols. in 60, Paris-Leipzig-Arnhem, 1901-1927.

Monumenta Germaniae Historica, 188 vols., incomplete, Hannoverae, 1826-, *Leges in 4.,* Sectio III (*Concilia*), Tom. II, pars II, et. A. Werminghoff, 1908.

Pallottini, S., *Collectio omnium Conclusionum et Resolutionum quae in causis propositis apud Sacram Congregationem Cardinalium S. Concillii Tridentini interpretum prodierunt ad eius institutione anno MDLXIV an annum MDCCCLX, Distinctis Titulis Alphabetico ordine per Materias digesta,* 17 vols., Romae, 1868-1895.

Potthast, A., *Regesta Pontificum Romanorum inde ab anno post Christum natum MCXCVIII, ad annum MCCIV,* 2 vols., Berolini, 1874-1875.

Rituale Romanum, Pauli V Maxima iussu editum et a Benedicto XIV auctum et castigatum, Baltimore, John Murphy, 1873.

Rituale Romanum Pauli V Pontificis Maximi iussu editum aliorumque Pontificum cura Recognitum atque Auctoritate Pii Papae XI ad normam Codicis Iuris Canonici accomodatum, 2. ed. *iuxta Typicam Vaticanam amplificata* I, New York: Benziger Brothers, 1925.

Schroeder, H. J., *Canons and Decrees of the Council of Trent,* St. Louis: Herder, 1941.

Thesaurus Resolutionum Sacrae Congregationis Concilii, 167 vols., Romae, 1718-1908.

Turner, C. H., *Ecclesiae Occidentalis Monumenta Iuris Antiquissima. Canonum et Conciliorum Graecorum Interpretationes Latinae*, Tom. I, Fasc. I, pars altera, Oxonii: e Typographia Clarendiana, 1904.

REFERENCE WORKS

Aertnys, J-Damen, C., *Theologia Moralis*, 13. ed., 2 vols., Taurini-Romae: Marietti, 1939.

Anglin, T. F., *The Eucharistic Fast*, The Catholic University of America Canon Law Studies, n. 124, Washington, D. C.: The Catholic University of America Press, 1941.

Aquinas, St. Thomas, *Summa Theologica*, 12. ed., 6 vols., Taurini: Marietti, 1937-1938.

Augustine, C., *A Commentary on the New Code of Canon Law*, 8 vols., Vol. IV, 2. ed., St. Louis: Herder, 1921.

———, *The Pastor according to the New Code of Canon Law*, 2. ed., St. Louis: Herder, 1924.

Ayrinhac, H. A., *Legislation of the Cacraments in the New Code of Canon Law*, New York: Longmans, Green and Co., 1928.

Ayrinhac, H. A., *Legislation of the Sacraments in the New Code of Canon Law*, New York: Benziger Brothers, 1936.

Barbosa, A., *Collectanea Doctorum tam Veterum quam Recentiorum in Ius Pontificium Universum*, 5 vols., Lugduni, 1641.

———, *De Officio et Potestate Parochi Descriptio*, ed. U. Giraldi a S. Cajetano, Romae, 1774.

Bastnagel, C. V., *The Appointment of Parochial Adjutants and Assistants*, The Catholic University of America Canon Law Studies n. 58, Washington, D. C.: The Catholic University of America, 1930.

Benedictus XIV (Prosper Lambertini), *De Sacrosancto Missae Sacrificio Libri Tres*, 2. ed., Romae, 1748.

———, *De Synodo Dioecesano*, 4 vols., Mechliniae, 1842.

Beste, U., *Introductio in Codicem*, 3. ed., Collegeville: St. John's Abbey Press, 1946.

Blat, A., *Commentarium Textus Codicis Iuris Canonici*, 5 vols. in 6, Vol. III, pars I (*De Sacramentis*), 2 ed., Romae: Ex Typographia Pontificia, 1924.

Bona, J. Cardinalis, *Rerum Liturgicarum Libri Duo*, Romae, 1671.

Bouix, D., *Tractatus de Parocho*, 3. ed., Parisiis, 1880.

Bouscaren, T.-Ellis, A., *Canon Law, A Text and Commentary*, Milwaukee: The Bruce Publishing Co., 1946.

Cappello, Felix M., *Tractatus Canonico-moralis de Sacramentis*, 5 vols., Vol. I. 4. ed., 1945; Vol. II, 4. ed., 1944; Vol. III, 2. ed., 1942; Vol. IV, 2. ed., 1947; Vol. V, 5. ed., 1947, Romae-Taurini: Marietti.

———, *Summa Iuris Canonici*, 3 vols., Vol. II, 3. ed., Romae: Universitas Gregoriana, 1939.

Catholic Encyclopedia, The, 15 vols. and 2 supplements, New York, 1907-1922.

Cavalieri, J. M., *Opera Omnia Liturgica seu Commentaria Authentica Sacrae Rituum Congregationis Decreta ad Romanum praesertim Breviarium, Missale et Rituale quomodolibet Attinentia*, 5 toms., in 1 vol., Basani, 1778.

Cavanaugh, W. T., *The Reservation of the Blessed Sacrament*, The Catholic University of America Canon Law Studies, n. 40, Washington, D.C.: The Catholic University of America, 1927.

Coronata, Matthaeus Conte a, *Tractatus Canonicus de Sacramentis*, 3 vols., Romae: Marietti, 1943-1945.

———, *Institutiones Iuris Canonici*, 5 vols., Vols. I-II, 2. ed., 1939; Vol. III, 2. ed., 1941; Vol. IV, 2. ed., 1945; Vol. V, 1936, Taurini: Marietti.

Corblet, J., *Histoire Dogmatique, Liturgique et Archéologique du Sacrement de l'Eucharistie*, 2 vols., Paris, 1885-1886.

Crotty, M., *The Recipient of First Holy Communion*, The Catholic University of America Canon Law Studies, n. 247, Washington, D.C.: The Catholic University of America Press, 1947.

Creusen, J., *Religious Men and Women in the Code*, 3. English ed. by A. Ellis, Milwaukee: The Bruce Publishing Co., 1940.

D'Annibale, J., *Summula Theologiae Moralis*, 5. ed., 3 vols., Romae: Ex Typographia Polyglotta, 1908-1909.

Davis, H., *Moral and Pastoral Theology*, 4. ed., 4 vols., London: Sheed and Ward, 1943.

De Azpilcueta, M. (Navarrus), *Consilia et Responsa iuxta Ordinem Decretalium*, Lugduni, 1594.

De Luca, J., *Theatrum Veritatis et Iustitiae seu Decisivi Discursus ad Veritatem editi in Forensibus Controversiis Canonicis et Civilibus*, 4 vols., Romae, 1706.

De Lugo, J., *Disputationes Scholasticae et Morales*, ed. nova, Parisiis: L. Vives, 1868-1869.

De Smet, A., *Tractatus Dogmatico-Moralis de Sacramentis in Genere, De Baptismo et Confirmatione*, ed. altera, Brugis: Beyaert, 1924.

Diana Coordinatus, 10 tomes in 5 vols., prepared by M. De Alcolea, Venetiis, 1728.

Dictionnaire de Théologie Catholique, 15 vols., Paris, 1903-1948.

Drumm, W., *Hospital Chaplains*, The Catholic University of America Canon Law Studies, n. 178, Washington, D. C.: The Catholic University of America Press, 1943.

Duchesne, L., *Christian Worship: Its Origin and Evolution*, translated by M. L. McClure, London: Society for Promoting Christian Knowledge, 1903.

Durieux, P., *The Eucharist, Law and Practice*, translated from the French by O. Dolphin, Chicago: The Lakeside Press, 1926.

Engel, L., *Collegium Universi Iuris Canonici servato ordine Decretalium*, ed. nova, Beneventi, 1760.

Fanfani, L., *De Iure Parochorum*, Romae: Marietti, 1924.

———, *De Iure Religiosorum ad normam Codicis Iuris Canonici*, 2. ed., Romae: Marietti, 1925.

Fermosini, N. R., *Opera Omnia*, 2. ed., 14 vols., Coloniae Allobrogum, 1741.

Ferreres, J., *Compendium Theologiae Moralis*, 14. ed., 2 vols., Barcinone: Ex Typis Eugenii Subirane, 1928.

Forcellini, A., *Lexicon Totius Latinitatis*, 6 vols., Patavii, 1940.

Fortescue, A., *The Mass: A Study of the Roman Liturgy*, New York: Longmans, Green and Co., 1922.

Gasparri, P., *Tractatus Canonicus de Eucharistia*, 2 vols., Parisiis, 1897.

Genicot, E.-Salsmans, I., *Institutiones Theologiae Moralis*, 2 vols., Bruxellis: Dewit, 1927.

Gonzales-Tellez, E., *Commentarium Perpetua in Singulos Textus quinque Librorum Decretalium Gregorii IX*, 5 toms., Lugduni, 1673.

Henry, J., *The Mass and Holy Communion: Interritual Law*, The Catholic Universi oytf America Canon Law Studies, n. 235, Washington, D. C.: The Catholic University of America Press, 1946.

Hostiensis, Cardinalis (Henricus de Segusio), *Commentaria in Quinque Libros Decretalium*, 3 vols., Venetiis, 1581.

Iorio, T., *Theologia Moralis*, 3 vols., Vol. III, 3. ed., Neapoli: D'Auria, 1947.

Jorio, D., *Comunione agl' Infermi*, Romae: Pustet, 1931.

Juenin, G., *Commentarius Historicus et Dogmaticus de Sacramentis in Genere et in Specie*, Lugduni, 1696.

Kelly, B., *The Functions Reserved to Pastors*, The Catholic University of America Canon Law Studies, n. 250, Washington, D. C.: The Catholic University of America Press, 1947.

Kilker, A., *Extreme Unction*, The Catholic University of America Canon Law Studies, n. 32, Washington, D. C.: The Catholic University of America, 1926.

King, J., *The Administration of the Sacraments to Dying Non-Catholics*, The Catholic University of America Canon Law Studies, n. 23, Washington, D. C.: The Catholic University of America, 1924.

Koudelka, C., *Pastors, Their Rights and Duties*, The Catholic University of America Canon Law Studies, n. 11, Washington, D. C.: The Catholic University of America, 1921.

Lamy, Thomas, *Dissertatio de Syrorum Fide et Disciplina in Re Eucharistica*, Lovanii: Universitatis Catholicae Lovaniensis 1859.

Laymann, P., *Theologia Moralis in Quinque Libros Distributa*, ed. nova, Venetiis, 1630.

Liddell, H. G.-Scott, R., *Greek-English Dictionary*, 2 vols., Oxford: The Clarendon Press, 1925.

Liguori, St. Alphonsus, *Theologia Moralis*, 4 vols., Taurini: Marietti, 1872.

Lohmuller, M., *The Promulgation of Law*, The Catholic University of America Canon Law Studies, n. 241, Washington, D. C.: The Catholic University of America Press, 1947.

Many, S, *Praelectiones de Missa cum Appendice de Sanctissimo Sacramento Eucharistiae*, Parisiis, 1903.

Marc, C.-Gestermann, F.-Raus, J. B., *Institutiones Morales Alphonsianae*, 18. ed., 2 vols., Lugduni: Typis Emmanuelis Vitte, 1927-1928.

Ménard, H., *Notae in S. Gregorii Librum Sacramentorum, Auctore D. Hugone Menardo, Monacho Benedictino—MPL*, LXXVIII, 263-582.

Merkelbach, B., *Summa Theologiae Moralis*, 3. ed., 3 vols., Romae: Descleé, 1939.

McFadden, Charles J., *Medical Ethics*, 2. ed., Philadelphia; F. A. Davis Company, 1949.

Michiels, G., *Normae Generales Iuris Canonici*, 2 vols., Lublin: Universitas Catholica, 1929.

Migne, P. J., *Patrologiae Cursus Completus, Series Latina*, 221 vols., Parisiis, 1844-1864.

———, *Patrologiae Cursus Completus, Series Graeca*, 161 vols., Parisiis, 1857-1866.

Noldin, H., *Summa Theologiae Moralis*, 5. ed., 3 vols., Oeniponte: F. Rauch, 1904.

Noldin, H.-Schmitt, A., *Summa Theologiae Moralis*, 3 vols., Vol. III, 26. ed., Ratisbonae, Romae et Neo Eboraci: Pustet, 1940.

O'Kane, J.-Fallon, M., *Notes on the Rubrics of the Roman Ritual*, revised ed., Dublin: James Duffy and Co., 1943.

Panormitanus (Nicholaus de Tudeschis), *Commentaria in quinque Decretalium Librum*, 5 vols., Venetiis, 1589.

Pilati, L., *Origines Iuris Pontificii ad Carolum Sextum*, Tridenti, 1739.

Pirhing, E., *Ius Canonicum Nova Methodo Explicatum*, 5 vols., ed. nova, Dilingae, 1722.

Prümmer, Dom. M., *Manuale Theologiae Moralis,* 7. ed., 3 vols., Friburgi-Brisgoviae: Herder and Co., 1933.

Ramstein, A., *A Manual of Canon Law,* Hoboken, N. J.: Terminal Printing Co., 1947.

Raus, P., *Institutiones Canonicae,* 2. ed., Lugduni: Vitte, 1931.

Regatillo, E., *Ius Sacramentarium,* 2 vols., Santander: Sal Terrae, 1945-1946.

Romani, S., *Institutiones Iuris Canonici,* 2 vols. in 3, Vol. II, Sectio prior, Romae: Editrice "Iustitia," 1944.

Rufinus, Magister, *Summa Decretorum,* ed. Heinrich Singer, Paderborn, 1902.

Rush, A. C., *Death and Burial in Christian Antiquity,* The Catholic University of America Studies in Christian Antiquity, n. 1, Washington, D. C.: The Catholic University Press, 1941.

Sabetti, A.-Barrett, T., *Compendium Theologiae Moralis,* 27. ed., New York: Pustet, 1919.

Schaefer, T., *De Religiosis ad normam Codicis Iuris Canonici,* 4. ed., Romae: Typis Polyglottis Vaticanis, 1947.

Schaff, P.-Wace, H., *The Nicene and Post-Nicene Fathers,* second series, 14 vols., New York: Scribners, 1900.

Schmalzgrueber, F., *Jus Ecclesiasticum Universum,* 5 vols. in 12, Romae, 1843-1845.

Schroeder, H. J., *Disciplinary Decrees of the General Councils, Text,* Translation and Commentary, St. Louis: Herder, 1937.

Shuhler, R. V., *Privileges of Religious to Absolve and Dispense,* The Catholic University of America Canon Law Studies, n. 186, Washington, D. C.: The Catholic University of America Press, 1943.

Stadler, J., *Frequent Holy Communion,* The Catholic University of America Canon Law Studies, n. 263, Washington, D. C.: The Catholic University of America Press, 1947.

Suarez, F., *Opera Omnia,* 28 vols., ed. nova, Parisiis: L. Vivès, 1856-1861.

Szal, I., *The Communication of Catholics with Schismatics,* The Catholic University of America Canon Law Studies, n. 264, Washington, D. C.: The Catholic University of America Press, 1948.

Tanquerey, A., *Synopsis Theologiae Dogmaticae,* 21. ed., 3 vols., Parisiis: Descleé et Socii, 1929.

The Casuist, A Collection of Cases in 5 vols., Vol. IV, revised ed., New York: Wagner, 1925.

Van Espen, Z. B., *Ius Ecclesiasticum Universum,* 2 vols., Lovanii et Lugduni, 1753.

Van Hove, A., *Prolegomena ad Codicem Iuris Canonici,* ed. altera auctior et emandatior, Mechliniae et Romae: H. Dessain, 1945.

———, *Tractatus de Sanctissima Eucharistia*, ed. altera, Mechliniae: H. Dessain, 1941.

Vasquez, G., *Libri Commentariorum in Tertiam Partem S. Thomae*, 4 toms. in 3 vols., Lugduni: Sumptibus Jacobi Cardon, 1630-1631.

Verano, G. F., *Iuris Canonici Universi Commentarium Paratitlaris*, 5 vols., Monachii, 1703-1708.

Vermeersch, A., *Theologia Moralis, Principia, Responsa, Consilia*, 4 vols., Vol. III, 3. ed., Romae: Universita Gregoriana, 1933.

Vermeersch, A.-Cruesen, I, *Epitome Iuris Canonici*, 3 vols., Vol. II, 6. ed., Mechliniae: H. Dessain, 1940.

Watkins, O. D., *History of Penance for the whole Church to A. D. 450, and for the Western Church from A. D. 450 to A. D. 1215*, 2 vols., New York: Longmans, Green and Co., 1920.

Wernz, F., *Ius Decretalium*, 6 vols., Vol. II, 3. ed., Romae et Prati, 1915.

Wernz, F.-Vidal, P., *Ius Canonicum ad normam Codicis Exactum*, 7 vols. in 8, Vol. IV, Pars I, Romae: Apud Aedes Universitatis Gregorianae, 1934.

Winslow, J., *A Commentary on the Apostolic Faculties*, New York: Field Afar Press, 1946.

Woywod, S., *A. Practical Commentary on the Code of Canon Law*, 10. printing, 2 vols., New York: Joseph F. Wagner, 1946.

Zitelli-Natali, Z., *Apparatus Iuris Ecclesiastici iuxta Recentissimos SS. Urbis Congregationum Resolutiones*, Romae, 1886.

Articles

Augustine, C., "Hospitals,—Their Chaplains, Confessors, Pastors," *ER*, LXVI (1922), 185-192.

Bride, A., "Viatique," *Dictionnaire de Theologie Catholique*, XV, 2842-2858.

Browe, P., "Die Kommunion in der Pfarrkirche," *Zeitschrift für katholische Theologie*, LIII (1929), 477-516.

Connell, F. J., "The Hospital Chaplain and the Administration of the Eucharist," *AER*, CXIX (1948), 19-27.

———, "The Hospital Chaplain and the Administration of Baptism and Penance," *AER*, CXVIII (1948), 254-264.

Connolly, J. F., "The Emergency Powers of Canons 1043, 1044, and 1045, and Some War-Time Considerations," *The Jurist*, V (1945), 20-53.

Coucke, V. J., "Casus de Viatico Suscipiendo," *Collationes Brugenses*, XXVI (1926), 457-461.

———, "De Ieiunio Eucharistico," *Collationes Brugenses*, XXXIV (1934), 380-386.

Mahoney, E. J., "Viaticum to the Unconscious," *CR*, XXXII (1949), 267-269.

Maroto, P., "Animadversiones de Ultimis Sacramentis Ministrandis," *Commentarium pro Religiosis*, XII (1931), 335-346.

O'Neill, P., "The Administration of Holy Viaticum, A Function Reserved to the Pastor," *IER*, 5. series, XXXVII (1931), 515-517.

O'Donnell, M. J., "Administration of the Viaticum to Soldiers Ordered to the Front," *IER*, 5. series, VI (1915), 625-627.

Schaaf, V., "Viaticum without Extreme Unction," *ER*, XCVII (1937), 298.

Schulte, A. J., "Viaticum," *The Catholic Encyclopedia*, XV, 397-399.

Schwienbacher, J., "The Administration of Viaticum in Cases of Cancer of the Esophagus," *The Casuist*, IV, 128-134.

Twomey, Louis J., "The Eucharistic Fast," *ER*, CII (1940), 405-430.

Umberg, J. B., "De Haereticis et Schismaticis in Mortis Periculo Constitutis," *Periodica*, XVIII (1928), 108-122.

Vermeersch, A., "De Iure Parochi et Iterata Viatici Ministratione," *Periodica*, XXII (1933), 213-215.

———, "Administratio Viatici Infirmo non Ieiuno," *Periodica*, XIV (1925), 102-112.

PERIODICALS

American Ecclesiastical Review, The, Vols. I-XXXII, Philadelphia, 1895-1905; *The Ecclesiastical Review*, Vols. XXXIII-CIX, Philadelphit, 1905-1943; *The American Ecclesiastical Review*, Vols. CX-, Washington, D.C., 1944-

Clergy Review, The, London, 1931-

Commentarium pro Religiosis, Romae, 1920-1934; ab anno 1935: *Commentarium pro Religiosis et Missionariis.*

Collationes Brugenses, Brugis Flandorum, 1896-

Homiletic and Pastoral Review, New York, 1900-

Irish Ecclesiastical Record, Dublin, 1864-

Le Canoniste Contemporain, Paris, 1878-1922; *Le Canoniste*, 1924-1926.

Periodica de Re Canonica et Morali utili praesertim Religiosis et Missionariis, Brugis, 1905-1926; ab anno 1927; *Periodica de Re Morali, Canonica, Liturgica.*

The Jurist, Washington, D.C., 1941-

Theologisch-praktische Quartalschrift, Linz, 1848-

Zeitscrift für Katholische Theologie, Innsbruck, 1877-

Abbreviations

AAS—*Acta Apostolicae Sedis.*
AER—*American Ecclesiastical Review.*
ASS—*Acta Sanctae Sedis.*
Bruns—*Canones Apostolorum et Conciliorum saec. IV-VII*, ed. Bruns.
CR—*Clergy Review.*
Coll. Lac.—*Acta et Decreta Conciliorum Recentiorum, Collectio Lacensis.*
Collect.—*Collectanea S. Congregationis de Propaganda Fide.*
CSEL—*Corpus Scriptorum Ecclesiasticorum Latinorum.*
Denzinger—*Enchirdion Symbolorum Definitionum de Rebus Fidei et Morum.*
ER—*The Ecclesiastical Review.*
Fontes—*Codicis Iuris Canonici Fontes cura* ... Gasparri editi.
Hardouin—*Acta Conciliorum et Epistolae Decretales ac Constitutiones Summorum Pontificum.*
HPR—*Homiletic and Pastoral Review.*
IER—*The Irish Ecclesiastical Record.*
Jaffé—*Regista Pontificum Romanorum* etc.
Mansi—*Sacrorum Conciliorum Nova et Amplissima Collectio.*
MGH—*Monumenta Germaniae Historica.*
MPL—Migne, *Patrologia Latina.*
MPG—Migne, *Patrologia Graeca.*
Pallottini—*Collectio Omnium Conclusionum et Resolutionum* etc.
Periodica—*Periodica de Re Morali, Canonica, Liturgica.*
Potthast—*Regesta Pontificum Romanorum inde ab anno post Christum natum MCXCVIII ad annum MCCCIV.*
S.C.C.—Sacra Congregatio Concilii.
S.C. de Prop. Fide—Sacra Congregatio de Propaganda Fide.
S.C. Ep. et Reg.—Sacra Congregatio Episcoporum et Regularium.
S.C. de Sacr.—Sacra Congregatio de Sacramentis.
S.C.S. Off.—Sacra Congregatio Sancti Officii.

BIOGRAPHICAL NOTE

JAMES J. HANNON was born January 13, 1920, at Headford, Co. Galway, Ireland. He attended the local National School and St. Jarlath's College, Tuam, where he received his secondary education. In September, 1939, he entered St. Patrick's Seminary, Carlow, where he was ordained to the Sacred Priesthood for the diocese of Natchez, Mississippi, on June 3, 1945. Arriving in the diocese on March 5, 1946, he engaged in parochial work at Biloxi and later at Pascagoula, Miss. In the fall of 1947 he entered The Catholic University of America to pursue graduate studies in the School of Canon Law. He received the Baccalaureate Degree in Canon Law in June, 1948, and the Degree of Licentiate in Canon Law in June, 1949.

ALPHABETICAL INDEX

Adult, term defined, 126
Apostates, 15, 17
Audientes, 18

Baltimore, II Plenary Council of
  gravity of obligation to administer Viaticum stressed by, 53
  gravity of precept to receive Viaticum stressed by, 44
  legislation of concerning children, 71
  directs that Viaticum be brought privately, 61
Battle—cf. danger of death
Bishops
  minister of Viaticum to, 120

Capital punishment
  administration of Viaticum to persons under, 72, 73
  Viaticum refused to persons under, 74
Case of necessity
  Minister of Viaticum in, 108
Catechism of the Council of Trent, 37ff.
Charon, 2
Children
  acquiring the use of reason, 70, 146
  as the recipients of Viaticum, 69, 70, 146-149
  dispositions of for reception of Viaticum, 148
Consistentes, 18
Coughing
  dangers of irreverence in, 68, 141-142
Councils
  Aix, 44
  Agde, 18
  Alba, 67
  Anse, 21
  Auxerre, 9
  Baltimore—cf. Baltimore
  Carthage III, 8, 9
  Carthage IV, 5
  Elvira, 16
  Epaon, 18
  Hippo, 8
  Lateran, IV General, 14
  Mainz, 21
  Nicea, I General, 3, 4, 10, 16
  Orange, 5, 6
  Oxford, 27
  Pavia, 21, 32
  Port of Spain, 44
  Quebec, II Provincial, 47
  Ravenna, 44
  Rheims, 47
  Saragossa, 13
  Tarragona, 23
  Toledo, 30
  Trent—cf. Trent
  Vaison, I Provincial, 5
  Vienna, 24
  York, 27

Deacon as minister of Viaticum, 109
Death, danger of, 45, 85
  causes of, 87
  element of time in, 92, 93, 95
  intrinsic and extrinsic causes of, 46, 86
  probable and proximate, 47, 85
Decree of Gratian, 7, 14, 18, 20, 21, 22, 25, 26
Decretals, 12, 22, 26
Delirious persons, 139
Doctors, 124, 125, 142

Esophagus, 143, 144
Eucharist—cf. Viaticum
  buried with the dead, 2, 8, 9
  brought to the sick privately, 60-61, 154

brought to the sick publicly, 60, 150
children as the recipients, 36, 38
deacon allowed to act as minister of, 25, 26, 51
lawful reception of, 127
minister of, 25, 51, 102
obligation to receive, 77, 78, 80
received under both species, 27
requisite intention for reception of, 129
reserved in private homes, 11, 12, 13
reserved under both species, 12
Extreme unction, 21, 46, 91, 115, 161

Familiares, 58, 114
Fast, Eucharist
conditions for exceptions to, 98
exceptions to, 33, 96, 97
required for administration of sacraments, 12

Genuflectentes, 18

High Church Anglicans, 130
Holy Communion—cf. Eucharist and Viaticum
Hospital Chaplains
rights of to administer Viaticum, 57, 118
rights of restricted by law, 118
rights of restricted by custom, 56
rights of related to pastors, 56, 117-120
simple mode of appointment of, 118

Insane persons, 38, 66, 67, 137, 138

Lapsi, 3
Last sacraments
order of, 31, 161
Lay persons as ministers of Viaticum, 111
Local interdict, 166

Manducatio, 143, 144
Mass
celebrated in homes of the sick, 62
celebrated while not fasting, 100
Viaticum administered during, 164-165

Non-Catholics, administration of sacraments to, 130-132
Notes on the Gregorian Sacramentary, 9, 30
Nurses, 124-125

Obligation to receive the Eucharist—cf. under Eucharist and Viaticum
Occult sinners, 135
Occupational hazards, 89-90
Oriental Catholics, 65, 167

Pastors
exceptions to right of, 107ff.
minister of Viaticum to, 59, 120
penalties against, 124
rights of, 52, 53, 56
those equivalent to, 104
Popes
Alexander VII, 62
Benedict XIV, 31, 43, 60, 70
Celestine I, 17
Eutychianus, 32
Felix III, 17
Clement V, 24
Gregory IX, 12
Gregory XIII, 56
Gregory XIV, 56
Gregory the Great, 30
Honorius III, 27, 55
Innocent I, 17
Leo X, 24
Leo XIII, 65
Martin V, 34
Paul III, 25
Paul V, 60

Pius IV, 55
Pius V, 55
Pius X, 65, 71
Siricius, 15
Sixtus V, 56
Pyx, 28
how carried, 60
how prepared, 156
materials used in, 29

Religious
conflict with parish priests, 23, 24
privileges granted, 23, 25
right to administer Viaticum, 58, 105
withdrawn from Episcopal jurisdiction, 57
withdrawn from Parochial jurisdiction, 57
Religious Houses
minister of Viaticum in, 113
Rite, 64, 166, 167

Saints
Alphonsus Liguori, 42, 70, 74
Ambrose, 10
Basil, 2
Benedict, 10
Cyprian, 3
Gregory the Great, 10
Gregory of Nazianzen, 2, 10
James of Edessa, 33
John Chrysostom, 12
Sancta, 11
Schismatics, 130
Seminary, minister of Viaticum in, 117, 119
Semifatui, 68, 140

Sick Room
requirements in, 156
vestments worn in, 157-158
Statuta Ecclesiae Antiqua, 5, 21
Styx, river, 2
Subdeacon as minister of Viaticum, 110
Surgical Operation, 89, 99

Trent, Council of
chief purposes of, 52
importance of, 35
legislation of, concerning Viaticum, 36-37

Unconscious persons, 139
Unworthy Catholics, 133

Viaticum
abuses in administration of, 63
administered by lay persons, 20
administered by deacon, 109
applied to Eucharist received at death, 4, 6
brought to the sick publicly, 27, 60, 150
conditions for fruitful reception of, 66
meaning of term, 1-3
origin of term, 1, 6
obligation to administer, 122, 123
obligation to receive anticipated, 49-50
precept to receive, 19, 43, 76, 79
received under species of wine, 30, 145
two-fold sense of, 75, 106
Vomiting, danger of irreverence in, 68, 141

CANON LAW STUDIES*

306. WATERS, REV. JOSEPH L., S.S.J., J.C.L., The Probation in Societies of Quasi-Religious.
307. REGAN, REV. MICHAEL J., J.C.L., Canon 16.
308. BYRNE, REV. HARRY J., J.C.L., Investment of Church Funds.
309. GALLAGHER, REV. THOMAS V., J.C.L., The Rejection of Judicial Witnesses and Testimony.
310. CHATHAM, REV. JOSIAH G., PH.D., S.T.L., J.C.L., Force and Fear as Invalidating Marriage: The Element of Injustice.
311. BROWN, REV. JAMES VICTOR, O.R.S.A., J.C.L., The Invalidating Effects of Force, Fear, and Fraud upon the Canonical Novitiate.
312. DUERR, REV. CHARLES J., B.A., J.C.L., The Judicial Notary.
313. GONZALEZ, REV. FRANCISCO J., O.S.A., J.C.L., De Parocho Religioso Eiusque Superiore Locali.
314. HANNON, REV. JAMES J., J.C.L., Holy Viaticum.
315. SADLOWSKI, REV. EDWIN L., J.C.L., The Sacred Furnishings of Churches.
316. SEGO, REV. ARTHUR A., J.C.L., Dispensation from the Interpellations.
317. WATERHOUSE, REV. JOHN M., J.C.L., The Power of the Local Ordinary to Impose a Matrimonial Ban.
318. FREIN, REV. EUGENE B., J.C.L., The Discretionary Power of the Defender of the Matrimonial Bond.
319. CARTON, REV. GEORGE A., J.C.L., The Time Factor in the Gaining of Indulgences.
320. WALSH, REV. JOHN J., C.S.Sp., J.C.L., The Jurisdiction of the Interritual Confessor in the United States and Canada.
321. UNTERKOEFLER, REV. ERNEST L., S.T.L., J.C.L., The Presiding Judge in Matrimonial Causes of First Instance.

* A complete list of the available numbers in the series will be found in earlier studies. Send orders to: The Catholic University of America Press, 620 Michigan Ave., N.E., Washington 17, D. C.

www.ingramcontent.com/pod-product-compliance
Lightning Source LLC
LaVergne TN
LVHW050235080826
844660LV00012B/535

* 9 7 8 0 8 1 3 2 2 4 8 9 3 *